Marco Polo (1254–1324) was the son of a Venetian merchant and traveler. In 1271, Marco, with his father and uncle, began a journey that four years later led to their being accepted at the court of Kublai Khan. During these years, they traveled extensively in Persia and China, through regions almost totally unknown to the Western world. In service to the Khan, Marco explored Tibet and Burma and many of the remote provinces of China; it is possible that he went to the southern parts of India. Participating in a military conflict between Genoa and Venice, he was taken prisoner in 1298. While in captivity, he dictated the *Travels of Marco Polo* to a fellow prisoner.

Milton Rugoff was a longtime editor for several publishing houses. He is the author of a number of books, including *A Harvest of World Folk Tales, Marco Polo's Adventures in China, The Great Travelers*, and *The Beechers: An American Family in the Nineteenth Century*, which was nominated for an American Book Award in 1982.

Howard Mittelmark is a writer, editor, and book critic. He lives in New York, City.

The Travels of
MARCO POLO

✳

Edited and with an Introduction by
MILTON RUGOFF

With a New Afterword by
HOWARD MITTELMARK

LONGWOOD PUBLIC LIBRARY

SIGNET CLASSICS

SIGNET CLASSICS
Published by New American Library, a division of
Penguin Group (USA) Inc., 375 Hudson Street,
New York, New York 10014, USA
Penguin Group (Canada), 10 Alcorn Avenue, Toronto,
Ontario M4V 3B2, Canada (a division of Pearson Penguin Canada Inc.)
Penguin Books Ltd., 80 Strand, London WC2R 0RL, England
Penguin Ireland, 25 St. Stephen's Green, Dublin 2,
Ireland (a division of Penguin Books Ltd.)
Penguin Group (Australia), 250 Camberwell Road, Camberwell, Victoria 3124,
Australia (a division of Pearson Australia Group Pty. Ltd.)
Penguin Books India Pvt. Ltd., 11 Community Centre, Panchsheel Park,
New Delhi - 110 017, India
Penguin Group (NZ), Cnr Airborne and Rosedale Roads, Albany,
Auckland 1310, New Zealand (a division of Pearson New Zealand Ltd.)
Penguin Books (South Africa) (Pty.) Ltd., 24 Sturdee Avenue,
Rosebank, Johannesburg 2196, South Africa

Penguin Books Ltd., Registered Offices:
80 Strand, London WC2R 0RL, England

Published by Signet Classics, an imprint of New American Library,
a division of Penguin Group (USA) Inc.

First Signet Classics Printing, December 1961
First Signet Classics Printing (Mittelmark Afterword), October 2004
10 9 8 7 6 5 4 3 2 1

Copyright © New American Library, a division of Penguin Group (USA) Inc.
Afterword copyright © Howard Mittelmark, 2004
All rights reserved

SIGNET CLASSICS and logo are tradmarks of Penguin Group (USA) Inc.

Library of Congress Catalog Card Number: 2004052535

Printed in the United States of America

Without limiting the rights under copyright reserved above, no part of this
publication may be reproduced, stored in or introduced into a retrieval system, or transmitted, in any form, or by any means (electronic, mechanical,
photocopying, recording, or otherwise), without the prior written permission
of both the copyright owner and the above publisher of this book.

If you purchased this book without a cover you should be aware that this
book is stolen property. It was reported as "unsold and destroyed" to the
publisher and neither the author nor the publisher has received any payment
for this "stripped book."

The scanning, uploading, and distribution of this book via the Internet or via
any other means without the permission of the publisher is illegal and punish-
able by law. Please purchase only authorized electronic editions, and do not
participate in or encourage electronic piracy of copyrighted materials. Your
support of the author's rights is appreciated.

CONTENTS

INTRODUCTION

IT IS difficult for us to conceive of a time when there existed highly developed civilizations that Europeans knew nothing about. We are aware that in certain periods travel was slow and tortuous and that robbers and hostile people added danger to difficulty. But few realize that for about seven hundred years—say from A.D. 550 to 1250—there was an almost complete lack of knowledge or curiosity about the world beyond the horizon. Of the many reasons for this the most obvious are the disintegration of the Roman Empire, barbarian invasions from the north of Europe, and beginning in the 8th century, Islam rising and standing astride the routes between East and West. The growth of Christianity may also have contributed by turning men's eyes away from this world and by inspiring the Crusades against the Saracens.

Thus, when Marco Polo was born in Venice in 1254, all of Asia east of Baghdad was, to Europeans, terra incognita, or a realm of fable. In ancient times, the Romans and Greeks had imported large quantities of silk, spices, furs, musk, rice, and other goods and products from the East. Although some of these always continued to find their way to Europe, the ancient caravan route called the Silk Road was cut by the 6th century A.D., and the memory of the old relationship soon grew dim. In time, the Byzantine Empire began to produce enough silk for Europe's curtailed needs, and in any event, no one in Europe seems to have cared where the spices or fine fabrics came from. If some particularly bold merchant, adventurer, or friar did penetrate the barriers from time to time, we have no record of the feat and almost no trace of the explorer.

Then, in 1243, scarcely a score of years before Nicolo and Maffeo Polo reached Cathay, Friar John of Plano Carpini, a Franciscan, was dispatched to try to convert the Mongols and to enlist their help—it was like getting devils to fight demons—against the Saracens. Carpini met Batu, Khan of the so-called Golden Horde, near the Black Sea, and later the Great Khan, Kuyuk, in Cathay; but although Keraits and other Nestorian Christians were scattered throughout Cathay, and although Kuyuk was not unsympathetic, Carpini's mission failed. A similar mission by William of Rubruck (or Rubruquis), a French Franciscan who visited the next Great Khan, Mangu, some eight years later, met with the same fate. Both Carpini and Rubruck left interesting journals of their travels, and these might well have become better known if Marco Polo's did not make them seem limited and quaint. Aside from these, and the uneven account by Rabbi Benjamin of Tudela of his wanderings across the Levant and India, and perhaps into China, in the 1160s and 1170s, there is, astonishingly, nothing.

That is why Marco Polo's *Description of the World,* now generally known as *The Travels of Marco Polo,* the record of what he saw and learned on his journey from Venice to Cathay, and throughout the Orient, between 1271 and 1295, is so remarkable. It would have been remarkable even if it had been a report only of unknown areas and primitive tribes. But it was immeasurably more than that—a systematic description of a variety of civilizations, including a few as highly developed as any in Europe, and at least one that was worthy of wonder. He told of a hundred practices and institutions that astonished his fellow Venetians, and a number that they did not even believe. Indeed, it is a measure of how remarkable his account was that so many doubted it.

How could they help doubting him when in one book he told of a potentate whose palace and pleasure pavilions dazzled, who clothed his nobles in bejeweled garments and his five thousand elephants in cloth of gold, and who had ten thousand falconers; of mighty mountain ranges so high there were no birds on them; of vast deserts so hot they turned dead bodies to dust; of a chief (the Old Man of the Mountain) who spirited his hashish-drugged victims into an artificial paradise; of black stones (coal) and a fountain of liquid (petroleum), both of which burned miraculously; of paper money; of a cloth (made of asbestos) that would not burn; of people who decorated their skin with designs (by tattooing); of prodigious white (polar) bears and of dogs that pulled sledges on snow; of great sheep (the *Ovis Poli,* named after him); of nuts (coconuts) as large as a man's head; of people who encased their teeth in gold; of a land (India) where the cattle were sacred; of jade-bearing rivers and of seabeds full of pearls; of an island (Sumatra) where the natives ate human flesh; of magicians who caused goblets of liquor to fly; of widows who were burned (in suttee) along with their husbands; of a city so large that its people used ten thousand pounds of pepper a day; of men who turned over their womenfolk to every strange guest; of "shark charmers" who protected pearl divers; of ships with watertight compartments; of naked dancing girls dedicated to the service of gods in (Hindu) shrines; of sorcerers who controlled the wind and the weather; of a courier system with 10,000 stations and 200,000 horses; of a country where the merchants would not lie even to save their lives; of great rivers teeming with boats; of a far northern land where all winter there was night and all summer there was day; and of a thousand other things equally incredible.

Where such later discoverers as Columbus and Cook only touched the shore of a continent and left the rest unknown, Polo filled in the map of Asia almost from end to end—and then peopled it.

The Influence of the Book

As curious as the opening of the channels to the East a few decades before Marco Polo's birth is their closing a few decades after his death in 1324. The explanation is that after Genghis Khan had established Mongol power in the early 13th century, the Great Khans, in their imperial condescension, or craft, or curiosity, tolerated and even protected the occasional Western visitor. But the Ming dynasty that forced the Mongols out of China in 1368 showed no such tolerance or curiosity. They shut the gates at the end of the road, and soon the roads themselves were made impassable all across Asia by wave after wave of marauding Turks.

Thus, for the next century and a half, until the Portuguese and the Spanish pushed their way into the Indies and the Spice Islands and got a foothold in India and China—and such individuals as the learned Jesuit, Father Ricci, established himself in China in the 1590s—the East sank back, as far as Europeans were concerned, into outer darkness. And if we except such feats as the overland trip to China by Benedict Goes, a Portuguese Jesuit, in 1603–1605, it would be another two and a half centuries before China would be completely "opened up" to the West. Even then, the opening of both China and Japan in the middle of the 19th century would be carried out by force. In the light of this, the present attitude of Communist China toward Westerners seems not so much a departure from tradition as a reversion to it.

Marco Polo's book was for all practical purposes not only the first to pull aside the veil that hid the East, but it was nearly the last for a long time to come. A few men followed in his steps during the early decades of the 14th century: Ibn Battuta, a North African Moslem who is said to have covered 75,000 miles during almost thirty years of roving from Spain to Cathay; and Friar Odoric, a saintly ascetic from the Udine area, who also reached the East. But we find ourselves turning from their journals, valuable as they may be, with a renewed respect for Marco Polo's scope, penetration, and ranging curiosity.

Marco's account should thus have burst upon his contemporaries as a kind of revelation. It did nothing of the kind. The Europeans of the 14th and 15th centuries, still children of the Middle Ages, were not particularly influenced or impressed. The majority, even among the literate, continued to be content with fragments of fable or fantasy. Even those who should have welcomed his report, the map makers and geographers, seem in general to have looked on his book as more romance than fact. Far from being a science, mapmaking was still an exercise of fancy, or religious devotion, or fear of the unknown. In the early Christian era—by which time such works as Ptolemy's atlas and the reports of Herodotus had been forgotten or disdained—a leading geographer of the early 5th century, Cosmas, thought the universe was a flat parallelogram and the earth a dome-shaped mountain with Jerusalem as center and summit. And as late as the 14th century another renowned geographer, Cardinal d'Ailly, concluded that Africa could not be far from India because both contained elephants.

A few cartographers, beginning with the maker of the excellent Catalan Atlas of 1375, appear to have appreciated and assimilated Polo's work. But it remained for the explorers of the Age of Discovery, and Christopher Columbus most of all, to register his influence most profoundly. One of the most interesting documents in the history of exploration is a Latin edition of Marco Polo's book in the Columbian Library in Seville. It belonged to Columbus and it contains no less than seventy marginal notes by the discoverer. There is little doubt that Polo's reports on the wealth of Cathay helped shape Columbus' vision and that Polo's estimates of distances—erroneous as they may have been—convinced the discoverer that it was possible to get to the "Indies" by sailing westward. In 1474, moreover, the Florentine cosmographer Toscanelli sent Columbus a map of the eastern part of Asia, including Zipangu (Japan) and the Indies, which he had based on Polo's descriptions, and encouraged the explorer to rely on it in any effort to sail westward.

What Columbus did not know, of course, was that the land mass of the Americas lay between him and his goal and that the distance westward to Cathay was far greater than he imagined. No one can say that Columbus would not have dreamed his dream if it had not been for Polo's book, but it surely persuaded him that at the end of the journey he would find such riches as would make all his efforts worthwhile.

MARCO'S VENICE

When Marco Polo went from Venice to the court of the emperor of Cathay, he passed from one peak of power and civilization to another. For the Venice into which Marco was born in 1254 was just entering its zenith. It was Queen of the Adriatic at a time when the Mediterranean was in fact as well as in name the center of the known world. Quick to profit in any way, Venice had become rich by equipping and transporting Crusaders and pilgrims to the Holy Land. In return for her help she had also won concessions of islands in the eastern Mediterranean from the Latin Emperor of Constantinople, Baldwin I. The high point of this aggrandizement came during the Fourth Crusade, in 1203, when Venice transported the Crusaders and then joined them in the barbaric sacking of Constantinople and the dismemberment of the Greek Empire. The booty, in loot and in fragments of empire, was enormous. It helped to make Venice in the next century the greatest commercial empire the world had known.

This was the Venice in which Marco Polo grew up. In its narrow streets and sudden squares, and on its crowded canals and tiny bridges, a host of traders from everywhere gathered and did business. The most prosperous—truly merchant princes—were already building those palaces along the Grand Canal that would make it seem a sea-born dream. The Basilica of St. Mark, begun in 829, rebuilt after a fire in 976, and given its Byzantine look in the 11th century, was, with its Oriental domes, its mosaics, its altarpiece made of six thousand jewels, and the great bronze horses surging from its façade (plunder from Constantinople), an education in itself. Around it washed an endless current of beggars and nobles, priests and prostitutes, pilgrims and rogues. For Venice was, like so many medieval cities, a study in violent contrasts: sumptuousness and filth, elegance and coarseness, asceticism and corruption, women who wore gorgeous silks but went unwashed, gilded palaces without sanitary facilities.

It was also a city of craftsmen; in one quarter or another young Marco could see the wizardry of the glass blowers, of the weavers of cloth of gold and crimson damask, the embroiderers, the goldsmiths, and the jewelers, and, if he made his way to the arsenal, the astonishing assembly line of the greatest shipyard in Europe.

Most fascinating of all were the quays, especially those crowded with goods from far-off places: with cinnamon, cloves, nutmeg, pepper, and ginger; with camphor in bamboo tubes; with muslin from Mosul and damask from Damascus; with myrrh, rhubarb, and sandalwood; with ivory, coral, and marble. And of course with slaves—Circassians, Turks, Russians, Tartars—brought from the Levant and on the way to the auction market. It was these slaves, more than all the goods or foreigners or details of architecture, that tinged Venice with the Orient. An attractive slave girl was worth thousands of dollars because she could also serve as a concubine, and thus the blood of many a Levantine or Caspian type was mingled with that of many a fine Venetian family.

Almost all of this, spices and marble and slaves, came by water. No wonder, then, that the Venetians looked on the sea with a kind of adoration, and once a year, on Ascension Day, took part in a ceremony wherein the people in their gondolas, led by the Doge in his resplendent bucentaur, went out on the lagoon and wed the waters with a ring.

From its vantage point midway in the Mediterranean, Venice linked Europe and Asia Minor and Africa, and its merchants were at home everywhere in the known world. In the known world—and, as the Polos were to show, in the unknown as well.

The Elder Polos and the First Journey

The true trailblazer in the Polo family was not Marco at all, but his father Nicolo and his uncle Maffeo. If they had put down their story as Marco did his—and if, of course, they had proved as curious and keen—their tale might well have been an even more remarkable one. For they made the great journey to Cathay, not once, but twice, leaving on the first trip at about the time Marco was born.

At that point Nicolo and Maffeo were already successful merchants. Like many others of their vocation they had concentrated their efforts in that terminus of Near Eastern trade, Constantinople. Despite the sacking of the city by Crusaders and Venetians in 1204, it was still the hub of the great caravan routes of Asia, its warehouses were again full of silks and spices, ebony and ivory, and its currency was accepted everywhere. Each nationality had its own quarter in the city, with the Venetians having the largest. It was in this section that the Polo brothers had established a branch. And it is there that our story really begins.

After a sojourn in Constantinople of perhaps as long as six years, Nicolo and Maffeo, hoping to do better, moved to Soldaia (Sudak) in the Crimea. But Soldaia was disappointing, and they went on to Bolgara, one of the capitals of Barka, Khan of the Western Tartars and a grandson of the great Genghis Khan. They prospered here, but when they sought to turn back, they found their way blocked by warring Tartar tribes. Literally following the path of least resistance, they made their way eastward to Bokhara, one of the great trade centers of Central Asia. But here they found the roads cut off in every direction. So they lingered patiently for three full years.

Then came the chance that changed their lives; an envoy from Hulaku, Khan of the Levant, arrived in the city on his way to the court of the Great Khan in Cathay. Fascinated by the two "Latins" who spoke the Mongol tongue, he urged them to accompany him. They had already been away from home eleven years, but the invitation must have seemed a matchless opportunity to cross Asia as the guests of the most powerful monarch on earth. No doubt they also surmised that it would prove profitable. They accepted, and after journeying for another entire year over steppe and desert and mountain, they arrived in about 1265 at the court of Kublai, the Great Khan and Supreme Lord of all the Mongols.

In his book, Marco gives us few details of the extraordinary journey made by his father and his uncle. To have done so would doubtless have meant his telling us of many things he would have to repeat concerning his own journey; but it is nonetheless a pity that we know so little of their experiences and encounters.

The Great Khan welcomed the Latins cordially. He talked to them again and again, asking them especially about the Pope and Christianity. Finally he gave them a letter inviting the Pope to send him a hundred learned missionaries who could undertake to prove the superiority of the Christian religion. This does not seem so surprising once we learn that there had long been tribes of Nestorian Christians (whose doctrine had been branded a heresy in 431) in the East, and that Kublai's own mother probably came from one of these. Beyond this, Kublai was evidently astute enough to want to learn all he could about so widespread and persuasive a doctrine.

The brothers started back at once and after many delays—as Marco casually reports—from floods and storms and snow and ice, they reached the Mediterranean seaport of Acre. To their dismay they found that the Pope, Clement IV, had died and that no successor had as yet been elected. In desperation they turned to a Papal legate, Tedaldo of Piacenza. He advised them to bide their time until a new Pope was elected.

So, after fifteen years of wandering and sojourning and wandering again, they came home to find Nicolo's wife dead, and his son Marco a lad of fifteen years.

JOURNEY TO THE EAST

We know nothing about Marco Polo's childhood. The evidence indicates that, like most boys of his time and place, he received little or no formal education. But Venice as a crossroads of the Mediterranean world, together with the travels of his father and his uncle, was surely education enough. When, two years after returning home, the elder Polos, weary of waiting for a Pope to be elected and fearful of disappointing the Great Khan, decided to start for Cathay again, Marco was ready. To the seventeen-year-old youth the prospect must have seemed like a dream.

But passing through the Aegean was no dream, and arriving at Acre, famous way station of Crusaders and pilgrims to the Holy Land, was certainly not. After a detour to Jerusalem to get some holy oil from the sepulcher of Jesus—as Kublai Khan had requested—they went to Layas and were about to start eastward when a courier came from their friend, the legate Tedaldo. The messenger informed them that Tedaldo himself had been elected Pope and that he wanted them to come to him at Acre.

The new Pope had remembered Kublai's request for missionaries, but instead of one hundred scholars, he could find only two members of the Order of Preaching Friars who would venture to accompany the Polos. And hardly had the five men started eastward when news of a Saracen force harrying the area before them caused the timid friars to turn tail and flee. The Polos were evidently undismayed: they represented the Pope on the one hand, and they carried a gold tablet inscribed by the Great Khan on the other hand. So they pushed on through Lesser Armenia (Cilicia) and Greater Armenia to the Baku region. Describing the area of Mt. Ararat, Marco relates the hoary legend of Noah's Ark at the top of it, but then he accurately describes the wells of Baku that produce an oil that burns. Such oil had been widely used as fuel in ancient Greece and Rome, but, Marco's note notwithstanding, it would not be put to use again until the 18th century.

Thereafter, the travelers must have come from time to time upon bands of nomad Mongols with their immense droves of horses, oxen, and sheep and with their huge tents mounted on carts as much as twenty feet wide and drawn by as many as twenty-two bullocks. Perhaps here too Marco got his first taste of the wanderers' favorite drink, the fermented mare's milk called kumiss, and began to pick up their strange tongue.

After that they came to Mosul and possibly Baghdad, although Marco's description of the latter does not convince us that he was there himself. Next there was Tabriz, with its pearl markets, Saba (whence came, Marco declares, the three Magi), Kerman, and then a place where they were ambushed by bandits. From there they proceeded southward to Hormuz, a port on the Persian Gulf. The travelers probably planned to continue by water from this port, but the ships seemed so unseaworthy and the hot wind so intolerable that they turned back to Kerman and the land route. After that they passed through deserts for many days and into the province of Tunocain, where Marco thought the women the most beautiful in the world.

Here he pauses to tell the fantastic story of the Old Man of the Mountain and the paradisaical gardens in which he initiated members of his band, called the Assassins.

Resuming the narrative of the journey, Marco describes their passage through Balach (Balkh) in Afghanistan, and Balashan (Badakhshan), land of huge rubies, where—we learn in passing—he lay ill for an entire year and was cured only by going into the mountains. Climbing higher and higher, they then moved across the lofty plateau of the Pamirs and passed into Kashmir, famous for its sorcerers. After these places came Kashgar and Khotan, where jade is dug from the dry riverbeds, and Lop, and then the vast and desolate Gobi (itself the Mongol word for desert), haunted by noises of drums and bells and the voices of evil spirits.

Struggling out of the desert, they began at last to see people with Chinese manners and customs. After describing Kamul, Bankul, and Kanchow, Marco, approaching the heart of Cathay, digresses to tell of the rise of Genghis Khan. Included in this account is the war between Genghis and Ung Khan, whom Marco, like Rubruck before him, confuses with the legendary "Prester John."

Finally, after three long years, they near the end of their journey. It is a happy end, for the Great Khan sends them an escort, and during the last forty days they travel in royal style. About May of 1275 they reach Shangtu, or Chandu (Coleridge's Xanadu), the summer retreat of the Great Khan Kublai, Lord of the Universe.

THE EMPIRE OF KUBLAI KHAN

When the Polos came to it, the empire of Kublai Khan, the greatest in extent the world has ever seen (it was six thousand miles from east to west and about two thousand at its widest from north to south), was scarcely three generations old. Less than eighty years before, the Mongols had been obscure horse nomads on the high prairies of Mongolia, southeast of Lake Baikal. Accustomed to endure every privation, to live in the saddle, to strike their enemies without mercy, they needed only to be disciplined as a military force and aroused by the taste of conquest to become invincible. A certain young chieftain named Temuchin gave them that discipline and that taste. By the time he was forty-four, in 1206, he had become Genghis (or Chinghiz) Khan, "The Universal Lord." His formula was simple: his force was horsemen—truly half man, half horse—who combined maximum mobility with iron stamina and discipline; his practice was to annihilate the enemy down to the very cats and dogs and to obliterate communities to a point where, in a few instances, horses could be grazed on the site; and his one aim in life was conquest. At his death in 1227 he was master of most of Asia from Peiping in the East to Georgia in the West and Afghanistan in the South.

Ogodai, the son who succeeded him, extended the empire southward into China. At the same time, Batu, the son of Ogodai's half-brother, Juchi, together with one of Genghis' old generals, Subotai, swept savagely westward, sacked Kiev and other Russian cities, burst into Poland and leveled Kracow. In the spring of 1241, in Hungary, they routed an army of one hundred thousand barons, knights and infantry, the best that eastern Europe could muster, and proceeded to devastate Pest on the Danube. By the following winter, one column, swinging south, reached Dalmatia, so that by December they stood on the shores both of the Danube and the Adriatic, eyeing Europe as a cat might eye a mouse.

It is hardly surprising that in their terror and ignorance, Europeans should have seen these "hordes" (from *ordu,* a nomad camp or troop) as fiends out of Tartarus, or hell, and distorted the name "Tatars" into "Tartars." Typical of the general reaction is that of the monk Matthew Paris, who wrote in his huge chronicle:

> In this year (1240), a detestable nation of Satan . . . the Tartars, broke loose from its mountain-environed home, and piercing the solid rocks, poured forth like devils. . . . They are thirsting for and drinking blood, tearing and devouring the flesh of dogs and men, dressed in oxhides, armed with plates of iron, thickset, strong, invincible.

At this supremely critical moment Ogodai died, and the heads of the clan were summoned to a meeting in Mongolia. While Europe hung in the balance, Batu and Subotai debated and then withdrew, Subotai going back to Mongolia, Batu retiring to his court on the Volga and the arms of his twenty-six wives. Had Ogodai not died, it is possible that the Mongols would have overrun Europe. What that would have meant to the history of the West, the reader is at liberty to imagine for himself.

By this time the Mongol empire had become so vast that although the eastern part remained the homeland, great segments came under the rule, more or less independent—and not without quarrels and clashes—of various members of the family. Ogodai's son Kuyuk was Great Khan only briefly, dying in 1248, and (after an interregnum in which Ogodai's widow Turakina guided the empire) another grandson of Genghis, Mangu, ruled from 1252 to 1259. Meanwhile Batu, Khan of the Golden Horde, remained Lord of the West (roughly European Russia), and Hulaku, another grandson of Genghis, became Lord of the Levant (from eastern Persia to the Mediterranean). It was Hulaku who in 1268 captured the last Caliph of Baghdad and did such destruction in that magnificent city that it never recovered. It was he too who took Damascus, Queen of Cities, and Jerusalem the Golden, and was threatening Egypt when once again the death of a Great Khan, this time Mangu, stopped what might have been a decisive blow. This time the fate of the Levant, of Moslem power, and the Crusades themselves hung in the balance. Like Batu before him, however, Hulaku turned back.

Meanwhile, another great figure was emerging in the East, Kublai, a younger brother of Mangu. Brought up partly under the influence of a few Chinese advisers, he had later been sent to extend Mongol dominion farther into China. And he had done so. But the more he saw of the Chinese way of life, the more he appears to have been influenced by it. The Sung emperors had ruled for over three centuries and had turned increasingly to the contemplation of spiritual values and an appreciation of the arts. Under their reign the great walled cities south of the Yangtze had grown ever greater. Only their taste for war had waned.

When Mangu died, Kublai, taking advantage of the dissension among the khans, caused himself to be declared Great Khan. Before long he had completed the conquest of China all the way to Canton and the southern seas, accomplishing much of this by cunning rather than force. His inclination was not to destroy but to assimilate what he found. Where Genghis had been the warrior, the ruthless conqueror, the military genius, Kublai was the astute statesman, the administrator, cultivator of values, sportsman, lover of refinement. By the time of his death in 1294, after thirty-five years on the throne, he had been transformed from a heroic to a divine figure, from a Khan of the Mongols to the Son of Heaven, inheritor of the Dragon Throne, before whom—as Marco Polo reports with awe—multitudes of courtiers fell prostrate when the cry arose: "Bow and adore!"

Marco was struck at every turn by Kublai's enlightened government: the reserve granaries for periods of scarcity (although something like it had been practiced in ancient times); the relief for the poor and the ill; the elaborate patrol against disorder and fire; the use of paper currency; the extraordinary post system; the beautification of roads by trees; the abolition of gambling; the completion of the Grand Canal from Peiping to Hangchow. Although Marco tended to respond more emphatically to such social and economic achievements, he did note Kublai's amazing toleration of all religions—Christian, Jewish, Moslem, and the Buddhism of the Tibetan lamas. His description of the summer palace conveys a sense of its beauty as architecture and decoration, but his main wonder is at its grandeur and opulence. And there is no hint whatever of one of the greatest distinctions of Sung civilization: its literature and painting.

The Mongol domination of such a civilization could not last. Just as in only three generations a nomad tribe had exploded into an empire of incredible extent, so in only three more it would disintegrate and be absorbed.

IN CATHAY

Kublai welcomed the travelers cordially, and almost immediately the nearly sixty-year-old monarch seems to have been impressed by the apt twenty-one-year-old whom the two Western merchants had brought back with them. Soon the Great Khan was sending him on missions; and Marco not only acquitted himself well but enlarged his reports with descriptions of novelties and curious customs such as Kublai delighted to read about. He gained such favor that he was made a governor of the large city of Yangchow, where he served for three years. But with the curious reticence that marks all his references to himself, Marco says nothing about his rule—and indeed gives us only a meager description of the city itself.

His missions included at least two major journeys, one southwestward to Yunnan and Burma and the other southward through eastern China and perhaps down into the southern seas. (The exact route of these is difficult to determine because his account of them incorporates information he had gathered on other trips or from other persons.) Out of the expedition to the southwest came such remarkable stories as that of the Golden King who surrounded himself only with maidens, of a place where the men preferred to marry those girls who had the most lovers, of the austere lives of the yogi of India, of a very strange beast (the crocodile), and of the childbirth custom of couvade. The other trip, which carried him deep into southeastern China, yielded descriptions of the immense traffic on the Yangtze and of the great cities of the province of Manzi. In Kinsai (Hangchow) he found a metropolis not only much larger than Venice, but one in which the excellence of the government and the civility of the people aroused him to twenty pages of praise and wonder.

THE JOURNEY HOME

At last, after seventeen years, the Polos began to think of returning to Venice; they can hardly be described as impatient since Nicolo and Maffeo had been home only

once in thirty-five years. Their wish to leave was also probably inspired by the fact that Kublai, who had protected
them from some of his more envious courtiers, was growing old. But the Great Khan would not let them go, saying—Marco tells us—that he loved them too much.

Once again totally unexpected good fortune took a
hand. This time it was three Persian ambassadors returning to their homeland with a princess royal, Kokachin, for Arghun II, Khan of Persia, whose favorite
wife had died not long before. The envoys and Kokachin
had made one start homeward but had turned back
when war had broken out among the tribes along the
caravan routes. Marco having just returned from a mission into the southern seas, the Polos had the shrewd
scheme of offering to guide the ambassadors back to
Persia by sea. Reluctantly, Kublai consented, but once
he had agreed, he had no less than fourteen ships fitted
out for them and gave them an imperial gold tablet that
would insure them safe passage.

As the party sets out from the great port of Zaitun
on the east coast, Marco takes the opportunity to give
us the history—rather garbled, unfortunately—of a certain very large island off the coast—Zipangu (Japan).
He follows that with descriptions of places touched at,
passed, or heard of on the voyage: Indo-China, Java,
Sumatra, Ceylon, India, and the so-called Male and Female Islands. He closes the section with notes on Madagascar and the Zanzibar area of East Africa, but it is
thought that he did not actually visit either. A fourth
and final segment (as later editors have divided the
book) includes an interesting account of Russia and the
Siberian arctic, together with a rather tedious history of
the wars between the Tartar chiefs.

After two and a half years of buffeting in the southern
ocean during which all but eighteen of the six hundred
passengers perished, the travelers arrived in Persia—only
to find that Arghun Khan had died. Fortunately, he had
left a grown son, Ghazan, who promptly agreed to take
the fair Kocachin off their hands. After an unexplained
delay of nine months, the Polos set out on the final,
the truly final lap of all their journeys, going by way
of Trebizond and Constantinople to the Mediterranean.

Sometime during the year 1295 they made their way slowly past the Aegean islands and up the Adriatic until the domes and spires of the proud and fabled city rising from the sea came into view. They had been away twenty-five years on the longest journey ever recorded, and the lad Marco was a man of forty-one.

Nearly everyone remembers the story of their return to the family mansion in the district of San Giovanni Grisostomo, for it has about it the air of a fairytale, or of the homecoming of Ulysses. As Ramusio, the 15th-century editor of the first printed edition, tells us, they came "with an indescribable something of the Tartar in their aspect and speech . . . their garments the worse for wear, of coarse cloth and cut after the fashion of the Tartars"; and no one recognized them.

Then there is the other story, which Ramusio says he got from an old man who had it from his grandfather, a neighbor of the Polos. This relates how when the relatives of the travelers continued to doubt their story, the three men arranged a family banquet, and cutting open the coarse garments they had worn on their return, poured out of them great quantities of rubies, sapphires, and emeralds, so that the guests were dazzled and dumbstruck. It is worthy of the *Arabian Nights,* and perhaps that treasury of Eastern romances inspired it, because such evidence as Marco's will (one of the few legal documents we have about him) indicates that when he died twenty-nine years later he was not more than moderately well off.

Still another very old tradition says that few who heard Messer Marco's stories took them literally and that he came to be called "Marco Milione" and the house he lived in "Corte di Milioni"—both names usually assumed to be jibes at the extravagant numbers in his stories. But it is hard to believe that a cascade of diamonds falling out of garments "cut after the fashion of the Tartars" would not have silenced such skepticism.

JAIL IN GENOA

Except for his capture in a naval battle and subsequent jailing in Genoa, the remainder of Messer Marco's life was something of an anticlimax. Once settled in Venice again, he must have felt that he could never do anything that would not seem insignificant next to his journey to Cathay. Probably he would have gone back—even as his father and uncle had gone back again—if he had not heard (so the Ramusio version says) that Kublai was dead.

Even the episode of the naval battle was hardly glorious. The fierce rivalry for the domination of trade, particularly in the eastern Mediterranean, that had raged for years between Venice and Genoa reached its climax in the 1290s. A series of savage clashes in Constantinople and on the sea culminated in 1298 in an engagement near Curzola, an island off the Dalmatian coast, in which a Venetian armada of one hundred galleys was decisively defeated. One story is that Messer Marco Polo was a "Gentleman Commander" of a galley in this battle and was captured along with seven thousand other Venetians; another is that he was taken in one of the earlier clashes. Whichever is true, he was carried off to "La Superba," as Genoa was called, and imprisoned, not in the dungeons with the common soldiers, but imprisoned nonetheless. Although it must have been a most humiliating experience for the veteran of the caravan routes of Asia, it is to that imprisonment and the enforced idleness that followed that we owe the book on which all of Marco Polo's fame rests.

For in that Genoa jail, Messer Marco's story evidently fascinated fellow prisoners, jailers, and (Ramusio declares) noble Genoan visitors alike. Among his audience in the prison was a certain fellow prisoner, Rustichello, who came from Pisa, which Genoa had humbled in 1290. Rustichello was a writer of metrical romances, and at some point he volunteered, or agreed, to put Marco's story into writing. For Rustichello it meant that he would for once be dealing not with a knight of chivalric legend but a living hero whose experiences were stranger than any invention of romance. So Marco sent for the notes he had left in Venice and began his remarkable narrative.

Not long after the completion of the manuscript, in about 1298, a treaty of peace was concluded between

Venice and Genoa, and Messer Marco, along with others, was released. It was thought that he then returned to Venice, married a certain Donata Badoèr, and settled down, rather belatedly, to the life of a well-to-do Venetian merchant. He is known to have had three daughters and several grandchildren, but no descendants have been traced beyond that. As so often happens with men who are not in the public eye, much of what we know of Messer Marco's later years comes from court records, especially of suits, and some of his biographers have therefore concluded that he became grasping and quarrelsome. Coupled with the story that neighbors ridiculed his tales, this may make him seem a somewhat embittered and neglected figure. In reality his manuscript was soon being copied widely and we have record of at least two distinguished men who sought him out: Pietro d'Abano, renowned professor at the University of Padua, and a French nobleman, representing Charles of Valois, who requested a copy of the manuscript when he passed through Venice in 1307. As for his supposed covetousness, we know of at least one magnanimous gesture: on his deathbed he gave freedom to Pietro, a Tartar who had long been one of his slaves—and whom he may have acquired in the East—and with it a handsome sum of money.

THE MAN AND HIS BOOK

Despite the fullness of Marco's book, it reveals little of his essential personality or character. Its judgments of customs and behavior are often conventional or rough generalizations. Again and again he speaks of people as "cruel" or "modest" or "mean-spirited" or "languid," but there is no example of these from his own experiences. Occasionally, as when he says that a certain place is a fine one for young men to visit because the natives gladly yield their women to strangers, the reader may well wonder what personal adventures lay behind his comment. It is only from the most casual references that we get any hint of some of his more extraordinary experiences: for example, the attack by bandits in which many in his party were either killed or captured, or the time he was ill for an entire year and had to go into the mountains to recuperate. These remain merely tantalizing glimpses. The fact is that this is a book not about Marco Polo but about what he saw; and there was, in any event, no tradition that would have encouraged him to indulge in personal revelations.

There are, of course, certain characteristics and interests that become apparent to any careful reader. Marco Polo was above all the merchant, with an eye for flourishing manufactures and profitable commodities, and with a strong tendency to measure people in terms of their wealth or industriousness; he was competent and tactful enough to carry out all kinds of commissions for the Great Khan; physically he was certainly hardy and not easily daunted; he was a keen observer, enterprising, curious, and enquiring. He was a Christian dutifully concerned with the spread of Christianity, and occasionally he (or perhaps some pious later editor) vouchsafes us a saint's legend or a miracle. He automatically dubs all Buddhists "idolaters," but nonetheless tells the story of the life of Gautama Buddha with understanding. He also appears to have had more than a casual interest in hunting, and his reports on curious sexual customs are notably explicit. But beyond this it is unsafe to go. Where manner of expression or tone might ordinarily be significant, in these pages it is not to be trusted since it may be the work of the scribe; for example, it is generally felt that the treatment of Mongol battles as though they were clashes between Christian knights of the age of chivalry is a Rustichello contribution.

As for Marco's accuracy and credibility, the studies of many scholars and the investigations of explorers such as Sven Hedin and Aurel Stein have gradually confirmed these to the point where only a handful of passages seem irredeemably gullible or superstitious. Among these are the legend of the cobbler whose faith moved a mountain; the roc, a bird that could carry off an elephant; dog-headed men in one place and dog-tailed men in another; an Island of Females inhabited by "Amazons"; and the tomb of Adam on Ceylon. But in all fairness it must be added that most of these are plainly secondhand and not vouched for.

As every editor has noted, there are some surprising omissions—the Great Wall, tea, the practice of footbinding, printed books, fishing with cormorants, chopsticks. But these can be explained as oversights or as circumstances that became so familiar in the course of twenty years that Marco forgot how strange or remarkable they could seem.

We have, in fact, come a long way from the days when, if we may believe certain traditional stories, Marco Polo's book was a synonym for extravagant claims and tall tales. We are now much more likely to believe the story that when friends urged him in his last hours to modify or retract some of his statements, he said: I did not write half the things I saw.

In style Marco's book may prove disappointing, especially to readers who come to it expecting a literary classic. The writer—whether Marco or a scribe—is wordy and repetitious; his prose is simply matter-of-fact, without grace, and almost without allusions to history, literature, or even the Bible.

But a narrative woven almost entirely of marvels evidently needs neither lining nor embroidery to enchant people of all ages and times. What Marco had in great measure was a sense of wonder, an eye for the exotic, the novel, and the spectacular, and the spirit that moves great discoverers. They permeate his best passages, such as his descriptions of the city of Kinsai and the wondrous palaces and dreamlike parks of Kublai Khan. It was one of these passages (in a translation by an Elizabethan, Samuel Purchas) that inspired the magic of Coleridge's "Kubla Khan," with its famous opening:

In Xanadu did Kubla Khan
A stately pleasure-dome decree:
Where Alph, the sacred river, ran
Through caverns measureless to man
    Down to a sunless sea.
So twice five miles of fertile ground
With walls and towers were girdled round:
And there were gardens bright with sinuous rills
Where blossomed many an incense-bearing tree . . .

Coleridge subtitled his poem "A Vision in a Dream," but the vision was Marco Polo's, and it was not a dream.

◆ ◆ ◆

A NOTE ON MANUSCRIPTS AND EDITIONS

It is probable that Marco Polo had Rustichello write, or rewrite, his account simply because he thought the scribe could do a better job, and do it more easily. He may also have thought that the Venetian dialect—which even an Italian from Pisa would have found difficult—was less suitable than French, which was not only the lingua franca of much of Europe but the language of such romances as Rustichello himself wrote. Because of this and because it has been shown that early copies of the manuscript in Latin or Italian were based on a French version, it is believed that the original version was in French. Much more significant than which came first is the fact that translations were soon made into Latin and various Italian dialects, and during the next century, into other languages, including Spanish, Bohemian, German, and even Irish. As many as 138 manuscripts have been uncovered, including one—containing new material—as late as 1934 (a Latin version called the Zelada Text, found in the Cathedral Chapter at Toledo, Spain).

So accustomed are we to thinking of our classics as printed books that we must be reminded that Marco Polo's work had to be circulated in manuscript for almost 180 years before the first printed edition appeared. That was a German version in 1477, only twenty-one years after Gutenberg's Bible. The effect of being copied and translated in manuscript form is that hardly any of the numerous printed editions are alike, each deriving from a different manuscript or combination of manuscripts. The most widely circulated English translation, made by William Marsden in 1818 and edited by Thomas Wright in 1854, was based on the Ramusio version. The edition with the most famous commentary is the two-volume work that Henry Yule, a great Orientalist, prepared in 1871 (revised in 1875, and again, with additional notes by Henry Cordier, in 1902, and reissued, with a volume of addenda by Cordier, in 1920). Yule's work, in which a page of text is sometimes followed by ten times its length in notes, is a treasury to which every student and editor of Polo's work is endlessly indebted.

But the uncovering of new material about Polo will never cease, and scholars such as Luigi Benedetto, who published in 1928 an edition based on all known manuscripts, and A. C. Moule and Paul Pelliot, who in 1934 brought out a composite edition incorporating the newly found Zelada manuscript, continue to make contributions to the study of the man and his book.

The aim of the present edition is to combine a readable text in modern English with the numerous notes that most first—or even second—readers find necessary. To this end I have used the Marsden-Wright text, chiefly because it remains among the fullest and richest. After collating it with translations—by Henry Yule, Aldo Ricci, A. C. Moule and Paul Pelliot, and R. E. Latham—of various other texts, I edited it line for line, mainly to eliminate redundant, stilted, or archaic locutions, and to clarify the considerable number of confusing or unintelligible passages. In my notes (the shorter ones are in brackets and the longer ones in footnotes) and in this Introduction I have drawn on the work of all the scholars mentioned above, and among others, of Percy Sykes, William Rockhill, Henry Hart, N. M. Penzer, Manuel Komroff, and Harold Lamb.

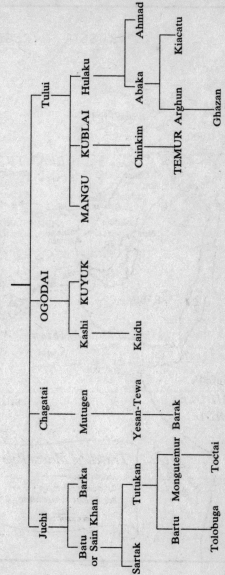

PRINCIPAL FIGURES OF THE HOUSE OF GENGHIS KHAN
(The names of the Great Khans are in capitals)

GENGHIS KHAN

Juchi — Chagatai — OGODAI — Tului

House of Juchi
(Khans of the West)

Batu or Sain Khan — Barka

Sartak — Tutukan

Bartu — Mongutemur — Toctai

Tolobuga

House of Chagatai
(Khans of Turkestan)

Mutugen

Yesan-Tewa

Barak

House of Ogodai
(Yuan Dynasty of China)

Kashi — KUYUK

Kaidu

House of Kublai
(Yuan Dynasty of China)

MANGU — KUBLAI — Hulaku

Chinkim

TEMUR

House of Hulaku
(Khans of the Levant)

Abaka — Ahmad

Arghun — Kiacatu

Ghazan

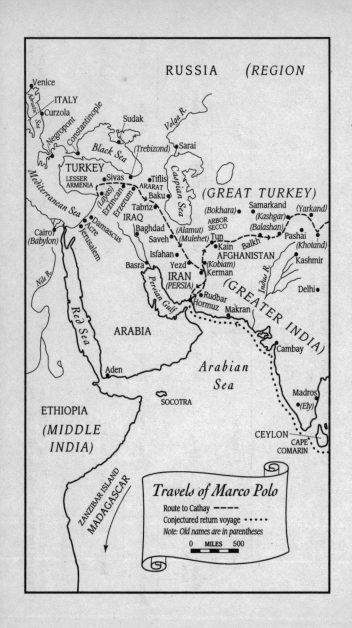

The Travels of
MARCO POLO

PROLOGUE

You emperors, kings, dukes, marquises, earls, and knights, and all other people desirous of knowing the diversity of the races of mankind, as well as of kingdoms, provinces, and regions of all parts of the East, read through this book, and you will find in it the greatest and most marvelous characteristics of the peoples especially of Armenia, Persia, India, and Tartary, as they are severally described in the present work by Marco Polo, a wise and learned citizen of Venice, who clearly states what things he saw and what things he heard from others. For this book will be a truthful one.

It must be known, then, that from the creation of Adam to the present day, no man, whether pagan, or Saracen, or Christian, or other, of whatever progeny or generation he may have been, ever saw or inquired into so many and such great things as this Marco Polo. Wishing in his private thoughts that the things he had seen and heard should be made public for the benefit of those who could not see them with their own eyes, he himself being in the year of our Lord 1298 in prison in Genoa, caused the things contained in the present work to be written by Master Rustichello, a citizen of Pisa, who was with him in the same prison. And he divided it into three parts.

3

CHAPTER 1

*How the Brothers Nicolo and Maffeo Polo Set Forth
from Constantinople to Traverse the World*

IT SHOULD be made known to the reader that at the time when Baldwin II was Emperor of Constantinople (where a magistrate representing the Doge of Venice then resided), and in the year of our Lord 1250,* Nicolo Polo, the father of the said Marco, and Maffeo, the brother of Nicolo, respectable and well-informed men, embarked in a ship of their own, with a rich and varied cargo of merchandise, and reached Constantinople in safety. After much deliberation, they determined to try to improve their trading business by continuing their voyage into the Euxine or Black Sea.

With this in view they made purchases of many fine and costly jewels, and taking their departure from Constantinople, navigated that sea to a port named Soldaia [Sudak, on the Crimean coast]. From there they traveled on horseback many days until they reached the court of a powerful chief of the Western Tartars, named Barka Khan [grandson of Genghis Khan and ruler of the Tartars of southern Russia], who dwelt in the cities of Bolgara and Assara [or Sarai]† and had the reputation of being one of the most liberal and civilized princes among the tribes of Tartary. He expressed much satisfaction at the arrival of these travelers, and received them with marks of distinction. In return for his courtesy, they laid before him the jewels they brought with them; and seeing that their beauty pleased him, they presented them to him. The liberality of this conduct aroused his admiration; and being unwilling that they should surpass him in generosity, he not only directed double the value of the jewels to be paid to them, but also made them several rich presents.

The brothers having remained for a year in the domin-

---

*This date seems to be several years too early, if (as Polo tells us) they left Venice just before Marco's birth. Some editors have changed this to 1260 and made that the date on which the travelers left Constantinople.
†Near present-day Tsarev, about 200 miles up the Volga. Bolgara, which had been the capital of the Bulgars, was about 800 miles up the river.

ions of this prince, they became desirous of revisiting their native country, but were hindered by the sudden breaking out of a war between Barka and a chief named Hulaku [another grandson of Genghis and brother of the Great Khans, Mangu and Kublai], who ruled over the Eastern Tartars. In a fierce and very bloody battle between their armies, Hulaku was victorious, in consequence of which, the roads being rendered unsafe, the brothers could not return by the way they came. They were advised that the only practical way to reach Constantinople was to proceed in an easterly direction by an unfrequented route so as to skirt the limits of Barka's territories.* Accordingly they made their way to a town named Oukaka, situated on the boundary of the Kingdom of the Western Tartars. Leaving that place and advancing still further they crossed the Tigris [actually the Volga], one of the four rivers of Paradise,† and came to a desert, the extent of which was seventeen days' journey, wherein they found neither town, castle, nor any substantial building, but only Tartars with their herds, dwelling in tents on the plain.

Having passed through this territory, they arrived at length at a well-built city, called Bokhara [a center of trade about 500 miles east of the Caspian Sea], in a province of that name. Belonging to the dominions of Persia, it is the noblest city of that kingdom and is governed by a prince named Barak. Unable to proceed further, they remained here three years.

CHAPTER 2

How the Brothers Were Persuaded to Visit the Court of the Great Khan

IT HAPPENED while these brothers were in Bokhara that a person of consequence and gifted with great talents made his appearance there. As ambassador from Hulaku, mentioned above, he was on the way to the Great Khan, supreme chief of all the Tartars, who lived

---

*And thus return to Constantinople by a roundabout route.
†Some church historians seem to have thought that the Tigris (Volga) flowed under the Caspian Sea on its way out of Paradise.

at the far edge of the continent in a direction between northeast and east. Never having had an opportunity of seeing any natives of Italy, he was highly gratified at meeting and conversing with these brothers, who had now become proficient in the Tartar language. After associating with them for several days and finding their manners agreeable, he proposed to them that they should accompany him to the Great Khan, who would be pleased by their coming to his court [at Peiping], which had not been visited by any person from their country. He added assurances that they would be honorably received and rewarded with many gifts. Convinced that their attempts to return home would expose them to the gravest risks, they agreed to this proposal; and commending themselves to the protection of the Almighty, they set out on their journey in the suite of the ambassador, attended by several Christian servants whom they had brought with them from Venice.

The course they took at first was between the northeast and north, and an entire year passed before they reached the imperial residence, in consequence of extraordinary delays resulting from snows and swollen rivers, which obliged them to halt until the snows had melted and the floods had subsided. They observed many noteworthy things on their journey, but these are here omitted, since they will be described by Marco Polo later in this book.

CHAPTER 3

How the Great Khan Sent the Two Brothers as His Envoys to the Pope

BEING introduced to the presence of the Great Khan, Kublai, the travelers were received by him with great hospitality and friendliness; and as they were the first Latins to visit that country, they were entertained with feasts and honored with other marks of distinction. Entering graciously into conversation with them, he made earnest inquiries concerning the western parts of the world, the Emperor of the Romans, and other Christian kings and princes. He wished to be informed of their relative importance, their possessions, the manner in which justice was administered in their kingdoms, and how they conducted themselves in warfare. Above all he questioned them about the Pope, the affairs of the Church, and the religious worship and doctrine of the Christians. Being well instructed and discreet men, they gave appropriate answers on all these points in the Tartar language, with which they were perfectly acquainted. The result was that the Great Khan, holding them in high esteem, frequently summoned them to talk with him.

When he had obtained all the information that the two brothers could give him, he was well satisfied. Having decided to use them as ambassadors to the Pope, he proposed to them, with many kind entreaties, that they should accompany one of his barons, named Kogatal, on a mission to the See of Rome.

His object, he told them, was to request his Holiness to send him a hundred men of learning, thoroughly acquainted with the principles of the Christian religion as well as with the seven arts.* They were to be qualified to prove to the learned of his dominions by just and fair argument that the faith professed by Christians is superior to, and founded upon more evident truth than, any other; that the gods of the Tartars and the idols worshiped in their houses are only evil spirits, and that they and the people of the East in general were under an error in revering them as divinities. He said, moreover, that he would be pleased if upon their return they should bring with them from Jerusalem some of the holy oil† from the lamp which is kept burning over the Sepulcher of our Lord Jesus Christ, whom he professed to hold in veneration and to consider the true God. Having heard these commands by the Great Khan they humbly prostrated themselves before him, declaring their willingness and instant readiness to perform to the utmost of their ability whatever might be the royal will. Upon which he caused letters to be written in the Tartar language in his

*These were usually considered to be rhetoric, logic, grammar, arithmetic, astronomy, music, and geometry.
†One Polo manuscript explains that he wanted it for his mother, who had become a Christian. But she is believed to have died long before.

name to the Pope of Rome, and these he turned over to them.

He likewise gave orders that they should be furnished with a golden tablet displaying the imperial cipher, according to the custom established by his majesty. By virtue of this, the bearer, together with his whole suite, are safely conveyed and escorted from station to station by the governors of all places within the imperial dominions, and are entitled, during the time of their stay in any city, castle, town, or village, to a supply of provisions and everything necessary for their accommodation. Thus honorably commissioned, they took leave of the Great Khan and set out on their journey, but had not proceeded more than twenty days when the officer named Kogatal, their companion, fell dangerously ill, and unable to proceed further, halted at a certain city. In this dilemma it was determined, upon consulting all who were present and with the approval of the man himself, that they should leave him behind.

In their journey they were greatly assisted by the royal tablet, which secured them attention in every place through which they passed. Their expenses were taken care of and escorts were furnished. But notwithstanding these advantages, so great were the natural difficulties they had to encounter—from extreme cold, snow, ice, and the flooding of rivers—that their progress was unavoidably tedious, and three years passed before they reached a seaport town, named Layas, in Lesser Armenia. Departing from there by sea, they arrived at Acre [an important seaport in northern Palestine] in the month of April, 1269, and there learned with dismay that Pope Clement the Fourth had recently died. A legate whom he had appointed, named Tedaldo of Piacenza, was at this time resident in Acre, and to him they gave an account of the mission they had been given by the Great Khan of Tartary. He advised them by all means to await the election of another pope, and when that had taken place, to carry out their embassy.

Approving of this, they determined to use the interval for a visit to their families in Venice. They accordingly embarked at Acre in a ship bound for Negropont [an island in the eastern Aegean Sea] and from there went on to Venice. There Nicolo Polo found that his wife, whom he had left with child at his departure, had died after having been delivered of a son. The boy had been named Marco and was now fifteen years of age. This is the Marco by whom the present work is composed and who will give therein an account of all those matters of which he has been an eyewitness.

CHAPTER 4

How the Two Brothers Again Departed from Venice on Their Way Back to the Great Khan and Took with Them Marco, Son of Messer Nicolo

IN THE meantime the election of a pope was delayed by so many obstacles that they remained two years in Venice, continually expecting it to take place. At length, becoming fearful that the Great Khan might be displeased at their delay, or might suppose they did not intend to revisit his country, they judged it wise to return to Acre; and on this occasion they took with them young Marco Polo. With the permission of the legate they made a visit to Jerusalem, and there provided themselves with some of the oil from the lamp of the Holy Sepulcher, as the Great Khan had requested. As soon as they were furnished with letters from the legate to the Khan testifying to their efforts to carry out his commission, and explaining that the Pope of the Christian Church had not as yet been chosen, they proceeded to the before-mentioned port of Layas.

Scarcely had they left, however, when the legate received messengers from Italy, dispatched by the College of Cardinals, announcing his own elevation [on September 1, 1271] to the papal chair. He thereupon assumed the name of Gregory the Tenth. Believing that he was now in a position to satisfy the wishes of the Tartar sovereign, he hastened to send letters to the King of Armenia, telling him of his election and requesting, in case the two ambassadors on their way to the Great Khan had not already quit his dominions, that he would give directions for their immediate return. These letters found them still in Armenia, and they promptly obeyed the summons to come once more to Acre. For this purpose the King furnished them with an armed galley, sending at the same time an ambassador with his congratulations to the pontiff.

Upon their arrival, his Holiness received them with honor and immediately dispatched them with papal letters, and with two friars of the Order of Preachers, learned men as well as profound theologians. One of them was named Friar Nicholas of Vicenza, and the other, Friar William of Tripoli. To them he gave authority to ordain priests, consecrate bishops, and grant absolution as fully as he could in his own person. He also entrusted them with valuable presents, including several handsome vases of crystal, to be delivered to the Great Khan in his name and along with his benediction. Having taken leave, they again steered their course to the port of Layas, where they landed, and from there proceeded into the country of Armenia.

Here they received news that the Sultan of Babylonia [that is, Babylon of Egypt, an old name for Cairo], named Bundokdari, had invaded the Armenian territory with a large army and had overrun and laid waste much of the country. Terrified at these accounts, the two friars determined not to proceed further; and turning over to the Venetians the letters and presents entrusted to them by the Pope, they placed themselves under the protection of the Master of the Temple [Knights Templars] and with him returned directly to the coast.

Nicolo, Maffeo, and Marco, however, undismayed by perils or difficulties—to which they had long been inured—crossed the borders of Armenia and continued on their journey. After crossing deserts of several days' march and many dangerous passes, they progressed so far in a direction between northeast and north that at length they had word of the Great Khan, who then had his residence in a large and magnificent city named Kemenfu [Shangtu, Chandu, or Xanadu, north of Peiping; it became Kublai's summer capital]. Their whole journey to this place occupied no less than three years and a half [1271 to 1275]; during the winter months they had of course made little progress. The Great Khan having been notified of their approach while they were still far off, and being aware of how much they must have suffered from fatigue, sent men to meet them a distance of forty days' journey, and gave orders to prepare in every place through which they were to pass whatever might be needed for their comfort. By these means, and through the blessing of God, they were conveyed in safety to the royal court.

CHAPTER 5

How the Brothers and Marco Presented Themselves Before the Great Khan

Upon their arrival they were honorably and graciously received by the Great Khan in a full assembly of his principal officers. When they drew near him, they paid their respects by prostrating themselves. He immediately commanded them to rise and to give him an account of their travels, with all that had taken place in their negotiation with his Holiness the Pope. To their story, which was clear and well-told, he listened with attentive silence. The letters and the presents from Pope Gregory were then laid before him, and upon hearing the former read, he commended the fidelity, zeal, and diligence of his emissaries; and receiving with due reverence the oil from the Holy Sepulcher, he gave directions that it should be preserved zealously. Upon his observing Marco Polo and inquiring who he was, Nicolo answered, "This is my son and your servant"; upon which the Great Khan replied, "He is welcome, and it pleases me much," and he caused him to be enrolled amongst his attendants of honor. And in recognition of their return he ordered a great feast and rejoicing; and as long as the brothers and Marco remained in the court of the Great Khan they were honored even above his own courtiers.

Marco was held in high esteem and respect by all belonging to the court. He soon learned and adopted the manners of the Tartars and acquired a proficiency in four different languages,* which he became qualified to

*It is thought that Marco knew Mongol, Turkish, Persian, and, although this is very doubtful, Chinese.

read and write. Finding him thus accomplished, his master was desirous of putting to use his talents for business and sent him on an important mission of state to a city named Karajan [or Karazan, in Yunnan, a province of southwest China], situated at a distance of six months' journey from the imperial residence. On this occasion he conducted himself with so much wisdom and prudence in the affairs entrusted to him that his services became highly acceptable. On his part, perceiving that the Great Khan took a pleasure in hearing accounts of whatever was new to him respecting the customs and manners of people, and the peculiar circumstances of distant countries, he tried wherever he went to obtain information on these subjects, and made notes of all he saw and heard in order to gratify the curiosity of his master.

In short, during the seventeen years that he continued in his service, he made himself so useful that he was employed on confidential missions to every part of the empire and its dependencies. And sometimes he also traveled on his own account, but always with the consent and sanction of the Great Khan. Thus it was that Marco Polo had the opportunity of acquiring a knowledge, either by his own observation or what he collected from others, of so many things, until his time unknown, respecting the eastern parts of the world, which he diligently committed to writing, as will later appear. And by this means he obtained so much honor that he aroused the jealousy of the other officers of the court.

CHAPTER 6

How Messers Nicolo, Maffeo, and Marco Asked Permission of the Great Khan to Leave

OUR Venetians, having now resided many years at the imperial court and in that time having amassed considerable wealth in jewels and in gold, felt a strong desire to revisit their native country; and, however honored and well treated by the sovereign, this sentiment was ever uppermost in their minds. It became even more decidedly their object when they thought of the very advanced age of the Great Khan, and the fact that his death, if it should occur before their departure, might deprive them of the assistance they would need to surmount the innumerable difficulties of so long a journey and reach their homes in safety.

Nicolo Polo accordingly took an opportunity one day, when he observed the Khan to be more than usually cheerful, of throwing himself at his feet, and appealed on behalf of himself and his family for permission to depart. But far from seeming disposed to comply, the Khan appeared hurt at the appeal, and asked what motive they could have for wishing to expose themselves to all the hazards of a journey in which they would probably lose their lives. If gain, he said, was their object, he was ready to give them double whatever they possessed and to gratify them with honors to the full extent of their desires; but that, from the regard he had for them, he must positively refuse their petition.

It happened about this period that a queen named Bolgana [Bulughan], the wife of Arghun, Sovereign of India [actually Persia], died, and her last request—which she repeated in a will—entreated her husband that no one might succeed to her place on his throne and in his affections who was not a descendant of her own family, which was now settled under the dominion of the Great Khan of Cathay. Wishing to comply with this solemn request, Arghun appointed three of his barons, discreet men, whose names were Ulatai, Apushka, and Koja, together with a numerous retinue, as his ambassadors to the Great Khan, with a request that the Khan find him a wife from among the relatives of his deceased queen. The application was taken in good part, and under the direction of his Majesty, choice was made of a damsel of seventeen, very beautiful and accomplished, whose name was Kokachin, and of whom the ambassadors highly approved. When everything was arranged for their departure, and a suite of attendants appointed to do honor to the future consort of King Arghun, they received a gracious farewell from the Great Khan and set out on their return by the way they had come. Having traveled for eight months, their progress was blocked and the roads shut against them by fresh wars that had broken out among the Tartar princes. Much against their will they were forced to turn back to the court of the Great Khan and tell him of the interruption they had met with.

About the time of their turning back, Marco Polo happened to arrive from a voyage he had made, with a few vessels under his command, to some parts of the East Indies [in some manuscripts, India], and reported to the Great Khan concerning the countries he had visited, with the details of his voyage, which, he said, was made with the utmost safety. This latter observation having reached the ears of the three barons, who were extremely anxious to return to their own country, from which they had now been absent three years, they sought a conference with our Venetians, whom they found equally desirous of going home. It was settled between them that the former, accompanied by their young Queen, should obtain an audience with the Great Khan and represent to him how conveniently and safely they might return by sea to the dominions of their master, a voyage that would be less costly than the journey by land and be performed in a shorter time—all this according to the experience of Marco Polo, who had lately sailed in those parts.

Should his Majesty incline to give his consent to their suggestion, they were then to urge him to allow the three Europeans, as persons skilled in navigation, to accompany them to the territory of King Arghun. On hearing this appeal, the Great Khan showed by his countenance that it was very displeasing to him, unwilling as he was to have the Venetians leave. Feeling nevertheless that he could not properly withhold his consent, he yielded. Had he not been forced by this peculiar situation, they would never have obtained permission to leave his service.

He sent for them, however, and addressed them with much kindness and friendliness, assuring them of his regard, and exacted from them a promise that when they had stayed some time in Europe and with their own family, they would return to him once more. With this in view he caused them to be given golden tablets ordering their free and safe conduct through every part of his dominions, with all necessary supplies for themselves and their attendants. He likewise gave them authority to act as his emissaries to the Pope, the kings of France and Spain [one Polo manuscript also mentions England], and the other Christian princes.

CHAPTER 7

How the Two Brothers and Messer Marco Left the Great Khan and Returned Home

AT THE same time preparations were made for equipping fourteen ships, each having four masts and nine sails, the construction and rigging of which would admit of a long description; but it is for the present omitted. Among these vessels there were at least four or five that had crews of 250 or 260 men. On them were embarked the barons, with the Queen under their protection, together with Nicolo, Maffeo, and Marco Polo. When they took leave of the Great Khan, he presented them with many rubies and other fine jewels. He also gave directions that the ships should be furnished with stores and provisions for two years.

After a voyage of about three months in a southerly direction, they arrived at an island named Java [actually Sumatra], where they saw various objects worthy of attention, of which notice shall be taken later in this work. Departing thence,* they spent eighteen months in the Indian seas before they could reach their destination in the territory of King Arghun; and also during this part of their voyage they had an opportunity of observing many things, which shall be related hereafter. But here it may be proper to mention that between the day of their sailing and that of their arrival, they lost, among the crews of the vessels and others, about six hundred persons; and of the three barons, only one, whose name was Koja, survived the voyage. But of all the ladies and female attendants only one died.

Upon landing they were informed that King Arghun had died some time before and that the government of the country was then administered, on behalf of his son, who was still a youth, by a person named Kiacatu. From

*Yule dates their departure from Sumatra in September 1292, and their arrival at Hormuz early in 1294.

him they asked instructions as to how they should dispose of the Princess, whom, by order of the late King, they had conducted thither. His answer was that they ought to present the lady to Casan [Ghazan], the son of Arghun, who was then at Arbor Secco, a place on the borders of Persia [in the province of Khorasan], where an army of sixty thousand men was assembled to guard certain passes against an invasion by the enemy.

Having done this, they returned to the residence of Kiacatu, because the road they were afterward to take lay in that direction. Here, however, they rested for the space of nine months. When they took their leave, he furnished them with four golden tablets, each of them a cubit [about 18 inches] in length, five inches wide, and weighing three or four marks of gold. Their inscription began with invoking the blessing of the Almighty upon the Great Khan, that his name might be held in reverence for many years, and threatening death and confiscating of goods to all who disobeyed. It directed that the three ambassadors, as his representatives, should be treated throughout his dominions with honor, that their expenses should be defrayed, and that they should be provided with the necessary escorts. All this was complied with fully and in many places they were protected by bodies of two hundred horsemen; nor could they have done without this, as the government of Kiacatu was unpopular and the people were disposed to insult them and cause trouble, which they would not have dared under the rule of their proper sovereign.

In the course of their journey our travelers received news that the Great Khan Kublai had departed this life, which put an end to all prospect of their revisiting those regions. Pursuing, therefore, their intended route, they at length reached the city of Trebizond, whence they proceeded to Constantinople, then to Negropont, and finally to Venice, at which place, enjoying health and riches, they arrived in the year 1295.

On this occasion they offered up their thanks to God, who had now been pleased to relieve them from such great fatigues, after having preserved them from innumerable perils. The foregoing narrative may be considered as a preliminary chapter, the object of which is to make the reader acquainted with the opportunities Marco Polo had, during a residence of so many years in the eastern parts of the world, of acquiring a knowledge of things he describes.

BOOK I

✳

OF REGIONS VISITED OR HEARD OF ON
THE JOURNEY FROM LESSER ARMENIA
TO THE COURT OF THE GREAT KHAN AT
SHANGTU

Book 1

❋

CHAPTER 1

Armenia Minor and the Port of Layas

IN BEGINNING the description of the countries Marco Polo visited in Asia, and of things which he observed therein, it is proper to distinguish two Armenias, the Lesser and the Greater. The king of Lesser Armenia dwells in a city called Sebastoz, and rules his dominions with strict justice. The towns, fortified places, and castles are numerous. There is an abundance of all the necessities of life, as well as of those things which contribute to comfort. Game, both beasts and birds, is plentiful. It must be said, however, that the air of the country is not remarkably healthy. In former times its gentry were esteemed expert and brave soldiers; but at the present day they are great drinkers, mean-spirited, and worthless.

On the seacoast is a busy city named Layas. Its port is frequented by merchants from Venice, Genoa, and many other places, who trade in spices and drugs of different sorts, silk and wool, and other rich commodities. Those who plan to travel into the interior of the Levant usually start from this port. The boundaries of Lesser Armenia are, on the south, the Promised Land, now occupied by the Saracens; on the north, Karaman, inhabited by Turkomans; towards the northeast, the cities of Kaisariah, Sevasta [Sivas], and many others subject to the Tartars; and on the western side, the sea, which extends to the shores of Christendom.

CHAPTER 2

Of the Province Called Turkomania

THE inhabitants of Turkomania [modern Anatolia] may be distinguished into three classes. The Turkomans, who reverence Mahomet and follow his law, are a primitive people and dull of intellect. They dwell among the mountains and in places difficult of access, where their object is to find good pasture for their cattle, as they live entirely upon animal food. There is here an excellent breed of horses, called Turki, and fine mules which are sold at high prices. The other races are Greeks and Armenians, who reside in the cities and fortified places, and gain their living by commerce and manufacture. The best and handsomest carpets in the world are woven here, and also silks of crimson and other rich colors. Among its cities are Kogni [Kuniyah], Kaisariah, and Sevasta, in which last Saint Blaise obtained the glorious crown of martyrdom. They are all subject to the Great Khan, Emperor of the Oriental Tartars, who appoints governors to them. We shall now speak of Greater Armenia.

CHAPTER 3

Of Armenia Major, of the Mountain Where the Ark of Noah Rested, and of a Remarkable Fountain of Oil

ARMENIA Major is a large province. Entering it, one comes to a city named Arzingan [Erzincan], where the inhabitants manufacture a very fine cotton cloth called bombazine, as well as many other fabrics which it would be tedious to enumerate. It possesses the handsomest and most excellent baths of warm spring water found anywhere. Its inhabitants are for the most part native Armenians, but under the dominion of the Tartars. In this province there are many cities, but Arzingan is the principal one and the seat of an archbishop; and the next in importance are Argiron and Darziz [Erzerum and Ercis]. It is very extensive, and in the summer season, the station of a part of the army of the Eastern Tartars, on account of the good pasture it affords for their cattle. But on the approach of winter they are obliged to change their quarters, the fall of snow being so very deep that the horses cannot find fodder, and for the sake of warmth and fodder they go southward. At a castle named Paipurth, which you meet with in going from Trebizond to Tauris [Tabriz], there is a rich silver mine.

In the central part of Armenia stands an exceedingly large and high mountain, upon which, it is said, Noah's Ark rested; and for this reason it is termed the Mountain of the Ark [Mt. Ararat in Eastern Turkey; its height is 16,696 feet]. Its base cannot be circled in less than two days. The ascent is impracticable on account of the snow towards the summit, which never melts, but goes on increasing with each successive fall. In the lower region, however, near the plain, the melting of the snow fertilizes the ground and encourages such an abundant vegetation that all the cattle which gather there in summer from the surrounding territory find a never-failing supply. Bordering upon Armenia to the southwest are the districts of Mosul and Maredin, which will be described hereafter, and many others too numerous to particularize. To the north lies Zorzania [Georgia], near the border of which there is a fountain of oil [probably the oil fields of Baku], which discharges so great a quantity of oil as to furnish loads for many camels. It is used not as food, but as an unguent for the cure of rashes in men and cattle, as well as other complaints; and it is also good for burning. In the neighboring country no other fuel is used in lamps, and people come from distant parts to procure it.*

---

*Petroleum was widely used by ancient Mediterranean peoples such as the Egyptians and the Romans, but almost completely abandoned in the Middle Ages.

CHAPTER 4

*Of the Province of Zorzania, the Pass Where
Alexander the Great Constructed the Iron
Gate and the Miraculous Fountain of Tiflis*

IN ZORZANIA the king is usually styled David Melik,
which in our language signifies David the King. One part
of the country is subject to the Tartars, and the other
part, in consequence of the strength of its fortresses, has
remained in the possession of its native princes. It is situated between two seas, of which that on the northern
[western] side is called the Greater Sea [Black], and the
other on the eastern side is called the Sea of Baku [Cas-
pian]. This latter is 2,800 miles in circuit, and is like a
lake, for it does not connect with any other sea. It has
several islands, with handsome towns and castles, some
of which are inhabited by people who fled before the
Grand Tartar when he laid waste the kingdom of Persia,
and who took shelter in these islands or in the fastnesses
of the mountains. Some of the islands are uncultivated.
This sea produces an abundance of fish, particularly stur-
geon and salmon at the mouths of the rivers, as well as
others of a large sort. The common wood of the country
is boxwood.

I was told that in ancient times the kings of the country were born with the mark of an eagle on the right
shoulder. The people are well made, bold sailors, expert
archers, and fair combatants in battle. They are Christians, observing the ritual of the Greek Church, and
wear their hair short, in the manner of the Western
clergy.

This is the province into which, when Alexander the
Great attempted to advance northwards, he was unable
to penetrate by reason of the narrowness and difficulty
of a certain pass. On one side this pass is washed by the
sea and on the other it is confined by high mountains
and woods for a distance of four miles; so that a very
few men were capable of defending it against the whole
world. Disappointed in this attempt, Alexander caused
a great wall to be constructed at the entrance of the pass
and fortified it with towers, in order to prevent those
who dwelt beyond it from molesting him. From its un-

usual strength the pass got the name of the Iron Gate,* and Alexander is commonly said to have enclosed the Tartars between two mountains.

It is not correct, however, to call these people Tartars, because in those days they were not Tartars, but of a people called Comanians, with a mixture of other nations. In this province there are many towns and castles. The necessities of life are abundant, and the country produces a great quantity of silk and engages in the manufacture of silk interwoven with gold. Here are found large vultures of a species named *avigi*. The inhabitants in general gain their livelihood by trade and handicrafts. The mountainous nature of the country, with its narrow and strong defiles, has prevented the Tartars from completing the conquest of it.

At a convent of monks dedicated to Saint Lunardo, the following miraculous events are said to take place. In a salt-water lake, four days' journey in circuit, upon the border of which the church is situated, the fish never make their appearance until the first day of Lent, and from that time to Easter eve they are found in vast abundance; but on Easter day they are no longer to be seen, nor during the remainder of the year. It is called the Lake of Geluchalat. The great rivers Herdil, Geihon, Kur, Araz [respectively, the Volga, Amu Daria, Kura, and Araxes], and many others empty into the aforementioned Sea of Baku, which is surrounded by mountains. Genoese merchants have recently begun to navigate it, and they bring from there the kind of silk called *ghellie*. In this province there is a handsome city named Tiflis, around which are suburbs and many fortified posts. It is inhabited by Armenian and Georgian Christians, as well as by some Mahometans and Jews; but these last are not numerous. The manufactures of silk and many other articles is carried on there. Its inhabitants are subjects of the Great Khan of the Tartars.

Although we speak only of a few of the principal cities in each province, it should be understood that there are many others, which it would be pointless to enumerate

*This has been identified as a wall at Derbend in the Caucasus, but Alexander's connection with it is considered merely a legend.

unless they happened to contain something remarkable. Having spoken of the countries bordering on Armenia to the north, we shall now mention those which lie to the south and to the east.

CHAPTER 5

Of the Province of Mosul and the People Named Kurds

MOSUL is a large province inhabited by various types of people, one group of which pay reverence to Mahomet and are called Arabians. The others profess the Christian faith, but not according to the canons of the Church, which they depart from in many instances, and are called Nestorians,* Jacobites, and Armenians. They have a patriarch whom they call Jacolit [the Arabic form of Catholic], and he consecrates archbishops, bishops, and abbots and sends them to all parts of India, to Baudas [Baghdad], or to Cathay, just as the Pope of Rome does in the Latin countries.

All those cloths of gold and of silk which we call muslins† are of Mosul manufacture, and all the great merchants, called Mossulini, who convey large quantities of spices and drugs from one country to another, are from this province.

In the mountainous parts there is a race of people named Kurds, some of whom are Christians and others Mahometans. They are all an unprincipled people whose occupation it is to rob merchants. In the vicinity of this province there are places named Mus and Mardin, where they produce in great abundance the cotton from which are made the cloth called buckram, and many other fabrics. The inhabitants are manufacturers and traders. They are all subjects of the king of the Tartars. We shall now speak of the city of Baudas.

---

*Named after a patriarch of Constantinople who was deposed as a heretic in 431 for maintaining that there were two persons, one divine and one human, in Jesus. The Nestorians founded churches throughout Asia, including one in China under the tolerant Emperor T'ai Tsung.
†Evidently not the cotton cloth called muslin today.

CHAPTER 6

Of the Great City of Baudas,
Anciently Called Babylon

BAUDAS [Baghdad] is a large city,* heretofore the residence of the Caliph, or Pontiff, of all the Saracens, as the Pope is of all Christians. A great river flows through the middle of it, by means of which the merchants transport their goods to and from the Indian Sea, the distance being computed at seventeen days' navigation, in consequence of the windings of its course. Those who undertake the voyage, after leaving the river, touch at a place named Kisi [Kais], whence they proceed to sea; but before reaching this anchorage they pass a city named Balsara [Basra], in the vicinity of which are groves of palm trees producing the best dates in the world.

In Baudas there are manufactured silks woven with gold, and also damasks, as well as velvets ornamented with the figures of birds and beasts. Almost all the pearls brought to Europe from India undergo the process of boring at this place. The Mahometan law is here regularly studied, as are also magic, physics, astronomy, geomancy, and physiognomy. It is the noblest and largest city in this part of the world.

The Caliph, who is understood to have amassed greater treasures than have ever been possessed by any other sovereign, perished miserably under the following circumstances. At the period when the Tartar princes began to extend their dominion, there were among them four brothers, of whom the eldest, Mangu, reigned in the royal seat. Having subdued the country of Cathay, and other districts in that quarter, they were not satisfied, but coveting further territory, they conceived the idea of Universal Empire, and proposed that they should divide the world amongst them. With this in view, it was agreed that one of them should proceed to the east, another should make conquests in the south, and the other two should direct their operations against the remaining quarters.

*The description of this fabulous city is here so brief that some scholars believe Polo did not visit it himself.

The southern portion fell to the lot of Hulaku, who assembled a vast army, and having subdued the provinces through which his route lay, proceeded in the year 1255 [actually 1258] to attack this city of Baudas. Being aware, however, of its great strength and the prodigious number of its inhabitants, he trusted rather to stratagem than to force for its reduction. In order to deceive the enemy with regard to the number of his troops, which consisted of a hundred thousand horsemen besides foot soldiers, he posted one division of his army on one side of the approach to the city, and another division on the other side, in such a manner as to be concealed by a wood. Then placing himself at the head of a third, he advanced boldly to within a short distance of the gate. The Caliph made light of a force apparently so inconsiderable, and confident of the effect of the usual Mahometan ejaculation, thought of nothing less than its entire destruction, and for that purpose marched out of the city with his guards. But as soon as Hulaku saw him approach, he feigned retreat, until he had drawn him beyond the wood where the other divisions were posted. By the closing in of these from both sides, the army of the Caliph was surrounded and broken. The Caliph was made prisoner, and the city surrendered to the conqueror. Upon entering it Hulaku discovered to his great astonishment a tower filled with gold. He called the Caliph before him, and reproached him with the greediness which had prevented him from spending his treasures on an army to defend his capital against the invasion with which it had long been threatened. He then gave orders for him to be shut up in this same tower without sustenance;* and there, in the midst of his wealth, the Caliph soon finished his miserable existence.

---

*One Polo manuscript says that Hulaku, seeing the vast hoard of gold, ordered the Caliph to eat the gold or starve, whereupon the captive "lingered for four days and then died like a dog."

CHAPTER 7

How the Caliph Took Counsel. to Slay All Christians

I JUDGE that our Lord Jesus Christ herein thought proper to avenge the wrongs of his faithful Christians, so abhorred by this Caliph. From the time of his accession in 1225, his daily thoughts were devoted to ways of converting those who resided within his dominions, or, on their refusal, in finding pretexts for putting them to death. Consulting with his learned men for this purpose, they discovered a passage in the Gospel which said: "If ye have faith as large as a grain of mustard seed, ye shall say unto this mountain—Move to yonder place, and it shall move," and rejoicing at the discovery, persuaded as he was that the feat was utterly impossible, he gave orders for assembling all the very numerous Nestorian and Jacobite Christians who dwelt in Baghdad.

To these the question was posed, whether they believed all that is asserted in the text of their Gospel to be true or not. They answered that it was true. "Then," said the Caliph, "if it be true, let us see which of you will give the proof of his faith; for certainly if there is not to be found one amongst you who possesses even so small a portion of faith in his Lord as to be equal to a grain of mustard seed, I shall be justified in regarding you henceforth as a wicked and faithless people. I allow you therefore ten days, by which time you must either remove the mountain now before you through the power of Him whom you worship, or embrace the law of our prophet. In either case you will be safe; otherwise you must all expect to suffer the most cruel death."

CHAPTER 8

How the Christians Were in Great Dismay

THE Christians, acquainted with his merciless disposition, as well as his eagerness to deprive them of their property, upon hearing these words, trembled for their lives; but nevertheless, having confidence in their Redeemer, and that He would deliver them, they gathered to deliberate on the course they ought to take. No other presented itself than that of imploring the Divine Being to grant them the aid of his mercy. To obtain this, every individual, great and small, prostrated himself night and day, shedding tears profusely, and doing naught but pray to the Lord. When they had thus persevered during eight days, a divine revelation came at length in a dream to a bishop of exemplary life, directing him to seek out a certain cobbler (whose name is not known) having only one eye. The bishop was told that he should summon the cobbler to the mountain, as a person capable through divine grace of causing it to move.

CHAPTER 9

How the One-eyed Cobbler Prayed for the Christians

HAVING found the cobbler and acquainted him with the revelation, he replied that he did not feel himself worthy of the undertaking, his merits not being such as to entitle him to such abundant grace. Implored, however, by the poor terrified Christians, he at length agreed. It should be understood that he was a man of strict morals and pious conversation, with a mind pure and faithful to his God, regularly attending the celebration of the Mass and other divine offices, fervent in works of charity, and strict in the observance of fasts.

It once happened that a handsome young woman, who came to his shop in order to be fitted with a pair of shoes, accidentally exposed a part of her leg while presenting her foot. The beauty of the leg excited in him momentary sinful thoughts. Calling to mind the words of the Gospel, "If thine eye offend thee, pluck it out and cast it from thee; for it is better to enter the kingdom of God with one eye than, having two eyes, to be cast into hell-fire," he immediately, with an instrument of his trade, scooped out his right eye. By this act you can judge the degree of his faith.

The appointed day having arrived, divine service was performed at an early hour, and a solemn procession was made to the plain where the mountain stood, the holy cross being borne in front. The Caliph, certain that it would prove a vain ceremony on the part of the Christians, chose to be present, accompanied by a number of his guards, for the purpose of destroying them in the event of the cobbler's failure.

CHAPTER 10

How the Prayer of the Cobbler Caused the Mountain to Move

HERE the pious artisan, kneeling before the cross and lifting his hands to heaven, humbly besought his creator to look compassionately down upon earth, and for the glory of his name, as well as for the support of the Christian faith, lend assistance to his people in the task imposed upon them, and thus manifest his power to those who mocked his law. Having concluded his prayer, he cried with a loud voice: "In the name of the Father, Son, and Holy Ghost, I command thee, O mountain, to remove thyself!"

Upon these words, the mountain moved, and the earth at the same time trembled in a wonderful and alarming manner.* The Caliph and all those by whom he was surrounded were struck with terror and dumbfounded. Many of the latter became Christians, and even the Caliph secretly embraced Christianity, always wearing a cross concealed under his garment, which after his death was found upon him; and because of this they did not entomb him in the shrine of his predecessors. In commemoration of this singular grace bestowed upon them by God, all the Christians, Nestorians, and Jacobites from that time forth have continued to celebrate in a solemn manner the return of the day on which the miracle took place; and they also keep a fast on the vigil.

---

*Stories of the miraculous moving of mountains were common and were told even among the Moslems.

CHAPTER 11

Of the Noble City of Tauris

TAURIS [Tabriz] is a large and very noble city belonging to the province of Iraq, which contains many other cities and fortified places; but this is the most eminent and most populous. The inhabitants support themselves principally by commerce and manufactures, which latter consist of various kinds of silk, some of them interwoven with gold, of high price. It is so advantageously situated for trade that merchants from India, from Baudas, Mosul, and Cremessor, as well as from different parts of Europe, come there to purchase and to sell a number of articles. Precious stones and pearls in abundance may also be procured here.

The merchants active in foreign commerce acquire considerable wealth, but the inhabitants in general are poor. They consist of a mixture of various nations and sects, Nestorians, Armenians, Jacobites, Georgians, Persians, and the followers of Mahomet, who form the bulk of the population and are those properly called Taurisians [Tabrizis]. Each group has its own language. The city is surrounded with delightful gardens, which produce the finest fruits.

The Mahometan inhabitants are treacherous and unprincipled. According to their doctrine, whatever is stolen or plundered from those of a different faith is justly taken, and the theft is no crime; while those who suffer death or injury at the hands of Christians are considered martyrs. If, therefore, they were not prohibited and restrained by the powers who now govern them, they would commit many outrages. These principles are common to all the Saracens. When they are at the point of death, their priest attends them and asks whether they believe that Mahomet was the true apostle of God. If their answer is that they do believe, their salvation is assured; and in consequence of this easy absolution, they have succeeded in converting to their faith a great proportion of the Tartars.

From Tauris to Persia is twelve days' journey.

CHAPTER 12

Of the Monastery of Saint Barsamo

Not far from Tauris is a monastery that takes its name from the holy Saint Barsamo and is famous for its devotion. There is here an abbot and many monks, who resemble the Order of Carmelites in their dress. That they may not lead a life of idleness, they employ themselves continually in the weaving of woollen girdles, which they place upon the altar of their saint during the celebration of divine service. And when they make the circuit of the provinces, soliciting alms—in the same manner as do the brethren of the Order of the Holy Ghost—they present these girdles to their friends and to persons of distinction, these being esteemed good for rheumatic pains, on which account they are devoutly sought after by everyone.

CHAPTER 13

Of the Country of Persia

Persia was anciently a large and noble province, but it is now in great part destroyed by the Tartars. In Persia there is a city called Saba [Saveh, just southwest of Teheran],* whence came the three Magi to adore Christ in Bethlehem; and the three are buried in that city in a fair sepulcher, and they are all three intact, even to their beards and hair. One was called Balthasar, the second Gaspar, and the third Melchior. Marco inquired often in that city concerning the three Magi, and nobody could tell him anything about them, except that the three were buried there in ancient times. After three days' journey you come to a castle called Palasata, which means the Castle of the Fire-Worshipers; and it is true that the inhabitants of that castle worship fire, and the following is given as the reason.

The men of that castle say that anciently three kings of that country went to adore a certain king who was newly born, and carried with them three offerings,

*According to Percy Sykes, Marco here wrongly identifies Saba with the Sheba from which, the Book of Isaiah says, the three Magi came.

namely, gold, frankincense, and myrrh: gold, that they might know if he were an earthly king; frankincense, that they might know if he were God; and myrrh, that they might know if he were a mortal man.

When these Magi were presented to Christ, the youngest of the three adored him first; and it appeared to him that Christ was of his stature and age. The middle one came next, and then the eldest; and to each he seemed to be of his own stature and age. Having compared their observations, they agreed to go to worship him all together, and then he appeared to all of them at his true age.

CHAPTER 14

What Happened When the Three Magi Returned to Their Own Country

WHEN they went away, the infant gave them a closed box, which they carried with them for several days; and then, becoming curious to see what he had given them, they opened the box and found in it a stone. This was intended as a sign that they should remain as firm as a stone in the faith they had received from him. When, however, they saw the stone, they marveled; and thinking themselves deluded, they threw the stone into a certain pit, and instantly fire burst forth in the pit. When they saw this, they repented bitterly of what they had done, and taking some of the fire with them they carried it home. And having placed it in one of their churches, they keep it continually burning, and adore that fire as a god, and make all their sacrifices with it. And if ever it should happen to be extinguished, they go for more to the original fire in the pit where they threw the stone, which is never extinguished, and they take of no other fire. And therefore the people of that country worship fire.*

Marco was told all this by the people of the country; and it is true that one of those kings was of Saba, and the second was of Dyava [Hawah], and the third was of

*This is but one of the many legends that have gathered around the brief account of the Magi given in St. Matthew.

the castle. Now we will treat of the people of Persia and their customs.

CHAPTER 15

Of the Eight Kingdoms of Persia and of the Breed of Horses and Asses Found There

IN PERSIA, which is a large province, there are eight kingdoms, the names of which are as follows: The first which you meet with upon entering the country is Kasibin [Kasvin]; the second, lying towards the south, is Kurdistan; the third is Lor [Luristan]; towards the north, the fourth is Shulistan; the fifth Spaan [Isfahan]; the sixth, Siras [Shiraz]; the seventh, Soncara [Shabankara]; the eighth, Timochain [Tun-o-Kain, that is, the two cities of Tun and Kain], which is at the extremity of Persia. All these kingdoms lie to the south, excepting Timochain, and this is to the north, near the place called Arbor Secco.

The country is distinguished for its excellent breed of horses, many of which are carried to India for sale, and bring high prices, not less in general than two hundred livres tournois [roughly, $1000]. It produces also the largest and handsomest breed of asses in the world, which sell—on the spot—at higher prices than the horses, because they are more easily fed, are capable of carrying heavier burdens, and travel farther in a day than either horses or mules, which cannot stand as much fatigue. The merchants, therefore, who in traveling from one province to another must pass through vast deserts and tracts of sand, where no kind of herbage is to be met with, and where, on account of the distance between wells or other watering places, it is necessary to make long journeys during the day, prefer asses because they get over the ground sooner and need less food. Camels also are used here, and these in like manner carry great weights and are maintained at little cost, but they are not so swift as the asses. The traders of these parts convey the horses to Kisi, to Ormus [Hormuz], and to other places on the coast of the Indian Sea, where they are purchased by those who plan to carry them to India. In consequence, however, of the greater heat of that country, they do not last many years, being natives of a temperate climate.

In some of these districts, the people are savage and bloodthirsty, making a common practice of wounding and murdering each other. They would not refrain from doing injury to the merchants and travelers, were they not in terror of the Eastern Tartars, who cause them to be severely punished. There is also a regulation that in all roads where danger is anticipated, the inhabitants shall be obliged, if required by merchants, to provide trustworthy guards for their guidance and security between one district and another, these to be paid at the rate of two or three groats for each loaded beast, according to the distance. They are all followers of the Mahometan religion.

In the cities there are merchants and numerous artisans, who manufacture a variety of stuffs of silk and gold. Cotton grows abundantly in this country, as do wheat, barley, millet, and several other sorts of grain, and also grapes and every species of fruit.

Should any one assert that the Saracens do not drink wine, being forbidden by their law, it may be answered that they salve their consciences on this point by persuading themselves that if they boil it over a fire, by which it is partly consumed and becomes sweet, they may drink it without infringing the commandment; for having changed its taste, they change its name, and no longer call it wine, although it is such in fact.

CHAPTER 16

Of the City of Yasdi

YASDI [Yezd] is a considerable city on the border of Persia, where there is much traffic. A species of cloth of silk and gold manufactured there is known as *yasdi,* and is carried thence by merchants to all parts of the world. Its inhabitants are of the Mahometan religion.

Those who travel from that city spend eight days in passing over a plain, in the course of which they find only three places that afford accommodation. The road lies through extensive groves of the date-bearing palm, in which there is abundance of game, including beasts as well as partridges and quails; and those travelers who are fond of the amusements of hunting may here enjoy excellent sport. A handsome breed of wild asses are also very numerous here. At the end of eight days you arrive at a kingdom named Kerman.

CHAPTER 17

Of the Kingdom of Kerman, Its Minerals, Manufacturers, and Falcons

KERMAN is a kingdom on the eastern borders of Persia, and was formerly governed by its own monarchs in hereditary succession; but since the Tartars have brought it under their dominion, they appoint governors to it at their pleasure. In the mountains of this country are found the precious stones we call turquoises. There are also veins of steel [probably iron] and of antimony in large quantities. They manufacture here in great perfection all the articles of military equipment, such as saddles, bridles, spurs, swords, bows, quivers, and every kind of arms used by these people. The women and young persons work with the needle, doing embroideries of silk and gold in a variety of colors and patterns, representing birds and beasts, with other ornamental devices. These are designed for the curtains, coverlets, and cushions of the sleeping places of the rich; and the work is executed with so much taste and skill as to be an object of admiration.*

In the mountainous parts are bred the best falcons that anywhere take wing. They are smaller than the peregrine falcon, reddish about the breast, belly, and under the tail, and their flight is so swift that no bird can escape them.

Upon leaving Kerman, you travel for seven days along a plain by a pleasant road, which is rendered still more delightful by the abundance of partridges and other game. You also meet frequently with towns and castles,

---

*Kerman is today known for its carpets as well as its shawls.

as well as scattered habitations, until at length you arrive at a mountain whence there is a considerable descent, which occupies two days. Fruit trees are found there in great numbers, the district having formerly been populated, though at present without inhabitants except for herdsmen attending their flocks. In the part of the country which you pass before you reach the descent, the cold is so severe that a man can barely manage to protect himself against it by wearing many garments and furs.

CHAPTER 18

Of the City of Kamandu and the District
of Reobarle, of Certain Birds Found There,
a Peculiar Kind of Oxen, and a Tribe of Robbers

AT THE end of the descent of this mountain, you arrive at a plain that extends in a southern direction to the distance of five days' journey; at the commencement of this there is a town named Kamandu [Kamadin], formerly a very large place and of much consequence, but not so at this day, having been repeatedly laid waste by the Tartars.

The neighboring district is called Reobarle [Rudbar]. The temperature of the plain is very warm. It produces wheat, rice, and other grains. On that part of it which lies nearest to the hills, dates, pomegranates, quinces, and a variety of other fruits, grow, among which is one called Adam's apple [probably a citrus fruit], which is unknown in our cool climate. Turtledoves are found here in vast numbers, attracted by the plenty of small fruits; but they are not eaten by the Mahometans, who abominate them. There are likewise many pheasants and francolins [a kind of partridge], which latter do not resemble those of other countries, their color being a mixture of white and black with red legs and beak.

Also among the cattle there are some of an uncommon kind, particularly a species of large white oxen [the zebu], with short, smooth coats—the effect of a hot climate—horns short, thick, and obtuse, and having between the shoulders a gibbous rising or hump, about the height of two palms. They are beautiful animals, and being very strong can carry great weights. When loading, they are accustomed to kneel down like the camel and then to rise up with the burden. We also find here sheep that are equal to an ass in size, with long thick tails, weighing thirty pounds and upwards, which are fat and excellent to eat.*

In this province there are many towns surrounded by lofty and thick walls of earth for the purpose of defending the inhabitants against the incursions of the Karaunas, who scour the country and plunder everything within their reach. In order that the reader may understand who these people are, it is necessary to mention that there was a prince named Nugodar [probably Nigudar], the nephew of Chagatai [a son of Genghis Khan], who was brother of the Great Khan Ogodai, and reigned in Turkestan. This Nugodar, while living at Chagatai's court, became ambitious of being himself a sovereign. Having heard that in India there was a province called Malabar, governed at that time by a king named Asidin Sultan, which had nòt yet been brought under the dominion of the Tartars, he secretly collected a body of about ten thousand men, the most profligate and desperate he could find; and leaving his uncle without giving him any hint of his intentions, proceeded through Balashan [Badakhshan] to the kingdom of Kesmur [Kashmir], where he lost many of his people and cattle from the difficulty and badness of the roads, and at length entered the province of Malabar. Coming thus upon Asidin by surprise, he took from him by force a city called Dely [Delhi], as well as many others in its vicinity, and there began to reign. The Tartars whom he carried thither, and who were men of light complexion, mixing with the dark Indian women, produced the race to whom the name of Karaunas is given, signifying in the language of the country a mixed breed; and these are the people who have since been in the habit of committing depredations, not only in the country of Reobarle, but in every other to which they have access.

In India they acquired the knowledge of magical and

*Fat-tailed sheep are well known in many parts of Asia.

diabolical arts, by means of which they are able to produce darkness, obscuring the light of day to such a degree that persons are invisible to each other, unless they
are close together.* Whenever they go on their preda-
tory excursions, they put this art into practice, and their
approach is consequently not perceived. This district is
the most frequent scene of their operations, because
when merchants assemble at Ormus [Hormuz] and wait
for those who are coming from India, they arrange in
winter to send their horses and mules (which are out of
condition from the length of their journey) to the plain
of Reobarle, where they find abundance of pasture and
become fat. The Karaunas, aware that this will take
place, seize the opportunity for a general pillage, and
make slaves of the people who attend the cattle, if they
have not the means of ransom. Marco Polo himself was
once enveloped in a darkness of this kind, but escaped
from it to the castle of Konsalmi. Many of his companions, however, were taken and sold, and others were put
to death.†

CHAPTER 19

Of the City of Ormus and the Hot
Wind That Blows There

AT THE end of the plain mentioned before as extending in a southern direction to a distance of five days'
journey, there is a descent for about twenty miles by a
road that is extremely dangerous because of the multitude of robbers by whom travelers are continually as-
saulted and plundered. This downward path conducts
you to another plain, very beautiful in appearance, two
days' journey in extent, which is called the plain of
Ormus. Here you cross a number of fine streams, and
see a country covered with date palms, among which are
found the francolin partridge, birds of the parrot kind,

---

*This is believed to refer to a kind of "dry fog" possibly combined
with a dust storm.
†It is characteristic of Polo's impersonal attitude throughout that he
should make such a casual reference to what was obviously an exciting
and tragic incident.

and a variety of others unknown to our climate. At
length you reach the border of the ocean, where upon
an island at no great distance from the shore, stands a
city named Ormus, whose port is frequented by traders
from all parts of India; these bring spices and drugs,
precious stones, pearls, gold cloth, elephants' tusks, and
various other articles of merchandise. These they dispose
of to other traders, by whom they are distributed
throughout the world. This city, indeed, is essentially
commercial, has towns and castles dependent upon it,
and is esteemed the principal place in the kingdom of
Kerman. Its ruler is Rukmedin Achomak, who governs
with absolute authority, but at the same time acknowl-
edges the King of Kerman as his liege lord. When any
foreign merchant happens to die within his jurisdiction,
he confiscates his property and deposits it in his treasury.

During the summer season the inhabitants do not remain in the city on account of the excessive heat, which
renders the air unwholesome, but retire to their gardens
along the shore or on the banks of the river, where with
a kind of osier-work they construct huts over the water.
These they enclose with stakes, driven into the water on
the one side, and into the shore on the other, making a
covering of leaves to shelter them from the sun. Here
they stay during the period in which there blows, every
day from about nine until noon, a land wind so intensely
hot as to hinder breathing and suffocate the person exposed to it. No one overtaken by it on the sandy plain
can escape from its effects. As soon as the approach
of this wind is noted by the inhabitants, they immerse
themselves to the chin in water and continue thus until
it ceases to blow.

In proof of the extraordinary degree of this heat,
Marco Polo says that he happened to be in these parts
when the following occurred. The ruler of Ormus having
neglected to pay his tribute to the king of Kerman, the
latter decided to enforce it at the season when the principal inhabitants are away from the city, upon the mainland, and for this purpose dispatched sixteen hundred
horsemen and five thousand foot soldiers through the
country of Reobarle in order to take them by surprise.
In consequence, however, of being misled by the guides,

they failed to arrive at their goal before nightfall, and halted to rest in a grove not far from Ormus; but upon recommencing their march in the morning, they were assailed by this hot wind and were all suffocated, not one escaping to carry the fatal news to his master. When the people of Ormus learned of this and went to bury the carcasses in order that their stench might not infect the air, they found them so baked by the intensity of the heat that the limbs, upon being handled, separated from the trunks,* and it became necessary to dig the graves close to the spot where the bodies lay.

The vessels built at Ormus are of the worst kind and dangerous for navigation, exposing the merchants and others who use them to great hazards. Their defects result from the failure to use nails in the construction because the wood is of too hard a quality and is liable to split or to crack like earthenware. When an attempt is made to drive a nail into it, it rebounds and is frequently broken. The planks are therefore bored as carefully as possible with an iron auger near the ends; wooden pins or trenails are then driven into them, and they are in this way fastened. After this they are bound, or rather sewed together, with a kind of rope yarn stripped from the husk of the Indian nuts [coconuts], which are large and are covered with a fibrous stuff like horsehair. This being steeped in water until the softer parts putrefy, the threads or strings remain, and of these they make a twine, which lasts long underwater, for sewing the planks. Pitch is not used for preserving the bottoms of vessels, but they are smeared with an oil made from the fat of fish, and then caulked with oakum. The vessel has no more than one mast, one helm, and one deck. When she has taken in her cargo, it is covered over with hides, and upon these they place the horses which they carry to India. They have no iron anchors, but instead employ another kind of ground-tackle, the consequence of which is that in bad weather—and these seas are very tempestuous—the ships are frequently driven on shore and lost.†

---

*This effect of the simoom is corroborated by later travelers.
†It is thought that the flimsiness of the vessels here may have dissuaded the travelers from going to India by sea.

The inhabitants of the place are of a dark color and are Mahometans. They sow their wheat, rice, and other grain in the month of November, and reap their harvest in March. They also gather the fruits in that month, with the exception of dates, which are collected in May. Out of these, along with other ingredients, they make a good kind of wine. When, however, it is drunk by persons not accustomed to it, it causes an immediate flux [diarrhea]; but upon their recovering from its first effects, it proves beneficial to them and helps make them fat.

The food of the natives is different from ours; for were they to eat wheaten bread and meat their health would be injured. They live chiefly upon dates and salted fish, such as the tunny, cepole, and others which from experience they know to be wholesome. Excepting in marshy places, the soil of this country is not covered with grass, because of the extreme heat, which burns up everything.

Upon the death of men of rank, their wives loudly bewail them once each day for four successive weeks. There are also people here who make such lamentations a profession and are paid for uttering them over the corpses of persons to whom they are not related.

Having spoken of Ormus, I shall for the present defer treating of India, intending to make it the subject of a separate Book, and now return to Kerman in a northerly direction. Leaving Ormus, therefore, and taking a different road to that place, you enter upon a beautiful plain, producing in abundance every article of food; and birds are numerous, especially partridges. But the bread made from wheat grown in the country cannot be eaten by those who have not accustomed their palates to it, having a bitter taste derived from the waters, which are all bitter and salty.* On every side you perceive warm, healing streams, good for the cure of skin ailments and other complaints. Dates and other fruits are very plentiful.

*Other theories are that this taste comes either from acorns or a bitter leguminous plant mixed in with the wheat.

CHAPTER 20

*Of the Great Desert Country Between Kerman and
Kobiam and of the Bitter Quality of the Water*

UPON leaving Kerman and traveling three days, you
reach the borders of a desert extending to a distance of
seven days' journey, at the end of which you arrive at
Kobiam [Kuhbanan]. During the first three days but little water is to be met with, and that little is impregnated
with salt,* and is as green as grass and so nauseating that
none can drink it. Should even a drop of it be swallowed,
frequent calls of nature will result; and the effect is the
same from eating a grain of the salt made from this
water. In consequence of this, persons who travel over
the desert are obliged to carry water along with them.
The cattle, however, are compelled by thirst to drink
such as they find, and a flux immediately ensues. In the
course of these three days not one habitation is to be
seen. The whole is arid and desolate. Cattle are not
found there because there is no sustenance for them. On
the fourth day you come to a river of fresh water, but
one which has its channel for the most part under-
ground. In some parts, however, there are abrupt openings, caused by the force of the current, through which
the stream becomes visible for a short space. Water is
abundant. Here the wearied traveler stops to refresh
himself and his cattle after the fatigues of the preceding
journey.† The circumstances of the latter three days resemble those of the former and bring him at length to
the town of Kobiam.

CHAPTER 21

Of Kobiam and Its Manufactures

KOBIAM is a large town, the inhabitants of which observe the law of Mahomet. They have plenty of iron and
ondanique ["Indian steel," famous for its use in swords].
Here they make mirrors of highly polished steel, of a

---

*This great salt desert had once been the bottom of a salt sea.
†Once again a casual reference suffices for what was surely a severe
ordeal.

large size and very handsome. Much antimony or zinc is found in the country, and they procure tutty which makes an excellent collyrium [eye salve], together with spodium, by the following process. They take the crude ore from a vein that is known to yield such as is fit for the purpose, and put it into a furnace. Over the furnace they place an iron grating formed of small bars set close together. The smoke or vapor ascending from the ore in burning clings to the bars, and as it cools becomes hard. This is the tutty; while the gross and heavy part, which does not ascend, but remains as a cinder in the furnace, becomes the spodium.

CHAPTER 22

Of the Journey from Kobiam to the Province of Timochain and of a Particular Species of Tree

LEAVING Kobiam you proceed over a desert of eight days' journey exposed to great drought; neither fruits nor any kind of trees are met with, and what water is found has a bitter taste. Travelers are therefore obliged to carry with them as much as may be necessary for their sustenance. Their cattle are forced by thirst to drink whatever the desert affords, which their owners try to render palatable to them by mixing it with flour.

At the end of eight days you reach the province of Timochain, situated towards the north, on the borders of Persia, in which are many towns and strong places. Here there is an extensive plain remarkable for a species of tree called the Tree of the Sun, and by Christians *Arbre Sec,* the dry or fruitless tree.* Its nature and qualities are these: It is lofty, with a large stem, and with leaves green on the upper surface, but white or bluish on the under. It produces husks or capsules like those in which the chestnut is enclosed, but these contain no fruit. The wood is solid and strong and of a yellow color resembling the box. There is no other species of tree

---

*Polo has here apparently confused two legends, one of the *Arbre Sol,* the Tree of the Sun, which figures in stories of Alexander the Great, and the other of the *Arbre Secco,* the Dry Tree, a familiar subject of Christian and Mahometan legend.

near it for the space of a hundred miles, excepting in one quarter, where trees are found within the distance of about ten miles. It is reported by the inhabitants of this district that a battle was fought there between Alexander, King of Macedonia, and Darius. The towns are well supplied with every necessity and convenience, the climate being temperate and not subject to extremes either of heat or cold. The people are of the Mahometan religion. They are in general a handsome race, especially the women, who in my opinion are the most beautiful in the world.

CHAPTER 23

Of the Old Man of the Mountain and His Palace and Gardens

HAVING spoken of this country, we shall now tell of the Old Man of the Mountain. The district in which his residence lay obtained the name of Mulehet [Alamut, in northern Persia], signifying, in the language of the Saracens, the place of heretics, and his people that of Mulehetites, or holders of heretical tenets; as we apply the term of Patharini to certain heretics amongst Christians. The following account of this chief Marco Polo testifies to having heard from sundry persons. He was named Alaodin, and his religion was that of Mahomet. In a beautiful valley enclosed between two lofty mountains he had built a luxurious garden, stored with every delicious fruit and fragrant shrub that could be procured. Palaces of various sizes and forms were erected in different parts of the grounds, ornamented with works in gold, with paintings, and with furnishings of rich silks. By means of small conduits in these buildings, streams of wine, milk, honey, and some of pure water, were seen to flow in every direction.

The inhabitants of these palaces were dainty and beautiful damsels, accomplished in the arts of singing, playing upon all sorts of musical instruments, dancing, and especially amorous dalliance. Clothed in rich dresses, they were seen continually sporting and amusing themselves in the garden and pavilions, their female guardians being confined within doors and never allowed to appear. The object which the chief had in view in forming a garden of this fascinating kind was this: that Mahomet having promised to those who should obey his will the enjoyments of Paradise, where every species of sensual gratification should be found, in the society of beautiful nymphs, he wanted it understood by his followers that he also was a prophet and the compeer of Mahomet, and had the power of admitting to Paradise such as he should choose to favor.

In order that no one might find his way into this delicious valley without his permission, he caused a strong and impregnable castle to be erected at the opening to it, through which the entry was by a secret passage. At his court, moreover, this chief entertained a number of youths, from the age of twelve to twenty years, selected from the inhabitants of the surrounding mountains, who showed a warlike disposition and appeared to possess the quality of daring courage. To them he was in the daily practice of holding forth on the subject of the paradise announced by the prophet, and of his own power of granting admission to it. At certain times he caused opium to be administered to ten or a dozen of the youths; and when they were unconscious he had them conveyed to the several apartments of the palaces in the garden.*

CHAPTER 24

How the Old Man Trained His Assassins

UPON awakening from the state of stupor, their senses were struck with all the delightful objects that have been described. Each saw himself surrounded by lovely dam-

*Although it seems entirely fantastic, and Marco's account is second-hand, this story is based on fact. The Old Man of the Mountain was Hasan-ben-Sabah, who was chief of a secret order of fanatics in northern Persia. They became known as the Assassins because of their addiction to the drug hashish, which induces an excitement amounting to fury. The modern application of the word comes from the Assassins' use of murder in carrying out their chief's orders.

sels, singing, playing, and captivating him with the most delightful caresses, serving him also with delicate foods and exquisite wines until, intoxicated with excess of enjoyment amid rivulets of milk and wine, he believed himself assuredly in Paradise, and unwilling to relinquish its delights.

When four or five days had thus been passed, they were thrown once more into a drugged state and carried out of the garden. Upon their being brought into his presence and questioned by him as to where they had been, their answer was, "In Paradise, through the favor of your highness"; and then before the whole court, who listened with curiosity and astonishment, they gave a circumstantial account of the scenes they had witnessed.

The chief thereupon addressing them, said: "We have the assurances of our prophet that he who defends his lord shall inherit Paradise, and if you show yourselves devoted to obeying my orders, that happy lot awaits you." Aroused to enthusiasm by words of this nature, all deemed themselves happy to receive the commands of their master and were ready to die in his service.

The consequence of this system was that when any of the neighboring princes, or others, offended this chief, they were put to death by these his disciplined assassins, none of whom felt terror at the risk of losing their own lives, which they held in little esteem, provided they could execute their master's will. On this account his tyranny became a matter of dread in all the surrounding countries.

He had also constituted two deputies or representatives of himself, one of whom had his residence in the vicinity of Damascus and the other in Kurdistan; and these pursued the plan he had established for training their young dependents. Thus there was no person, however powerful, who, having been exposed to the enmity of the Old Man of the Mountain, could escape assassination.

CHAPTER 25

How the Old Man Came by His End

HIS territory being within the dominions of Hulaku, the brother of the Great Khan Mangu, that prince learned of his atrocious practices as above related, as well as of his employing people to rob travelers as they passed through his country, and in the year 1252 sent one of his armies to besiege this chief in his castle. It proved, however, so capable of defense, that for three years no impression could be made upon it, until at length he was forced to surrender from want of provisions; and being made prisoner was put to death. His castle was dismantled and his Garden of Paradise destroyed. And from that time there has been no Old Man of the Mountain.*

CHAPTER 26

*Of a Fertile Plain of Six Days' Journey
Succeeded by a Desert of Eight*

LEAVING this castle, the road leads over a spacious plain, and then through a country broken up into hill and dale, where there is grass and pasture, as well as fruits in great abundance, whereby the army of Hulaku was enabled to remain so long upon the ground. This country extends to a distance of full six days' journey. It contains many cities and fortified places, and the inhabitants are of the Mahometan religion. An arid desert then commences, extending forty or fifty miles, and it is necessary that the traveler provide himself with water at the outset. As the cattle find no drink until this desert is passed, the greatest expedition is necessary that they may reach a watering place.

At the end of the sixth day's journey, one arrives at a town named Sapurgan [Shibarghan], which is plentifully supplied with every kind of provision and is celebrated for producing the best melons in the world. These are preserved in the following manner. They are cut spirally

*Actually a remnant of the sect, styled Ismaili, has survived into modern times. Its leader today is Aga Khan IV.

in thin slices, as we do the pumpkin, and after they have
been dried in the sun, are sent in large quantities to be
sold to neighboring countries; there they are in great
demand, being sweet as honey. Game, both of beasts
and birds, is also plentiful there. Leaving this place, we
shall now speak of another, named Balach [Balkh], a
large and magnificent city.

CHAPTER 27

Of the City of Balach

BALACH was formerly larger, but has sustained much
damage from the Tartars, who in their frequent attacks
have partly demolished its buildings. It contained many
palaces constructed of marble, and spacious squares, still
visible, although in a ruinous state. It was in this city,
according to the report of the inhabitants, that Alexander
took to wife the daughter of King Darius. The Mahometan religion prevails here also.

The dominion of the lord of the Eastern Tartars extends to this place; and to it the limits of the Persian
empire extend in a northeastern direction.

Upon leaving Balach and holding the same course for
twelve days, you traverse a country that is destitute of
every sign of habitation, the people having all fled to
strong places in the mountains in order to safeguard
themselves against the attacks of lawless marauders by
whom these districts are overrun. Here are extensive waters and game of various kinds. Very large and numerous lions are also found in these parts. Provisions,
however, are scarce in the hilly tract passed during these
twelve days, and the traveler must carry with him food
sufficient both for himself and his cattle.

CHAPTER 28

Of the Castle Named Thaikan and the
Salt Hills of Scassem

AFTER those twelve days' journey you reach a castle
named Thaikan [Talikan], where a great market for corn
is held, it being located in a fine and fruitful country.

The hills that lie to the south of it are large and lofty. They all consist of white salt, extremely hard, with which the people, to a distance of thirty days' journey round, come to provide themselves, for it is esteemed the purest that is found in the world; but it is at the same time so hard that it cannot be detached by anything but iron picks. The quantity is so great that all the countries of the earth might be supplied by it. Other hills produce almonds and pistachio nuts, in which products the natives carry on a considerable trade.

Leaving Thaikan and traveling three days, still in a northeast direction, you pass through a well-inhabited country, very beautiful and abounding in fruit, corn, and vines. The people are Mahometans, and are bloodthirsty and treacherous. They are given also to debauchery, and to excess in drink, to which the excellence of their sweet wine encourages them. They wear nothing on the head but a cord about ten spans in length, which they wind around it. They are keen sportsmen and take many wild animals, wearing no other clothing than the skins of the beasts they kill, of which their shoes are also made. They are all taught to prepare the skins.

During a journey of three days there are cities and many castles, and at the end of that distance you reach a town named Scassem [Ish Kasham], governed by a chief whose title is equivalent to that of our barons or counts; and among the mountains he possesses other towns and strong places. Through the middle of this town runs a river of tolerable size. Here are found porcupines, which roll themselves up when the hunters set their dogs at them, and with great fury shoot out the quills or spines with which their skins are furnished, wounding both men and dogs.

The people of this country have their own peculiar language. The herdsmen who attend the cattle live among the hills in caverns they form for themselves; nor is this difficult, the hills consisting not of stone, but only of clay. Upon departing from this place you travel for three days without seeing any kind of building, or meeting with any of the necessities required by a traveler, excepting water; but for the horses there is sufficient pasture. You are therefore obliged to carry with you

every article which you may need on the road. At the
end of the third day you arrive at the province of
Balashan.

CHAPTER 29

Of the Province of Balashan, the Precious Stones
Found There, and the Dress
the Women Wear

IN the province of Balashan [or Badakhshan], the people are Mahometans and have their own peculiar language. It is an extensive kingdom, being in length full
twelve days' journey, and is governed by princes, in hereditary succession, who are all descended from Alexander by the daughter of Darius, king of the Persians. All
these have borne the title in the Saracenic tongue of
Zulkarnen, which is the equivalent of Alexander.

In this country are found the precious stones called
balas rubies, of fine quality and great value, and so called
from the name of the province. They are embedded in
the high mountains, but are sought for only in one
named Sikinan [Sighinan]. In this the king causes mines
to be worked in the same manner as for gold or silver;
and through this channel alone they are obtained, no
person daring under pain of death to make an excavation for the purpose, unless as a special favor he obtains
his majesty's permission.

Occasionally the king gives them as presents to strangers who pass through his dominions, as they cannot be
purchased from others and cannot be exported without
his permission. Since he believes his credit is dependent
on these rubies, his object in these restrictions is to keep
them in high esteem and maintain their high price; for
so great is their abundance that if they could be dug for
indiscriminately, and if everyone could purchase and
carry them out of the kingdom, they would soon be of
little value. Some he sends as gifts to other kings and
princes; some he delivers as tribute to his superior lord;
and some also he exchanges for gold and silver. These
he allows to be exported.

There are also mountains in which are found veins

of lapis lazuli, the stone which yields the azure color (ultramarine), here the finest in the world. The mines of silver, copper, and lead are also very productive. It is a cold country.

The horses bred here are of a superior quality and have great speed. Their hoofs are so hard that they do not require shoeing. The natives are in the habit of galloping them down inclines where other animals could not or would not venture to run. They say that not long ago there were still found in this province horses of the strain of Alexander's celebrated Bucephalus, which were all foaled with a particular mark on the forehead. The whole of the breed was owned by one of the king's uncles, who, upon his refusal to yield them to his nephew, was put to death. Enraged by the murder, the widow then caused them all to be destroyed; and thus the race was lost to the world.

In the mountains there are falcons of the species called saker, which are excellent birds and of strong flight; and plenty of lanners as well. There are also goshawks of a perfect kind, and sparrow hawks. The people of the country are expert at hunting both beasts and birds. Good wheat is grown there, and a species of barley without the husk. There is no oil of olives, but they press an oil from certain nuts and from the grain called sesame, which resembles the seed of flax, excepting that it is light-colored; and the oil this yields is better and has more flavor than any other. It is used by the Tartars and other inhabitants of these parts.

In this kingdom there are many narrow passes and natural strong points which leave the inhabitants with little fear of any foreign power trying to invade them. The men are good archers and excellent sportsmen. They generally clothe themselves in the skins of wild animals, other materials for the purpose being scarce. The mountains afford pasture for innumerable sheep, which ramble about in flocks of four, five, and six hundred, all wild; and although many are taken and killed, there does not appear to be any lessening in their numbers.

These mountains are so exceedingly lofty that it requires from morning till night to ascend to the top of them. Between them there are wide plains clothed with grass and trees, and large streams of the purest water spurting through clefts in rocks. In these streams are trout and many other fine sorts of fish. On the summits of the mountains the air is so pure and healthy that when those who dwell in the towns and in the plains and valleys below find themselves attacked with fevers or inflammations, they immediately take to the hills, and remaining for three or four days, recover their health. Marco Polo affirms that he himself experienced its excellent effects; for having been confined by sickness in this country for nearly a year, he was advised to seek a change of air by ascending the hills. There he soon got well.*

A peculiar fashion of dress prevails among the women of the upper class: they wear below their waists, in the manner of drawers, a kind of garment in which they use, depending on their means, eighty or sixty ells of fine cotton cloth. This they gather or plait in order to increase the apparent size of their hips, the women with the bulkiest hips being considered the most handsome.

CHAPTER 30

Of the Province of Pascia

LEAVING Balashan and traveling in a southerly direction for ten days, you reach the province of Pascia, the people of which have their own peculiar language. They worship idols; are of a dark complexion, and of evil disposition. They are skilled in the art of magic and in the invocation of demons, a study to which they continually apply themselves. They wear in their ears pendent rings of gold and silver, adorned with pearls and precious stones. The climate of the province is in some parts extremely hot. The food of the inhabitants is meat and rice.

---

*Thus, again casually, are we given one of the few intimate glimpses of the hardships Marco underwent. If this illness delayed him here for a year, it is easy to understand why it took him three and a half years to make the entire journey.

CHAPTER 31

*Of the Province of Kesmur, and of
Its Inhabitants Who Are Skilled in
Magic, and of a Class of Hermits*

KESMUR [Kashmir] is a province seven days distant from Pascia. Its inhabitants also have their own peculiar language. They are adepts beyond all others in the art of magic,* to such a degree that they can compel their idols, although dumb and deaf, to speak. They can likewise obscure the day, and perform many other miracles. They are preeminent among the idolatrous nations,† and from them come the idols worshiped in other parts.

From this country there is communication by water with the Indian Sea.

The natives are of a dark complexion, but by no means black; and the women, although dark, are very beautiful. Their food is meat, with rice and other grains; yet they are in general of temperate habits. The climate is moderately warm. In this province, besides the capital, there are many other towns and strong places. There are also woods, desert tracts, and difficult passes in the mountains, which insure the inhabitants against invasion. Their king is not tributary to any power.

They have among them a particular class of devotees who live in communities, observe strict abstinence in regard to eating, drinking, and the intercourse of the sexes, and refrain from every kind of sensual indulgence in order that they may not give offense to the idols whom they worship. These persons live to a considerable age. They have several monasteries, in which certain superiors exercise the functions of abbots, and they are held in great reverence by the mass of the people. The natives of this country do not deprive any creature of life, nor shed blood, and if they are inclined to eat meat, it is necessary that the Mahometans who reside among them should slay the animal. The coral that is brought here

---

*Marco had been greatly impressed by the Kashmirian conjurers at the court of the Great Khan.
†Kashmir was a center of Buddhism and sent forth missionaries who spread the doctrine in Tibet and Central Asia.

from Europe is sold at a higher price than in any other part of the world.

If I were to proceed in the same direction, it would lead me to India; but I have judged it proper to reserve the description of that country for a third Book; and shall therefore return to Balashan, intending to pursue from there the straight road to Cathay [southern China], and to describe, as has been done from the beginning of the work, not only the countries through which the route lies, but also those in its vicinity.

CHAPTER 32

*Of the Province of Vokhan, of an Ascent
for Three Days, and the Effect of the
Great Elevation upon Fires*

LEAVING the province of Balashan and traveling in a direction between northeast and east, you pass many castles and habitations, on the banks of the river, belonging to the brother of the king of that place, and after three days' journey, reach a province named Vokhan. This extends in length and width to a distance of three days' journey. The people are Mahometans, have a distinct language, are civilized in their manners, and are considered valiant in war. Their chief holds his territory as a fief dependent upon Balashan. They have various ways of taking wild animals.

On leaving this country, and proceeding three days, still in an east-northeast course, ascending mountain after mountain, you at length arrive at a point of the road where you may well think the surrounding summits to be the highest lands in the world.* Here, between two ranges, you see a large lake, from which flows a handsome river [a tributary of the upper Oxus River], that follows a course along an extensive plain covered with the richest verdure. Such indeed is its quality that the leanest cattle turned out upon it would become fat in the course of ten days.

*The Pamir region, called by natives the "roof of the world," is a lofty plateau where the Hindu Kush, the Tien Shan, and the Himalayan mountain systems meet.

In this plain there are wild animals in great numbers, particularly sheep of a large size,* having horns, three, four, and even six palms in length. Out of these the shepherds make ladles and vessels for holding their victuals; and with the same materials they construct fences for enclosing their cattle and safeguarding them against the wolves, with which, they say, the country is filled, and which destroy many of these wild sheep or goats. Their horns and bones being found in large quantities, heaps are made of them at the sides of the road for the purpose of guiding travelers when the road is buried in snow.

For twelve days the course is along this elevated plain, which is named Pamer [Pamir Plateau], and as during all that time you do not meet with any habitations, it is necessary to make provision at the outset accordingly. So great is the height of the mountains that no birds are to be seen near their summits; and however extraordinary it may be thought, it is affirmed that from the rareness of the air, fires when lighted do not give the same heat as in lower locations, nor produce the same effect in cooking food.

After having performed this journey of twelve days, you have still forty days to travel in the same direction, over mountains, and through valleys, in endless succession, passing many rivers and tracts of desert, without seeing any habitations or verdure. Every article of provision must therefore be carried along. This region is called Belor. Even amid the highest of these mountains, there lives a tribe of savage, ill-disposed, and idolatrous people, who subsist upon the animals they can destroy and clothe themselves with the skins.

CHAPTER 33

Of the City of Kashgar

AT length you reach a place called Kashgar, which, it is said, was formerly an independent kingdom; but it is now subject to the dominion of the Great Khan. Its

---

*This is the Great Sheep of Pamir, named *Ovis Poli* in honor of Marco—although William of Rubruck had described it almost fifty years before.

inhabitants are of the Mahometan religion. The province
is extensive and contains many towns and castles, of
which Kashgar* is the largest and most important. The
language of the people is peculiar to themselves. They
subsist by commerce and manufacture. They have handsome gardens, orchards, and vineyards. An abundance
of cotton is produced there, as well as flax and hemp.
Merchants from this country travel to all parts of the
world; but in truth they are a wretched, sordid race,
eating badly and drinking worse. Besides the Mahometans, there are among the inhabitants several Nestorian
Christians, who are permitted to live under their own
laws and to have their churches. The extent of the province is five days' journey.

CHAPTER 34

Of the City of Samarkand and the Miraculous Column in the Church of St. John the Baptist

SAMARKAND† is a noble city, adorned with beautiful
gardens and surrounded by a plain in which are produced all the fruits that man can desire. The inhabitants,
who are partly Christians and partly Mahometans, are
subject to a nephew of the Great Khan, with whom,
however, he is not upon amicable terms; on the contrary,
there is perpetual strife and frequent wars between
them. This city lies toward the northeast. A miracle is
said to have taken place there under the following circumstances. Not long ago, a prince named Chagatai, who
was a brother [actually uncle] to the then reigning Great
Khan, became a convert to Christianity. This greatly delighted the Christian inhabitants of the place, who under
the favor and protection of the prince, proceeded to
build a church, and dedicated it to St. John the Baptist.
It was so constructed that all the weight of the roof,
being circular, should rest upon a column in the center;

*A city in the extreme southwest of China.
†Now in the southwest Soviet Union. Although his uncle and father
had probably passed through it on their first journey (they had taken
a more northerly route), there is no evidence that Marco himself was
ever there.

beneath this, as a base, they fixed a square stone, which, with the permission of the prince, they had taken from a temple belonging to the Mahometans, who dared not prevent them from doing so. But upon the death of Chagatai, the son who succeeded him showing no disposition to become a Christian, the Moslems had influence enough to obtain from him an order that their opponents should restore the stone to them. Although the latter offered to pay them a compensation in money, the Moslems refused to listen to the proposal because they hoped that its removal would cause the church to tumble down.

In this difficulty the afflicted Christians had no other resource than with tears and humility to recommend themselves to the protection of the glorious St. John the Baptist. When the day arrived on which they were to make restitution of the stone, it came to pass that through the intercession of the saint, the pillar raised itself from its base to the height of three palms in order to facilitate the removal of the stone; and in that situation, without any kind of support, it remains to the present day. Enough being said of this, we shall now proceed to the province of Karkan [Yarkand].

CHAPTER 35

Of the Province of Karkan, the Inhabitants of Which Are Troubled with Goiters

DEPARTING thence, you enter the province of Karkan, which extends to a distance of five days' journey. Its inhabitants, for the most part Mahometans, with some Nestorian Christians, are subjects of the Great Khan. Provisions are here in abundance, as is also cotton. The people are expert artisans. They are in general afflicted with swellings in the legs as well as tumors in the throat resulting from the water they drink. In this country there is nothing further that is worthy of note.

CHAPTER 36

Of the City of Kotan

FOLLOWING a course between northeast and east, you next come to the province of Kotan [Khotan], the extent of which is eight days' journey. It is under the dominion of the Great Khan, and the people are Mahometans. It contains many cities and fortified places,* but the principal city, and the one that gives its name to the province, is Kotan. Everything necessary for human life is here in the greatest plenty. It likewise yields cotton, flax, hemp, grain, wine, and other articles. The inhabitants cultivate farms and vineyards and have numerous gardens. They support themselves also by trade and manufactures, but they are not good soldiers. We shall now speak of a province named Peyn.

CHAPTER 37

Of the Province of Peyn, the Chalcedony and Jasper Found in Its River, and a Peculiar Custom with Regard to Marriages

PEYN [Pem] is a province of five days' journey in extent and is in the direction of east-northeast. It is under the dominion of the Great Khan, and contains many cities and strong places, the principal one of which is likewise named Peyn. Through this flows a river, and in its bed are found many of those stones called chalcedony and jasper [varieties of Chinese jade]. All kinds of provision are obtained here. Cotton also is produced in this country.

The inhabitants live by manufacture and trade. They have this custom, that if a married man goes to a distance from home to be absent twenty days, his wife has a right, if she is inclined, to take another husband; and the men, on the same principle, marry wherever they happen to reside.† All the before-mentioned provinces,

*In 1895 the Swedish explorer Sven Hedin here discovered the sites of two ancient cities long buried in the sand.
†Yule reported that the custom of "temporary marriages" was still common in the halting-places of caravans in Central Asia.

that is to say, Kashgar, Kotan, Peyn, and as far as the Desert of Lop, are within the limits of Turkestan. Next follows the province of Charchan.

CHAPTER 38

Of the Province of Charchan

CHARCHAN is also a province of Turkestan, lying in an east-northeast direction. In former times it was flourishing and productive, but it has been laid waste by the Tartars. The people are Mahometans. Its chief city is likewise named Charchan. Through this province run several large streams, in which chalcedony and jasper are also found, these are carried to Cathay for sale, and such is their abundance that they form an important article of commerce.

The area from Peyn to this district, as well as throughout its whole extent, is all sand, and the water is for the most part bitter and unpalatable, although in a few places sweet and good. If a hostile army of Tartars passes through these places, the inhabitants are plundered of their goods; and if a friendly one, their cattle are killed and devoured. For this reason, when they become aware of the approach of any body of troops, they flee with their families and cattle into the sandy desert, going a distance of two days' journey toward some spot where they can find fresh water, and by that means survive. From the same fear, when they collect their harvest, they deposit the grain in caverns among the sands, taking monthly from the store as much as may be needed. Nor can any persons besides themselves find the places they use for this purpose, because their footprints are soon effaced by the wind.

Upon leaving Charchan the road runs for five days over sands, where the water is generally, but not in all places, bad. Nothing else occurs here that is worthy of remark. At the end of these five days you arrive at the city of Lop, on the borders of the great desert.

CHAPTER 39

*Of the Town of Lop, the Vast Desert, and the
Strange Noises Heard on It*

THE town of Lop is situated toward the northeast,
near the commencement of the Great Desert,* which is
called the Desert of Lop. It belongs to the dominions of
the Great Khan, and its inhabitants are of the Mahometan religion. Travelers who intend to cross the desert
usually halt for a considerable time at this place in order
to rest from their fatigue as well as to make the necessary preparations for their further journey. For this purpose they load a number of stout asses and camels with
provisions and with their merchandise. Should the former be consumed before they have completed the passage, they kill and eat both kinds of animals; but camels
are commonly here employed in preference to asses, because they carry heavy burdens and require less food.

Provisions for a month should be laid in, that time
being required for crossing the desert even in the nar-
rowest part. To travel it in the direction of its length
would prove a vain attempt, as little less than a year
would be needed, and to carry stores for such a period would
be impracticable. During these thirty days the journey
is invariably over either sandy plains or barren mountains; but at the end of each day's march you stop at a
place where water is procurable, not indeed in sufficient
quantity for large numbers, but enough to supply a hundred persons, together with their beasts of burden.† At
three or four of these halting-places the water is salt
and bitter, but at the others, amounting to about
twenty, it is sweet and good. In this tract neither beasts
nor birds are met with, because there is no kind of food
for them.

It is asserted as an established fact that this desert is
the abode of many evil spirits which lure travelers to

---

*This is the Gobi (the Mongol word for "desert"), which stretches
eastward for 1,000 miles. The Polos actually kept to the mountains at
the southern edge of the desert.
†In the early 1900s the Swedish explorer Sven Hedin helped end a
controversy concerning the location of the Lake of Lop Nor by showing
that it "wanders" as its tributary silts up and finds a new channel.

their destruction with the most extraordinary illusions. If during the daytime any persons remain behind on the road, either when overtaken by sleep or delayed by natural functions, until the caravan has passed a hill and is no longer in sight, they are startled to hear themselves called by their names, and in a tone of voice to which they are accustomed. Supposing the call to come from their companions, they are led away by it from the road, and not knowing in what direction to advance, are left to perish. In the nighttime they are persuaded they hear the march of a large cavalcade of people on one side or the other of the road, and concluding the noise to be that of their party, they direct their steps to the quarter whence it seems to come. But at break of day they find they have been misled and drawn into danger. Sometimes during the day these spirits assume the appearance of their traveling companions, address them by name, and try to lead them out of the proper road. It is said also that some persons while crossing the desert have seen what appeared to be a body of armed men advancing toward them, and fearful of being attacked and plundered have taken to flight. Having thus abandoned the right path, and not knowing how to regain it, they perish miserably of hunger. Marvelous indeed and almost beyond belief are the stories related of these spirits of the desert, which are said at times to fill the air with the sounds of all kinds of musical instruments, and also of drums and the clash of arms, obliging the travelers to close their line of march and to proceed in more compact order.* They also find it necessary to take the precaution, before they stop for the night, to agree on a sign pointing out the course they are to take, and to attach a bell to each of the beasts of burden so that they may be more easily kept from straggling. Such are the excessive troubles and dangers that are inevitably met in crossing this desert.

---

*The illusion of singing, musical instruments, and voices is not uncommon in deserts; it is said to be produced by the shifting of sand among dunes.

CHAPTER 40

Of the Province of Tangut, the City of Sachion,
and the Ceremony of Burning the Dead

WHEN the journey of thirty days across the desert has
been completed, you arrive at a city called Sachiu [Sa-
chau] which belongs to the Great Khan. The province is
named Tangut. The people are worshipers of idols.
There are Turkomans among them, and a few Nestorian
Christians and Mahometans. Those who are idolators
have a language distinct from the others. This city lies
toward the east-northeast. They are not a commercial,
but an agricultural people, having much wheat.

There are in this country a number of monasteries and
abbeys which are filled with idols of various kinds. To
these, which they regard with the profoundest reverence,
they offer sacrifices; and on the birth of a son, they recommend him to the protection of one of their idols. In
honor of this deity the father rears a sheep in his house
until the end of a year, and then, on the idol's holiday,
they conduct their son, together with the sheep, into its
presence, and there sacrifice the animal. They boil the
flesh, then lay it before the idol, and stand in front of it
until they have finished a long prayer in which they beg
the idol to preserve the health of their child; and they
believe that during this interval it has sucked in all the
savory juices of the meat. The remaining substance they
then carry home, and assembling all their relations and
friends, eat it with much devout festivity. Finally, they
collect the bones and preserve them in handsome urns.
The priests of the idol have for their portion the head,
the feet, the intestines, and the skin, together with part
of the flesh.

With respect to the dead, too, these idolators have
special ceremonies. Upon the death of a person of rank,
whose body they plan to burn, the relations call together
the astrologers and tell them the year, day, and hour in
which he was born, whereupon these proceed to examine
the horoscope; and having ascertained the constellation
or sign, and the planet presiding therein, declare the day
on which the funeral ceremony shall take place. If it
should happen that the same planet is not then in the

ascendant, they order the body to be kept a week or more, and sometimes even for six months, before they allow the ceremony to be performed. In the hope of a favorable aspect, and dreading unfavorable influence, the relations do not dare to burn the corpse until the astrologers have prescribed the proper time.

It being therefore often necessary that the body remain long in the house, they guard against the consequences of putrefaction by preparing a coffin made of boards a palm in thickness, well fitted together and painted, in which they deposit the corpse, and along with it sweet-scented gums, camphor, and other drugs. The joints or seams they smear with a mixture of pitch and lime, and the whole is then covered with silk. During this period the table is spread every day with bread, wine, and other provisions, which remain long enough for the dead one to eat a meal, as well as for the spirit of the deceased—which they suppose is present—to satisfy itself with the aroma of the victuals. Sometimes the astrologers tell the relations that the body must not be taken from the house through the main door because they have discovered from the aspect of the heavens, or otherwise, that this would be unlucky, and it must therefore be taken out from a different side of the house. In some instances, indeed, they oblige them to break through the wall and convey the corpse through that opening, persuading them that if they refuse to do so, the spirit of the dead will be incensed against the family and do them some injury.* Accordingly, when any misfortune befalls a house, or any person belonging to it meets with an accident or a loss or an untimely death, the astrologers attribute the event to a funeral not having taken place during the ascendancy of the planet under which the dead relative was born, but on the contrary, under an evil influence, or to its not having been conducted through the proper door.

As the ceremony of burning the body must be performed outside the city, they erect at intervals along the road on which the procession is to pass small wooden

---

*This is still practiced and one traveler tells of a family who broke through a wall on to a main street.

buildings with a portico which they cover with silk; and under each of these the body is set down. They place before it meats and liquors, and this is repeated until they reach the appointed spot, believing as they do that the spirit is thereby refreshed and acquires energy to attend the funeral pyre. Another ceremony also is performed on these occasions. They provide pieces of paper made of the bark of a certain tree, upon which are painted the figures of men, women, horses, camels, pieces of money, and dresses, and these they burn along with the corpse in the conviction that in the next world the deceased will enjoy the services of the servants, cattle, and all the articles depicted on the paper. Throughout these proceedings, all the musical instruments belonging to the place are sounded with an incessant din.

Having told of this city, others lying toward the northwest, near the head of the desert, shall now be mentioned.*

CHAPTER 41

Of the District of Kamul and Some Peculiar Customs Respecting the Entertainment of Strangers

KAMUL is a district within the great province of Tangut; it is subject to the Great Khan, and contains many towns and castles, of which the principal city is also named Kamul. This district lies in between two deserts; that is to say, the Great Desert already described and another of smaller extent, being only about three days' journey across. The inhabitants are worshipers of idols and have their own peculiar language. They subsist on the fruits of the earth, which they possess in abundance, and are able to supply the needs of travelers. The men are addicted to pleasure, and attend to little else besides playing upon instruments, singing, dancing, reading, writing, according to the custom of the country, and the pursuit, in short, of every kind of amusement.

*Because Kamul does not lie in the line of travel which the Polos were following, there is some doubt that Marco visited it—or the next province with which he deals—at this time.

When strangers arrive and desire lodging and accommodation at their houses, it affords them the highest gratification. They give positive orders to their wives, daughters, sisters, and other female relations to indulge their guests in every wish, while they themselves leave their homes and retire into the city. The stranger lives in the house with the females as if they were his own wives, and they send him whatever necessities may be desired; but it should be understood that they expect payment for these. Nor do they return to their houses so long as the strangers remain in them. This abandonment of the women of their family to casual guests, who are permitted the same privileges and the same indulgences as if the women were their own wives, is regarded by these people as an honor to themselves and as adding to their reputation. They consider the hospitable reception of strangers, who (after the perils and fatigues of a long journey) need relaxation, an action agreeable to their deities, calculated to draw down the blessing of increase upon their families, to augment their wealth, and to earn them safety from all dangers, as well as a successful issue to all their undertakings. The women are very handsome, very sensual, and fully disposed to conform in this respect to the command of their husbands.

It happened that when Mangu Khan held his court in this province, he learned of the above scandalous custom and issued an edict strictly commanding the people of Kamul to give up this disgraceful practice, and forbidding individuals to furnish lodging to strangers, but to make them stay at inns. In grief and sadness the inhabitants obeyed for about three years; but finding that the earth ceased to yield the accustomed fruits and that many misfortunes befell their families, they resolved to send a deputation to the Great Khan to beg him to permit them to resume the observance of a custom solemnly handed down to them by their ancestors from remotest times—especially since their failure to offer this hospitality to strangers had brought ruin on their families. The Khan, having listened to this application, replied: "Since you appear so anxious to persist in your own shame, let it be as you desire. Go, live according to your base customs and manners, and let your wives continue to receive the beggarly wages of their prostitution." The deputies returned home with this answer to the great delight of all the people, who, to the present day, observe their ancient practice.

CHAPTER 42

Of the City of Chinchitalas

NEXT to the district of Kamul follows that of Chinchitalas [Ghingintalas], which in its northern part borders on the desert and is in length sixteen days' journey. It is subject to the Great Khan and contains cities and several strong places. Its inhabitants are of three religious sects: a few of them confess Christ, according to the Nestorian doctrine; others are followers of Mahomet; and a third worship idols. There is in this district a mountain where the mines produce steel, and also zinc or antimony.

Also found here is a substance of the nature of the salamander, for when woven into cloth and thrown into the fire, it does not burn.* The following mode of preparing it I learned from one of my traveling companions named Zurficar, a very intelligent Turkoman, who directed the mining operations of the province for three years. The fossil substance procured from the mountain consists of fibers not unlike those of wool. After being exposed to the sun to dry, this is pounded in a brass mortar and is then washed until all the earthy particles are separated from it. Having thus cleansed and detached the fibers from each other, they then spin them into thread and weave the thread into cloth. In order to render the texture white, they put it into the fire and allow it to remain there about an hour; when they draw it out it has not been injured by the flame and is as white as snow. By the same process they afterward clean it whenever it becomes dirty.

Of the salamander in the form of a serpent, which is supposed to exist in fire, I could never discover any traces in the eastern regions. It is said that they preserve at Rome a napkin woven from this material, sent as a

*This has been identified as asbestos.

gift from a Tartar prince to the Roman Pontiff as a wrapper for the sudarium of Jesus Christ.

CHAPTER 43

Of the District of Succuir, Where Rhubarb Is Produced

UPON leaving the district last mentioned, and proceeding for ten days east-northeast through a country where there are few habitations and little that is worthy of remark, you arrive at a district named Succuir [Sukchu], in which are many towns and castles, the principal one being likewise named Succuir. The inhabitants are in general idolaters, with some Christians. They are subject to the dominion of the Great Khan. This district, together with the two last named, are in the province of Tangut.

Throughout all the mountainous parts of it the most excellent kind of rhubarb is produced in large quantities; and merchants, who buy loads of it, convey it to all parts of the world. It is a fact that when they take that road, they cannot venture among the mountains with any beasts of burden excepting those accustomed to the country, on account of a poisonous plant growing there. If eaten by them, this causes the hoofs of the animal to drop off. Those of the country, however, being aware of its dangerous quality take care to avoid it. The people of Succuir depend for subsistence upon the fruits of the earth and the meat of their cattle, and do not engage in trade. The district is perfectly healthy, and the complexion of the natives is brown.

CHAPTER 44

Of Campichu and of Its Idols and Marriage Customs

CAMPICHU [Kanchow], the chief city of the province of Tangut, is large and magnificent, and has jurisdiction over all the province. The bulk of the people worship idols [that is, of Buddha], but there are some who follow the religion of Mahomet, and some Christians. The latter have three large and handsome churches in the city. The idolaters have many religious houses, or monasteries and abbeys, built like those in our country, and in these there are a multitude of idols, some of wood, some of stone, and some of clay. They are all highly polished, gilded, and carved in a masterly style. Among these are some of very large size, some small. The former are fully ten paces in length and are lying down; the small figures stand behind them and look like disciples in the act of reverent salutation. Both great and small are held in extreme veneration. Those persons amongst the idolaters who are devoted to the services of religion [the lamas of Tibetan Buddhism] lead more virtuous lives, according to their ideas of morality, than the other classes. They abstain from the indulgence of carnal and sensual desires. The unrestricted intercourse of the sexes is not in general considered by these people a serious offense. Their maxim is that if the advances are made by the female, the connection does not constitute an offense, but it is held to such when the proposal comes from the man.

They employ an almanac in many respects like our own, according to the rules of which, during five, four, or three days in the month [Buddhist Sabbaths or fast days], they do not shed blood, nor eat flesh or fowl— just as we do in regard to Friday, the Sabbath, and the vigils of the saints.

The laity take as many as thirty wives, some more, some fewer, according to their ability to maintain them; for they do not receive any dowry with them, but on the contrary, settle upon their wives dowers of cattle, slaves, and money. The first wife always retains the highest rank in the family and if the husband sees that anyone among them does not behave well to the rest, or if she becomes otherwise disagreeable to him, he can send her away. They take to their beds cousins by blood, and even espouse their mothers-in-law. Many other mortal sins are regarded by them with indifference, and they live in this respect like the beasts of the field.*

In this city Marco Polo remained, along with his father and uncle, about the space of one year, which their business required.

---

*Similar matrimonial practices are later attributed to the Tartars, too.

CHAPTER 45

*Of the City of Ezina and a Desert Extending
Forty Days' Journey Toward the North*

Leaving this city of Campichu and traveling for
twelve days in a northerly direction, you come to a city
named Ezina, at the commencement of the sandy desert
and within the province of Tangut. The inhabitants are
idolaters. They have camels and much cattle of various
sorts. Here you find lanner falcons and many excellent
sakers. The fruits of the soil and the meat of the cattle
supply the wants of the people, and they do not concern
themselves with trade. Travelers passing through this city
lay in a store of provisions for forty days, because upon
their leaving it to go northwards, it takes that long to
cross a desert in which there are no dwellings nor any
inhabitants, except a few among the mountains and in
some valleys during the summer. In these areas, frequented by wild asses and other wild animals, they find
water and pine woods. Having passed this desert, the
traveler arrives at a city, on the northern side of it,
named Karakorum.

CHAPTER 46

*Of the City of Karakorum, the First in Which
the Tartars Had a Settled Residence*

The city of Karakorum is about three miles in circumference* and is the first place in which the Tartars established their residence in remote times. It is surrounded
with a strong rampart of earth, since there is not a good
supply of stone in that part of the country. On the outside of the rampart stands a huge castle in which is located the handsome palace of the governor of the place.

The circumstances under which these Tartars first
began to exercise dominion shall now be related. They
dwelt in the northern regions of Chorcha and Bargu
[south and east of Lake Baikal], but without settled habitations—that is, without towns or fortified places—but

---

*This and the next nine chapters are a digression having little to do
with the journey itself.

where there were extensive plains, good pasture, large rivers, and plenty of water. They had no sovereign of their own, and were tributary to a powerful prince, who, as I have been informed, was called Ung Khan,* which is thought by some to be the same as Prester John† in ours. To him the Tartars paid the tenth part of their cattle in tribute.

In time the tribe multiplied so exceedingly that Ung Khan, that is, Prester John, becoming fearful, conceived the plan of dividing them up into groups and having each group live in a different area. With this in view, whenever a pretext was available, such as a rebellion in one of his provinces, he would draft three or four out of every hundred of these people and use them in quelling it. And thus their power was gradually decreased. He also dispatched them on other expeditions and sent some of his principal officers to see that his orders were carried out.

At length the Tartars, becoming aware that he was trying to reduce them to slavery, resolved to band together, and seeing that their complete ruin was being planned, decided to move from the areas they had inhabited. They proceeded in a northerly direction across a vast desert until they felt they were at a safe distance, and then they refused to pay Ung Khan the customary tribute.

CHAPTER 47

Concerning Genghis, First Khan of the Tartars, and His War with Ung Khan

SOME time after the migration of the Tartars to this place, and about the year of our Lord 1187, they proceeded to elect as their king one named Genghis Khan, a man of proved integrity, great wisdom, commanding

---

*According to Yule, he was probably the head of the Keraits of Mongolia, who had been converted to Nestorian Christianity. He was first identified, or confused, with Prester John by Friar William of Rubruck, a French Franciscan, in 1255.
†Prester (Priest or Presbyter) John was a legendary figure originally reported to be a Christian prince ruling somewhere in Asia or, in later versions of the tale, in Ethiopia.

eloquence, and celebrated valor. He began his reign with
so much justice and moderation that he was beloved and
revered as their deity rather than their sovereign. The
fame of his great and good qualities spreading over that
part of the world, all the Tartars, however far off, placed
themselves under his command. Finding himself thus at
the head of so many brave men, he became ambitious
to emerge from the deserts and wildernesses by which
he was surrounded, and gave them orders to equip themselves with bows and such other weapons as they were
accustomed to use in their pastoral life. He then proceeded to make himself master of cities and provinces;
and such was his reputation for justice and other virtues
that wherever he went he found the people disposed to
submit to him, and to think themselves fortunate to have
his protection and favor. In this manner he got possession of about nine provinces. Nor is his success surprising when we consider that at this period each town and
district was governed either by the people themselves or
by a petty king or lord; and since they had no general
confederacy, it was impossible for them separately to
resist so formidable a power. After subjugating these
places, he appointed such worthy governors to them that
the inhabitants did not suffer either in their persons or
their properties.

Seeing how well his enterprises went, he resolved to
attempt still greater things. With this view he sent ambassadors to Prester John with a message (which he knew
would not be heeded by that prince) demanding* his
daughter in marriage. Upon receiving the proposal, the
monarch indignantly exclaimed: "How does Genghis Khan
presume to ask for my daughter's hand when he knows
he is only a servant of mine! Leave instantly," he said,
"and let him know from me that if he repeats such a
demand I shall put him to a shameful death." The ambassadors on receiving this reply departed straightway, hastened to their master, and related all that Prester John
had ordered them to say, keeping nothing back.

---

*Actually Genghis Khan proposed, in 1202, a marriage between his son
and Ung Khan's daughter.

CHAPTER 48

How Genghis Mustered His People to March Against Prester John

ENRAGED at this reply, Genghis Khan collected a very large army, at the head of which he entered the territory of Prester John, and encamping on a great plain called Tenduk, sent a message warning him to defend himself.

CHAPTER 49

How Prester John Marched to Meet Genghis

PRESTER John advanced likewise to the plain with a vast army, and took his position at a distance of about ten miles from the other. At this juncture Genghis Khan commanded his astrologers and magicians to tell him which of the two armies would win in the approaching conflict. Upon this they took a green reed, and dividing it lengthways into two parts, they wrote on one part the name of their master, and on the other the name of Prester John. They then placed them on the ground at some distance from each other, and gave notice to the king that while they were uttering their incantations the two pieces of reed, through the power of their idols, would advance toward each other, and that the victory would fall to that monarch whose piece should be seen to mount the other.

The whole army was assembled to witness this ceremony, and while the astrologers were reading their books, they perceived the two pieces begin to approach each other, and after a brief interval they saw the one marked with the name of Genghis Khan place itself on top of the other.*

---

*Using reeds or twigs for the purpose of divination was not uncommon as far back as Herodotus.

CHAPTER 50

The Battle Between Genghis Khan and Prester John

UPON witnessing this, the king and his band of Tartars marched with exultation to attack the army of Prester John, broke through its ranks, and entirely routed it. Prester John himself was killed, his kingdom fell to the conqueror, and Genghis Khan espoused his daughter. After this battle he continued for six years to make himself master of additional kingdoms and cities until at length, in the siege of a castle named Thaigin, he was struck in the knee by an arrow, and dying of the wound,* was buried in the Altai Mountains.

CHAPTER 51

Of Six Successive Emperors of the Tartars and Their Burial Ceremonies

GENGHIS Khan was succeeded by Kuyuk Khan,† the third was Batu Khan, the fourth Alacou Khan, the fifth Mangu Khan, the sixth Kublai Khan, who became greater and more powerful than all the others, inasmuch as he inherited all that his predecessors possessed, and afterwards, during a reign of nearly sixty years, took over the remainder of the world.

The title of Khan, or Kaan, is equivalent to emperor in our language. It has been an invariable custom that all the Great Khans and chiefs of the race of Genghis, their first Lord, should be carried for burial to a certain lofty mountain named Altai; and wherever they happen to die, although it be a hundred days' journey, they are nevertheless brought here.

While they are removing the bodies of these princes, it is likewise the custom for those who form the escort to sacrifice such persons as they chance to meet on the

---

*Since the battle with Ung Khan occurred in 1203 and Genghis did not die until 1227, he outlived Ung by twenty-four, not six, years.
†Genghis was in fact succeeded by his son Ogodai, and then his grandsons Kuyuk, Mangu, and Kublai. Batu, brother of Kublai, was ruler of the Russian Tartars.

road, saying to them, "Depart for the next world, and there attend upon your deceased Lord." They do this in the belief that all whom they thus slay do actually become his servants in the next life. They do the same also with horses, killing the best of the stud in order that he may have the use of them. When the corpse of Mangu Khan was transported to this mountain, the horsemen who accompanied it slew upwards of twenty thousand persons who fell in their path.

CHAPTER 52

Of the Wandering Life of the Tartars, of Their Domestic Manners, Their Food, and the Virtue of Their Women

Now that I have begun speaking of the Tartars, I will tell you more about them. The Tartars never remain in one place, but as the winter approaches move to the plains of a warmer region in order to find sufficient pasture for their cattle. In summer they frequent cold areas in the mountains, where there is water and vegetation, and where their cattle are free from horseflies and other biting insects. During two or three months they progressively climb to higher ground to seek fresh pasture, the grass in any one place not being adequate to feed the multitudes of their herds and flocks.

Their huts or tents are formed of rods covered with felt, and being perfectly round, and neatly put together, they can gather them into one bundle and make them up as packages, which they carry along with them upon a sort of cart with four wheels. When they have occasion to set them up, they always face the entrance to the south. Besides these carts they have a better kind of vehicle upon two wheels, also covered with black felt, and so effectually as to protect those within it from wet throughout a whole day of rain.* These are drawn by oxen and camels, and serve to carry their wives and children, their utensils, and such provisions as they require.

*Rubruck reported that one which he measured was no less than twenty feet wide.

It is the women who attend to their trading concerns, who buy and sell, and provide everything necessary for their husbands and their families, the time of the men being entirely devoted to hunting, hawking, and matters that relate to the military life. They have the best falcons in the world and also the best dogs.

They subsist entirely upon flesh and milk, eating the game they catch, and a certain small animal called Pharaoh's mice [the jerboa], which is not unlike a rabbit and which is found during the summer season in great abundance in the plains. But they likewise eat meat of every description, including horses, camels, and even dogs, provided they are fat. They drink mares' milk, which they prepare in such a manner that it has the qualities and flavor of white wine.

Their women are not excelled for chastity and decency of conduct, nor for love and duty to their husbands. Infidelity to the marriage bed is regarded by them as a vice not merely dishonorable, but of the most infamous nature. It is also wonderful to see the loyalty of the husbands toward their wives, among whom, although there are perhaps ten or twenty, there is a unity and accord that is very praiseworthy. No offensive language is ever heard, their attention being fully occupied with their own affairs and their domestic duties, such as providing food for the family, the management of servants, and the care of the children, who are cared for in common.

The men are allowed as many wives as they want. Their expense to the husband is not great, and on the other hand the benefit he derives from their training and the work they do is considerable. For each, he first makes payment to the mother. The first wife has the most privileges and is held to be the most truly legitimate, and this extends also to the children borne by her. In consequence of this unlimited number of wives, they have more children than any other people. Upon the death of the father, the son may take for himself the wives he leaves behind, with the exception of his own mother. They cannot marry their sisters, but upon the death of their brothers they can take their sisters-in-law. Every marriage is solemnized with great ceremony.

CHAPTER 53

Of the God of the Tartars and of Tartar Dress

THE doctrine and faith of the Tartars are these: They believe in a deity whose nature is sublime and heavenly. To him they burn incense and offer up prayers for the enjoyment of intellectual and bodily health. They also worship another, named Natigay, whose image, covered with felt or other cloth, every individual preserves in his house. Next to this deity they set images of a "wife" and "children," placing the former on his left side, and the latter before him. They consider him the divinity who presides over their earthly concerns, protects their children, and guards their cattle and their grain. They show him great respect, and at their meals they never fail to take a fat morsel of the flesh and with it grease the mouth of the idol and at the same time the mouths of its wife and children. They then toss out of the door some of the liquid in which the meat has been dressed, as an offering to the other spirits. This done, they consider that the deity and his family have had their proper share, and proceed to eat and drink without further ceremony.

The wealthy Tartars dress in cloth of gold and silks, with skins of the sable, the ermine, and other animals, all in the richest fashion.

CHAPTER 54

Concerning the Tartar Customs of War

THEIR arms are bows, iron maces, and in some instances, spears; but the first of these is the weapon at which they are the most expert, being accustomed from childhood to use it in their sports. They wear armor made from buffalo hides and those of other beasts, dried by fire and thus rendered extremely hard and strong. They are brave in battle, almost to desperation, setting little value upon their lives and exposing themselves without hesitation to all manner of danger. Their disposition is cruel.

They are capable of enduring every kind of privation, and when there is a necessity for it, can live for a month on the milk of their mares [kumiss, a favorite drink of Asiatic nomads] and upon such wild animals as they may chance to catch. Their horses are fed upon grass alone, and do not require barley or other grain. The men are trained to remain on horseback for two days and nights without dismounting and to sleep in that position while their horses graze. No people upon earth can surpass them in fortitude under difficulties, nor show greater patience under privation of every kind. They are most obedient to their chiefs and are maintained at little cost. It is because of these qualities, so essential to the making of a soldier, that they are fitted to subdue the world—as in fact they have done to a considerable portion of it.

When one of the great Tartar chiefs proceeds on an expedition, he puts himself at the head of an army of a hundred thousand horsemen and organizes them in the following manner. He appoints an officer to the command of every ten men, and others to command a hundred, a thousand, and ten thousand men, respectively. Thus ten of the officers commanding ten men take their orders from the one who commands a hundred; of these, each ten, from him who commands a thousand; and each ten of these latter, from him who commands ten thousand.

By this arrangement each officer has only to attend to the management of ten men or ten groups of men; and all are implicitly obedient to their respective superiors. Every company of a hundred men is dominated by a *tuc,* and ten of these constitute a *toman.* When the army goes into battle, a body of two hundred men is sent two days' march in advance, and parties are stationed on each flank and in the rear in order to prevent a surprise. When their goal is far off they carry but little with them, and then chiefly what is needed for their encampment and for cooking. They subsist for the most part upon milk. Each man has, on the average, eighteen horses and mares; and as soon as one wearies, his rider changes to another. In case of rain they are provided with small tents made of felt. Should it be necessary, they can march for ten days without lighting a fire or taking a meal. During this time they subsist upon the blood drawn from their horses, each man opening a vein in one of his own cattle and drinking from it.

They also make use of milk thickened and dried to the state of a paste (or curd), which is prepared in the following manner. They boil the milk, and skimming off the rich or creamy part as it rises to the top, put it into a vessel as butter; as long as that remains in the milk, it will not become hard. The latter is then exposed to the sun until it dries. Upon going into battle they carry with them about ten pounds for each man, and every morning half a pound of this is put into a leather flask with as much water as is thought necessary. As they ride, these flasks are violently shaken up and a thin porridge is produced, upon which they make their dinner.

When these Tartars come to engage in battle, they never mix with the enemy, but keep hovering about him, firing arrows first from one side and then from the other, occasionally pretending to fly, and during their flight shooting arrows backwards at their pursuers, killing men and horses as easily as if they were fighting face to face. In this sort of warfare the adversary imagines he has gained a victory when in fact he has lost the battle; for the Tartars, noting the damage they have done him, wheel about, and renewing the fight, overpower his remaining troops and make them prisoners in spite of their utmost exertions. Their horses are so well trained that upon a given signal, they instantly turn in any direction. By such rapid maneuvers they have won many victories.

All that has been here related concerns the early Tartar chiefs; at the present day they are much degenerated. Those who dwell in Cathay, forsaking their own laws, have adopted the customs of the people who worship idols, and those who inhabit the eastern provinces [the Levant] have adopted the manners of the Saracens.

CHAPTER 55

Of the Laws and of an Imaginary Kind of Marriage Between Deceased Children

JUSTICE is administered by them in the following manner. When a person is convicted of a robbery not meriting the punishment of death, he is condemned to receive a certain number of strokes with a rod—seven, seventeen, twenty-seven, thirty-seven, forty-seven, or as many as one hundred and seven, according to the value of the article stolen and circumstances of the theft. Many die from this punishment. When a man is condemned to death for stealing a horse or other article, the sentence is executed by cutting his body in two with a sword. But if the thief can pay nine times the value of the property stolen, he escapes all further punishment.

It is usual for every chief of a tribe or other person possessing cattle, such as horses, mares, camels, oxen, or cows, to distinguish them by his mark and then to allow them to graze at large in any part of the plains or mountains, without herdsmen to look after them. If any of them should happen to mix with the cattle of other proprietors, they are restored to the person whose brand they bear. Sheep and goats, however, have shepherds to tend them. Their cattle of every kind are good-sized, fat, and exceedingly handsome.

When one man has had a son, and another man a daughter, although both have been dead for some years, they have a custom of arranging a marriage between their deceased children, and of bestowing the girl upon the youth. At the same time they paint upon pieces of paper human figures representing servants with horses and other animals, dresses of all kinds, money, and furniture; and all these, together with the marriage contract, which is regularly drawn up, they commit to the flames in order that, through the smoke, these things may be conveyed to their children in the other world and that they may become husband and wife in due form. After this ceremony, the fathers and mothers consider themselves mutually related, just as if a real connection had taken place between their living children.

Having thus given an account of the manners and customs of the Tartars, although not yet of the brilliant acts and enterprises of their Great Khan, who is Lord of all the Tartars, we shall now return to our former subject, that is, to the wide plain which we were crossing when we stopped to relate the history of this people.

CHAPTER 56

*Of the Plain of Bargu, Its Inhabitants,
the Ocean, and the Falcons in This Country*

UPON leaving Karakorum and the mountains of
Altai—the burial place, as has been said, of the imperial
Tartar family—you proceed in a northerly direction
through a country called the plain of Bargu [around
Lake Baikal in Siberia], extending to a distance of about
forty days' journey. The people who dwell there are
called Makrit, a rude tribe who live upon the flesh of
animals, the largest of which are like stags;* and these
they also use for the purpose of traveling. They likewise
feed upon the birds that live in their numerous lakes and
marshes, as well as upon flesh. At the molting season, or
during the summer, the birds seek these waters, and
being then unable to fly for lack of feathers, they are
taken by the natives without difficulty. This plain borders on the ocean [Lake Baikal] at its northern extremity. The customs and manners of the people resemble
those of the Tartars that have been described, and they
are subjects of the Great Khan. They have neither corn
nor wine; and although in summer they live on what
they can catch, in winter the cold is so excessive that
neither birds nor beasts can remain there. Upon traveling forty days, as was said, you reach the ocean. On a
mountain near this, as well as in the neighboring plains,
vultures and peregrine falcons have their nests. Neither
men nor cattle are found there, and of birds there is
only a species called *bargherlak,* and the falcons which
prey on them. The former are about the size of a partridge, have tails like the swallow, and claws like those
of the parrot, and are swift of flight. When the Great
Khan wants a brood of peregrine falcons, he sends to
this place for them. Gerfalcons are found in such numbers in an island lying off the coast that his Majesty may
be supplied with as many of them as he pleases. It must
not be supposed that the gerfalcons sent from Europe
for the use of the Tartars go to the court of the Great
Khan. They go only to some Tartar or other chief of the

*These are evidently reindeer.

Levant, bordering on the countries of the Comanians and Armenians. This island is situated so far to the north that the North Star appears to be behind you, and to have in part a southerly bearing.

Having thus spoken of the regions in the vicinity of the Northern Ocean, we shall now describe provinces lying nearer to the residence of the Great Khan, returning to that of Campichu, which has already been mentioned.

CHAPTER 57

*Of the Kingdom of Erginul and the Province
of Sinju, and of the Customs of That
Country and the Beauty of the Women*

UPON leaving Campichu [Kanchau]* and proceeding five days' journey toward the east, in the course of which travelers are frequently terrified at night by the voices of spirits, they reach a kingdom named Erginul [Koko Nor], subject to the Great Khan and included in the province of Tangut. Within the limits of this kingdom are several principalities, the inhabitants of which are, in general, idolaters, with some few Nestorian Christians and worshipers of Mahomet.

Among many cities and strong places, the principal one is Erginul. Proceeding thence in a southeasterly direction, the road takes you to Cathay [the medieval name for northern China], and on that route you find a city called Singui, in a district of the same name. It has many towns and castles, also belonging to Tangut and under the dominion of the Great Khan. The population of this country consists chiefly of idolaters; but there are also some Mahometans and Christians. Here are found many wild cattle [wild yaks] that, in point of size, may be compared to elephants. Their color is a mixture of white and black, and they are very beautiful. The hair on their bodies lies flat, excepting upon the shoulders, where it stands up to the height of about three palms. This hair, or rather wool, is white and more soft and delicate than

---

*Polo here returns to the description of his journey.

silk. Marco Polo carried some of it to Venice as a great curiosity, and such it was esteemed by all who saw it. Many of these cattle, taken wild, have been domesticated, and the breed produced between them and the common cow are noble animals and better able to resist fatigue than any other kind. They are accustomed to carry heavier burdens and to do twice as much work as the ordinary sort, being both active and powerful.

It is in this country that the finest and most valuable musk is procured. The animal which yields it is not larger than the female goat, but in form resembles the antelope. It is called *gudder* in the Tartar language. Its coat is like that of the larger kind of deer: its feet and tail are those of the antelope, but it does not have horns. It has four projecting teeth or tusks, each three inches in length, two in the upper jaw pointing downward, and two in the lower jaw pointing upward; they are small in proportion to their length and as white as ivory. Upon the whole it is a handsome creature. The musk is obtained in the following manner. At the time when the moon is at the full, a bag or sac of coagulated blood forms around the navel. Those whose occupation it is to take the animal avail themselves of moonlight for that purpose, cut off the membrane, and afterwards dry it, with its contents, in the sun. It provides the finest musk and produces that powerful perfume. Great numbers are caught, and the meat is esteemed good to eat. Marco Polo brought with him to Venice the dried head and the feet of one of them.

The inhabitants of this country occupy themselves in trade and manufacture. They have grain in abundance. The extent of the province is twenty-five days' journey. Pheasants are found in it that are twice the size of ours, but somewhat smaller than the peacock, and with tail feathers eight or ten palms in length. There are also other pheasants, in size and appearance like our own, as well as a great variety of other birds, some of which have beautiful plumage.

The inhabitants are idolaters. In person they are inclined to be fat, and their noses are small. Their hair is black, and they have scarcely any beard, or only a few scattered hairs on the chin. The women of the upper class are similarly free from superfluous hairs; their skin is fair and they are well formed. The men like female company; and according to their laws and customs, they may have as many wives as they please, provided they are able to maintain them. If a young woman is poor but attractive, and a rich man wants to marry her, he must make valuable presents to her parents and relations, beauty alone being the quality held in high esteem. We shall now take leave of this district, and proceed to speak of another, situated further to the eastward.

CHAPTER 58

Of the Province of Egrigaia and the City of Kalachan

DEPARTING from Erginul, and proceeding easterly for eight days, you come to a country named Egrigaia [Ninghia, located where the Great Wall and the Yellow River meet], still belonging to the great province of Tangut, and subject to the Great Khan. In this country there are many cities and castles, the principal one of which is called Kalachan. The inhabitants are in general idolaters; but there are three churches of Nestorian Christians. In this city they manufacture beautiful camlets [a fabric], the finest known in the world, of the hair of camels and likewise of white wool. These are a beautiful white, for they also have white camels. They are purchased by the merchants in considerable quantities and carried to many other countries, especially to Cathay.

Leaving this province, we shall now speak of another situated toward the east, and shall thus enter the territory of Prester John.

CHAPTER 59

Of the Province of Tenduk, Which Is Governed by Princes of the Race of Prester John

TENDUK, belonging to the territory of Prester John, is an eastern province, with many cities and castles. It is subject to the rule of the Great Khan, all the princes of that family having remained dependent since Genghis, the first emperor, subdued the country. The capital is likewise named Tenduk [Tokoto]. The greater part of the inhabitants are Christians. The king now reigning, named George, holds his country as a fief of the Great Khan; not, indeed, the entire country of the original Prester John, but a portion of it. The Khan always gives his daughters, and other females of the royal family, in marriage to him and other princes of his house.

In this province the stone that produces azure coloring is found in abundance and is of fine quality. Here likewise they manufacture fabrics of camels' hair. The people gain their livelihood by agriculture, trade, and mechanical work. Among the inhabitants, however, there are both worshipers of idols and followers of the law of Mahomet as well as Christians. The rule of the province is in the hands of the Christians. There is likewise a class of people known by the name of *Argon,* because they result from a mixture of two races, namely, those natives of Tenduk who are idolaters [that is Buddhists] and the Mahometans. The men of this country are fairer complexioned and better looking than those in the other countries of which we have been speaking. They are also better trained and more skillful traders.

In this province of Tenduk was located the principal seat of government of the sovereigns styled Prester John, when they ruled over the Tartars of this and the neighboring countries, which their successors still occupy. George, the present king, is the fourth in descent from Prester John, of whose family he is regarded as the head. There are two regions in which they exercise dominion; and in our part of the world they are known as Gog and Magog,* but by the natives as Ung and Mongul. In each of these there is a distinct race: in Ung they are Gog, and in Mongul they are Tartars.

Traveling seven days through this province in an east-

---

*Much has been made of Polo's failure to mention the Great Wall of China, though he surely knew it well. There is no explanation for this unless we accept Yule's supposition that Polo has it in mind here. According to this theory, Gog and Magog (those who threaten Israel in the Old Testament) were thought of as the Tartars; and since the Alexander legend said he had built a rampart to shut them out, Polo would here be thinking of the Great Wall because it was such a rampart.

erly direction, toward Cathay, you pass many towns inhabited by idolaters, as well as by Mahometans and Nestorian Christians. They gain their living by trade and manufacture, weaving, gold cloths ornamented with mother-of-pearl, and silks of diverse textures and colors, not unlike those of Europe, together with a variety of woolen cloths.

These people are all subjects of the Great Khan. One of the towns, Sindachu, is celebrated for the manufacture of all kinds of arms and every article for the equipment of troops. In the mountainous part of the province there is a place called Ydifu [Yuchow] in which is a rich mine of silver, whence large quantities of that metal are obtained. There are also plenty of birds and beasts.

CHAPTER 60

Of the City of Chagan Nor, and of Cranes, Partridges, and Quails

LEAVING the city and province last mentioned and traveling three days, you arrive at a city named Chagan Nor, which signifies the White Pool. At this place the Khan has a great palace, which he is fond of visiting because it is surrounded by lakes and streams which are the haunt of many swans. There is also a fine plain, where cranes, pheasants, partridges, and other birds are found in great numbers. He derives the greatest amusement from sporting with gerfalcons and hawks, the game most abundant here.

Of the cranes they reckon five species. The first sort are entirely black as coals and have long wings. The second sort have wings still longer than the first, but are white, and the feathers of the wings are full of eyes, round like those of the peacock but of a gold color and very bright; the head is red and black and well formed; the neck is black and white, and the general appearance of the bird is very handsome. The third sort are of the size of ours. The fourth are small cranes, having the feathers prettily streaked with red and azure. The fifth are of a gray color, with the head red and black, and are of a large size.

Near this city is a valley frequented by great numbers of partridges and quail, for whose food the Great Khan causes millet and other grains that attract such birds to be sown along the sides of it every season, and gives strict command that no person shall reap the seed. Many keepers are also stationed there to see that the game is not taken or destroyed, as well as to spread the millet for the birds during the winter. So accustomed are they to this feeding, that when the grain is scattered and the man whistles, they immediately assemble from every quarter. The Great Khan also directs that a number of small buildings be prepared for their shelter during the night; in consequence of these attentions, he always finds abundant sport when he visits this country. Even in the winter, when on account of the severity of the cold he does not stay there, he has camel loads of the birds sent wherever his court may happen to be.

CHAPTER 61

Of the Great Khan's Beautiful Palace in the City of Shandu and the Ceremonies Performed There

DEPARTING from the city last mentioned and proceeding three days' journey in a northeasterly direction, you arrive at a city called Shandu [Shangtu],* built by the Great Khan Kublai, now reigning. In this he caused a palace to be erected of marble and other handsome stones, admirable for the elegance of its design as well as for the skill of its execution.

The halls and chambers are all gilt and very handsome. One front faces the interior of the city, and the other toward the wall; and from each extremity of the building runs another wall to such an extent as to enclose sixteen miles of the adjoining plain, to which there is no entrance but through the palace. Within the bounds of this royal park there are rich and beautiful meadows,

*Kublai's summer residence, about 200 miles north of Peiping as the crow flies. Kublai founded it in 1256.

watered by many rivulets,* where a variety of animals of the deer and goat kind are pastured to serve as food for the hawks and other birds employed in the chase, whose pens are also in the grounds. The number of these birds is more than two hundred, without counting the hawks; and the Great Khan goes in person once every week to inspect them. Frequently, when he rides about this enclosed forest, he has one or more small leopards carried on horseback behind their keepers; and when he feels like ordering them to be slipped, they instantly seize a stag, goat, or fallow deer, which he gives to his hawks, and in this manner he amuses himself.

In the center of these grounds is a beautiful grove of trees, in which he has built a Royal Pavilion supported upon a colonnade of handsome pillars, gilt and varnished. Round each pillar a dragon, likewise gilt, entwines its tail, while its head supports the projection of the roof, and its talons, or claws, are extended to the right and left. The roof, like the rest, is of bamboo cane, and so well varnished that no wetting can injure it. The bamboos used for this purpose are three palms in girth and ten to fifteen paces in length, and being cut at the joints, are split into two equal parts, so as to form gutters, and with these (laid concave and convex) the pavilion is covered. But to secure the roof against the wind, each of the bamboos is tied at the ends to the frame. The building is supported on every side like a tent by more than two hundred very strong silken cords, or, because of the lightness of the materials, it might otherwise be overturned by the force of high winds. The whole is constructed with so much ingenuity that all the parts may be taken apart, removed, and set up again, at his Majesty's pleasure. He has selected this spot for his recreation on account of its mild temperature and healthful air, and he accordingly makes it his residence during three months of the year, namely, June, July, and August. Every year, on the twenty-eighth day of the moon,

*It was while reading this passage in an old translation that Samuel Taylor Coleridge fell asleep and had a vision in a dream which he described in the opening lines of his "Kubla Khan."

in August, it is his custom to proceed to an appointed place in order to perform certain sacrifices in the following manner.

It should be added that the Khan keeps up a stud of about ten thousand horses and mares, which are white as snow. Of the milk of these mares no person can presume to drink who is not of the family descended from Genghis Khan, with the exception only of one other family, named Horiat, to whom that monarch gave the privilege, in reward for valorous deeds performed in battle and in his own presence. So great, indeed, is the respect shown to these horses that even when they are at pasture in the royal meadows or forests, no one dares to place himself before them or otherwise hinder their movements. The astrologers whom he entertains in his service, and who are deeply versed in the diabolical art of magic, have pronounced it his duty annually, on the twenty-eighth day of the moon in August, to scatter in the wind the milk taken from these mares in propitiation of all the spirits and idols whom they adore. On such occasion these astrologers, or magicians as they may be termed, sometimes display their skill in a wonderful manner; for if it should happen that the sky becomes cloudy and threatens rain, they ascend the roof of the palace where the Great Khan resides and by incantations prevent the rain from falling and halt the tempest. The sorcerers who perform these miracles are from Tibet and Kashmir, two nations of idolaters more profoundly skilled in magic than any others. They persuade the people that these works are effected through the holiness of their lives and their penances. They exhibit themselves in a filthy and indecent state, and are without respect for themselves, or for those who see them. They go about with their faces unwashed and their hair uncombed, living altogether in a squalid style. They are addicted, moreover, to this beastly and horrible practice: when any culprit is condemned to death, they carry off the body, prepare it on a fire, and devour it. But they do not eat the bodies of persons who die a natural death.

Besides the marvels before mentioned, by which they are distinguished from each other, they are likewise termed Bakshi [Buddhist begging priests, called lamas in

Tibet], which applies to their religious sect, or order. So expert are they in their infernal art that they can do whatever they will; and one instance shall be given, although it may be thought to exceed the bounds of credibility. When the Great Khan sits at meals in his hall of state—as will be described in the following book—the table which is placed in the center is elevated to a height of about eight cubits; and at a distance from it stands a large buffet, where all the drinking vessels are arranged. Now, by means of their supernatural art, they cause the flagons of wine, milk, or any other beverage to fill the cups spontaneously, without being touched by the attendants, and the cups to move through the air the distance of ten paces until they reach the hand of the Great Khan! As he empties them, they return to the place whence they came; and this is done in the presence of such persons as are invited by his Majesty to witness the performance.*

When the festival days of their idols draw near, these Bakshi go to the palace of the Great Khan, and thus address him: "Sire, be it known to your Majesty that if honors and offerings are not paid to our deities, they will afflict us with bad seasons, with blight on our grain, pestilence on our cattle, and with other plagues. On this account we beg your Majesty to grant us a certain number of sheep with black heads, together with so many pounds of incense and aloes wood, in order that we may perform the customary rites with due solemnity." Their words, however, are not spoken directly to the Great Khan, but to certain great officers, who then tell him about it. Upon receiving it he never fails to comply with the whole of their request. Accordingly, when the day arrives, they sacrifice the sheep; and by pouring out the liquor in which the meat has been cooked, in the presence of their idols, perform the ceremony of worship.

In this country there are great monasteries and abbeys, so extensive indeed that they might pass for small cities, some of them containing as many as two thousand

---

*Indian magicians have been celebrated for tricks of this kind from Marco's time down to those present-day troupes in which a performer throws a rope into the air, climbs it, and disappears.

monks,* who are devoted to the service of their divinities, according to the established religious customs of the people. These are clad in a better style of dress than the other inhabitants. They shave their heads and their beards, and celebrate the festivals of their idols with the utmost possible solemnity, including bands of singers and burning tapers. Some of this class are allowed to take wives.

There is likewise another religious order, the members of which are named Sensin [probably Sien-seng, ascetic Taoist priests], who observe strict abstinence and lead very austere lives, having no other food than bran, which they mix in warm water.† That is their food: bran, and nothing but bran; and water for their drink. This sect sometimes pay adoration to fire, and are considered by the others as heretics, because they do not worship idols. There is a material difference between the rules of the two orders: the last described never marry in any instance. They shave their heads and beards like the others, and wear hempen garments of a black and blue color; but even if the material were silk, the color would be the same. They sleep upon coarse mats, and suffer greater hardships in their mode of living than any people in the world.

We shall now quit this subject, and proceed to speak of the wonderful acts of the Supreme Lord of Lords, the great Emperor of the Tartars, Kublai Khan.

---

*Polo does not exaggerate. Some of the Tibetan lamaseries, such as those at Kumbum and Lhasa, have housed upwards of 5,000 lamas.
†Probably the staple of Tibetan diet called *tsamba,* which consists of parched barley, often mixed in hot tea.

Book II

✳

Of the Great Kublai Khan and
of Provinces Visited on
Journeys Westward and Southward

PART 1

THE GREAT KHAN KUBLAI, HIS CAPITAL, COURT, AND GOVERNMENT

CHAPTER 1

Of the Deeds of Kublai Khan, the Emperor Now Reigning

IN THIS book it is our design to tell you of the great achievements of the Great Khan now reigning, who is styled Kublai Khan. The latter title means in our language Lord of Lords, and surely he has every right to such a title, for in respect to number of subjects, extent of territory,* and amount of revenue, he surpasses every sovereign that has ever been or now is in the world; nor has any other been served with such implicit obedience by those whom he governs. This will be made so evident in the course of our work as to satisfy everyone of the truth of our assertion.

CHAPTER 2

The Revolt of Nayan, Uncle of the Great Khan

KUBLAI KHAN, it should be understood, is the direct and legitimate descendant of Genghis Khan, the first emperor and the rightful sovereign of the Tartars. He is the sixth [actually the fifth] Great Khan, and began his reign in the year 1256 [really 1260]. He obtained the sovereignty by his valor, virtues, and prudence, in opposition

---

*Kublai's empire extended from the China Sea as far west as Poland.

to his brothers, who were supported by many of the great officers and members of his own family. But the succession was his in law and right.

It is forty-two years from the time he began to reign to the present year, 1298, and he is fully eighty-five years of age.* Before he ascended the throne he had served as a volunteer in the army, and endeavored to take part in every enterprise. Not only was he brave and daring in action, but in judgment and military skill he was considered the most able and successful commander that ever led the Tartars to battle. From that period, however, he ceased to take the field in person, and entrusted the expeditions to his sons and his captains—excepting in one instance, the occasion of which was as follows.

A certain chief named Nayan, who, although only thirty years of age, was kinsman to Kublai, had succeeded to the dominion of many cities and provinces, which enabled him to bring into the field an army of 300,000 horsemen. His predecessors, however, had been vassals of the Great Khan. Motivated by youthful vanity upon finding himself at the head of so great a force, he resolved to throw off his allegiance and seize the sovereignty. With this in view he privately dispatched messengers to Kaidu, another powerful chief, whose territories lay toward Greater Turkey [Turkestan]. Although a nephew of the Great Khan, Kaidu was in rebellion against him, and was his bitter enemy as a result of fear of punishment for former offenses.

To Kaidu, therefore, the propositions made by Nayan were highly satisfactory, and he promised to bring to Nayan's assistance an army of a hundred thousand horsemen. Both princes immediately began to assemble their forces, but this could not be done so secretly as not to come to the knowledge of Kublai.

---

*Marco did not know that Kublai had died in 1294 at the age of seventy-eight, about two years after the Polos had left China.

CHAPTER 3

How the Great Khan Marched Against Nayan

Upon hearing of their preparations, the Great Khan lost no time in occupying all the passes leading to the countries of Nayan and of Kaidu in order to prevent them from learning of the measures he was himself taking. He then gave orders for mustering, with the utmost speed, all the troops stationed within ten days' march of the city of Khan-balik [or Kanbalu, now part of Peiping]. These amounted to 360,000 horsemen, to which was added 100,000 foot soldiers, consisting of those who were usually around him, and principally his falconers and domestic servants.

In the course of twenty days they were all in readiness. Had he assembled the garrisons kept up for the constant protection of the different provinces of Cathay, it would have required thirty or forty days. During this time the enemy would have learned of his arrangements, and would have united and occupied such strong positions as would best suit their designs. His object was by prompt action to anticipate the preparations of Nayan, and by falling upon him while he was alone, destroy his power with more certainty than after he should have been joined by Kaidu.

It may be proper here to observe, while on the subject of the armies of the Great Khan, that in every province of Cathay and of Manzi, as well as in other parts of his dominions, there were many disloyal and seditious persons, who were always ready to break out in rebellion against their sovereign. On this account it became necessary to keep armies stationed at a distance of four or five miles from all large cities, and ready to enter them at their pleasure. The Great Khan makes it a practice to change these armies every second year, and the same with respect to the officers who command them. By means of such precautions the people are kept in quiet subjection, and no movement or outbreak of any kind can be attempted. The troops are maintained not only from the pay they receive out of the imperial revenues of the province, but also from the cattle and their milk, which belong to them individually and which they send into the cities for sale. In this manner they are distributed over the country in various places, to a distance of thirty, forty, and even sixty days' journey. If even half of these corps were to be collected in one place, the statement of their number would appear incredible.

Having formed his army in the manner described, the Great Khan proceeded toward the territory of Nayan; and by forced marches, continued day and night, he reached it at the end of twenty-five days. So prudently was the expedition managed that neither that prince himself nor any of his dependents were aware of it, all roads being guarded in such a manner that no persons who attempted to pass could escape arrest.

CHAPTER 4

Of the Battle That the Great Khan Fought with Nayan

UPON arriving at a certain range of hills, on the other side of which was the plain where Nayan's army lay encamped, Kublai halted his troops and allowed them two days of rest. During this interval he called upon his astrologers to ascertain by their art, and declare in front of the whole army, which side would win. They declared that Kublai's forces would be victorious. Confident of success, they ascended the hill with cheerful willingness the next morning, and confronted the army of Nayan; they found the enemy poorly posted, without advance parties or scouts, while the chief himself was asleep in his tent with one of his favorite wives. Upon awaking, Nayan hastened to form his troops as best he could, lamenting that he had not started to join Kaidu sooner.

Kublai took his station in a large wooden castle, borne on the backs of four elephants, whose bodies were protected with coverings of thick leather hardened by fire, over which were housings of cloth of gold. The castle contained many crossbowmen and archers, and above it flew the imperial banner, adorned with representations of the sun and moon.

His army, which consisted of thirty battalions of horsemen, each battalion containing ten thousand men

armed with bows, he disposed in three grand divisions.
Those which formed the left and right wings he extended
in such a manner as to outflank the army of Nayan. In
front of each battalion of horsemen were placed five
hundred infantry armed with short lances and swords,
who, whenever the cavalry made a show of flight, were
trained to mount behind the riders and accompany them,
alighting again when they returned to the charge, and
killing with their lances the horses of the enemy.

As soon as the order of battle was arranged, an infinite number of wind instruments of various kinds were
sounded, and these were succeeded by singing, according
to the custom of the Tartars before they engage in a
fight. The battle begins at a signal given by the cymbals
and drums, and there was such a beating of these instruments and such singing, that it was wonderful to hear.

By order of the Great Khan, this signal was first given
to the right and left wings, and the great drums of Kublai
Khan began to sound. Then a fierce and bloody conflict
began. The air was instantly filled with a cloud of arrows
that poured down on every side, and vast numbers of
men and horses were seen to fall to the ground. The
loud cries and shouts of the men, together with the noise
of the horses and the weapons, were such as to inspire
terror in those who heard them. Once their arrows had
been discharged, the warring parties engaged in close
combat with their lances and swords, and with maces
shod with iron. Such was the slaughter, and so large the
heaps of the bodies of men, and more especially of
horses, that it became impossible for either side to advance upon the other.

The fortune of the day remained for a long time unde-
cided, victory wavering between the contending armies
from morning until noon; for so zealous was the devotion of Nayan's people to the cause of their master, who
was most liberal and indulgent toward them, that they
were all ready to meet death rather than turn their backs
to the enemy. At length, however, Nayan, perceiving
that he was nearly surrounded, attempted to save himself
by flight, but was presently made prisoner and conducted
into the presence of Kublai, who ordered him put to
death.

CHAPTER 5

*How the Great Khan Caused Nayan
to Be Put to Death*

THIS was carried into execution by wrapping Nayan in two carpets, which were violently shaken until the spirit had departed from the body. The reason for this peculiar treatment is that the sun and the air should not witness the shedding of the blood of one who belonged to the imperial family. Those of his troops that survived the battle came to make their submission and swear allegiance to Kublai. They were inhabitants of the four noble provinces of Chorza [Manchuria], Kauli [Korea], Barskol, and Sikintinju.

Nayan, who had privately undergone the ceremony of baptism but never made open profession of Christianity, thought proper on this occasion to bear the sign of the cross in his banners, and he had in his army a vast number of Christians who were left among the slain. When the Jews* and the Saracens perceived that the banner of the cross was overthrown, they taunted the Christian inhabitants, saying, "Behold the state to which your banners and those who followed them are reduced!"

On account of this derision the Christians were compelled to lay their complaints before the Great Khan, who ordered the former to appear before him and sharply rebuked them. "If the cross of Christ," he said, "has not proved advantageous to the party of Nayan, it was consistent with reason and justice, inasmuch as Nayan was a rebel against his lord, and to such wretches it could not give its protection. Let none therefore presume to charge the God of the Christians with injustice, for he is the perfection of goodness and of justice."

---

*There had been Jews in China for well over a century. According to its inscriptions, the synagogue at K'ai-feng was built in 1163 by Jews who had come from Persia. They were treated with tolerance but dwindled until, by the end of the 19th century, worship had ceased and almost all their traditions had died out.

CHAPTER 6

*Of the Return of the Great Khan to the City
of Khan-balik and of the Honor He
Does Christians and Jews*

THE Great Khan, having won this signal victory, returned with great pomp and triumph to the capital city
of Khan-balik. This took place in the month of November, and he continued to reside there during February
and March, in which latter was our festival of Easter.
Being aware that this was one of our principal solemni-
ties, he commanded all the Christians to attend him, and
to bring with them their Book which contains the four
Gospels of the Evangelists.

After causing it to be repeatedly perfumed with incense in a ceremonious manner, he devoutly kissed it,
and directed that the same should be done by all his
nobles who were present. This was his usual practice
upon each of the principal Christian festivals, such as
Easter and Christmas; and he observed the same at the
festivals of the Saracens, Jews, and idolaters.

Upon being asked his motive for this conduct, he said:
"There are four great Prophets who are reverenced and
worshiped by the different classes of mankind. The
Christians regard Jesus Christ as their divinity; the Saracens, Mahomet; the Jews, Moses; and the idolaters,
Sakyamuni-Burkhan [Buddha], the most eminent among
their idols. I do honor and show respect to all four, so
that I may be sure of invoking whichever among them
is in truth supreme in Heaven."* But from the manner
in which his Majesty acted toward them, it is evident
that he regarded the faith of the Christians as the truest
and the best, its professors being enjoined to do nothing
that was not filled with virtue and holiness. By no means,
however, would he permit them to bear the cross before
them in their processions, because upon it so exalted a
being as Christ had been scourged and put to death. It
may perhaps be asked by some, why, if he showed such

---

*This astonishing tolerance is generally explained as partly the practice
of the great house to which Kublai belonged and partly the condescension of an astute prince, secure in his power and authority.

a preference for the faith of Christ, he did not embrace it and become a Christian? He gave Nicolo and Maffeo his reason for not doing so when, on his sending them as his ambassadors to the Pope, they ventured to talk to him about it. "Wherefore," he said, "should I become a Christian? You yourselves must perceive that the Christians of these countries are ignorant, incompetent persons, who are unable to perform anything miraculous; whereas you see that the idolaters can do whatever they will. When I sit at table the cups that were in the middle of the hall come to me filled with wine and other beverages, spontaneously and without being touched by human hand, and I drink from them. They have the power of controlling bad weather and causing it to retreat whence it came, with many other wonderful gifts of that nature. You are witnesses that their idols have the faculty of speech and predict whatever is required.

"If I become a convert to the faith of Christ and profess myself a Christian, the nobles of my court and other persons who do not incline to that religion will ask me what caused me to receive baptism and embrace Christianity. 'What extraordinary powers,' they will say, 'what miracles have been displayed by its ministers? Whereas the idolaters declare that what they exhibit is performed through their holiness and the influence of their idols.'

"To this I shall not know what answer to make, and I shall be considered to be in grievous error, while the idolaters, who by means of their profound art can effect such wonders, might without difficulty bring about my death. But return to your Pope, and request him in my name to send hither a hundred persons learned in your law, who, being confronted with the idolaters, shall have power to counter them and show that they themselves are endowed with similar art, but refrain from exercising it because it is derived from evil spirits, and thus shall compel them to give up such practices in their presence. When I witness this, I shall ban them and their religion, and shall allow myself to be baptized. All my nobles will then also receive baptism, and this will be imitated by my subjects in general. In the end the Christians of these parts will exceed those in your own country."

From this it must be evident that if the Pope had sent

out persons duly qualified to preach the gospel, the Great Khan would have embraced Christianity, for it is certain that he had a strong leaning toward it.

To return to our subject, we shall now speak of the rewards and honors he bestows on such as distinguish themselves in battle.

CHAPTER 7

Of the Rewards Granted to Those Who Distinguish Themselves in Battle

THE Great Khan appointed twelve of his most intelligent nobles to acquaint themselves with the conduct of the officers and men of his army, particularly on expeditions and in battles, and to present reports to him. On the basis of their respective merits he advances them in his service, raising those who commanded a hundred men to the command of a thousand, and presenting many with vessels of silver, as well as the customary tablets or warrants of authority.

The tablets given to those commanding a hundred men are of silver; to those commanding a thousand, of gold or of silver gilt; and those who command ten thousand receive tablets of gold, bearing the head of a lion, the former weighing 120 *saggi* [about 20 ounces and about 3 ½ x 12 inches in size], and these with the lion's head, 220. On the tablet is an inscription to this effect: "*By the power and might of the great God, and of the great grace which He hath accorded to our Emperor, be the name of the Khan blessed; and let all such as disobey him be slain and destroyed.*" The officers who hold these tablets have special privileges, and in the inscription is specified the duties and the powers of their respective commands.

He who is at the head of a hundred thousand men, or the commander in chief of a grand army, has a golden tablet weighing 300 *saggi,* with the inscription mentioned above, and at the bottom is engraved the figure of a lion, together with the sun and moon. He exercises also the privileges of his high command as set forth in this magnificent tablet. Whenever he rides in public, an umbrella* is carried over his head, denoting the rank and authority he holds; and when he is seated, it is always upon a silver chair.

The Great Khan likewise confers upon certain of his nobles tablets on which are represented figures of the gerfalcon, in virtue of which they have the power to take with them as their guard of honor the whole army of any great prince. They can also use the horses of the imperial stud at their pleasure, and can appropriate the horses of any officers of lower rank.

CHAPTER 8

Of the Figure of the Great Khan, His Four Principal Wives, and the Annual Selection of Young Women for Him

KUBLAI, who is styled the Great Khan, or Lord of Lords, is of middle stature, that is, neither tall nor short. His limbs are well formed, and there is a just proportion in his whole figure. His complexion is fair and occasionally suffused with red, like the bright tint of the rose, which adds much grace to his countenance. His eyes are black and handsome, his nose well shaped and prominent.

He has four wives of the first rank, who are considered legitimate, and upon the decease of the Great Khan, the eldest born son of any one of these succeeds to the empire. They all bear the title of empress and have their separate courts. None of them has fewer than three hundred young female attendants of great beauty, together with a multitude of youths as pages and eunuchs, as well as ladies of the bedchamber; so that the number of persons belonging to each of their courts amounts to ten thousand.

When his Majesty desires the company of one of his empresses, he either sends for her or goes himself to her chamber. Besides these, he has many concubines provided for his use by a province of Tartary named Kung-

---

*Umbrellas were familiar from antiquity in China and known in ancient Greece and Rome; they were not introduced into England before the early 18th century.

urat, the inhabitants of which are distinguished for beauty of features and fairness of complexion. Every second year, or oftener, as suits his pleasure, the Great Khan sends thither his officers, who select one hundred or more of the handsomest of the young women, according to the standards of beauty set forth in their instructions.

They make their selection as follows. Upon their arrival, these commissioners give orders for assembling all the young women of the province and appoint qualified persons to examine them. These examiners, upon careful inspection of each of them, that is to say, of the hair, countenance, eyebrows, mouth, lips, and other features, as well as the symmetry of these, estimate their value at seventeen, eighteen, twenty, or more marks, according to the degree of beauty. If the Great Khan asked for those who were rated at, perhaps, twenty or twenty-one marks, these are then selected from the rest and they are conveyed to his court.

Upon their arrival in his presence, he causes a new examination to be made by a different set of inspectors, and a further selection takes place, after which thirty or forty are retained for his own chamber. These are committed to the care of certain elderly ladies of the palace, whose duty it is to observe them attentively during the night, to ascertain that they have not any concealed imperfections, that they sleep tranquilly, do not snore, have sweet breath, and are free from any unpleasant scent. Having undergone this rigorous scrutiny, they are divided into parties of five, each taking turn for three days and three nights, in his Majesty's inner apartment, where they are to perform every service that is required of them, and he does with them as he likes.

When this term is completed, they are relieved by another party, and so on, until all have taken their turn, whereupon the first five recommence their attendance. While one serves in the inner chamber, another is stationed in the outer apartment. If his Majesty should have need for anything, such as drink or food, the former relays his commands to the latter, who immediately gets whatever is needed. In this way the duty of waiting upon his Majesty's person is performed exclusively by these young females. The remainder, who have received a lower rating, are assigned to the different lords of the household; under whom they are instructed in cookery, in dressmaking, and other suitable work; and when any person belonging to the court expresses an inclination to take a wife, the Great Kahn bestows upon him one of these damsels, along with a handsome dowry. In this manner he provides for all of them among his nobility.

It may be asked whether the people of the province do not feel themselves aggrieved in having their daughters thus forcibly taken from them by the sovereign. They certainly do not; on the contrary, they regard it as a favor and an honor; and those who are the fathers of handsome children feel highly gratified if he deigns to choose their daughters. "If," say they, "my daughter is born under an auspicious planet and to good fortune, his Majesty can best fulfill her destinies by matching her nobly; which it would not be in my power to do." If, on the other hand, the daughter misbehaves, or a mishap befalls her and she is disqualified, the father attributes the disappointment to the evil influence of her stars.

CHAPTER 9

Of the Great Khan's Sons by His Four Wives

THE Great Khan has had twenty-two sons by his four wives, the eldest of whom, named Chinghis [actually Chinkim], was supposed to succeed his father as emperor; and this was confirmed to him during the lifetime of his father. But he died leaving a son, whose name is Temur and who is to succeed to the dominion. The disposition of this prince is good, and he is endowed with wisdom and valor; of the latter he has given proofs in several successful battles.

Besides these, his Majesty has twenty-five sons by his concubines, all of them brave soldiers, having been continually active in military affairs. These he has placed in the rank of nobles. Of his legitimate sons, seven are at the head of extensive provinces and kingdoms, which they govern with wisdom and prudence, as might be expected of the children of one whose great qualities have not been surpassed by any person of the Tartar race.

CHAPTER 10

Of the Palace of the Great Khan

THE Great Khan usually resides during three months of the year, namely December, January, and February, in the great city of Khan-balik in the northeastern extremity of the province of Cathay. Here, on the southern side of the new city, is the site of his vast palace, the form and dimensions of which are as follows.

It is a square enclosed with a wall and deep ditch, each side being eight miles in length,* and having at an equal distance from each extremity an entrance gate for the throngs of people coming there from all quarters. Within this enclosure there is, on all four sides, an open space one mile in breadth, where the troops are stationed. This is bounded by a second wall, enclosing a square of six miles, with three gates on the south side and three on the north, the middle portal of each being larger than the other two and always kept shut, except when the emperor himself enters or departs. Those on each side always remain open for the use of other people.

In the middle of each section of these walls is a handsome and spacious building (consequently within the enclosure there are eight such buildings), in which are deposited the royal military stores, one building being devoted to each class of stores. Thus, for instance, the bridles, saddles, stirrups, and other equipment of cavalry occupy one storehouse; the bows, strings, quivers, arrows, and other articles belonging to archery occupy another; cuirasses, corselets, and other armor formed of leather, a third storehouse; and so of the rest. Within this walled enclosure there is still another, of great thickness and full twenty-five feet in height. The battlements, or notched parapets, are all white. This forms a square four miles in extent, each side being one mile, and it has six

*This seems to be the outermost and perhaps the city wall.

gates, distributed like those of the former enclosure. It likewise contains eight large buildings, similarly arranged, which are appropriated to the wardrobe of the emperor. The spaces between the one wall and the other are ornamented with many handsome trees and contain meadows in which are kept various kinds of beasts, such as stags, the animals that yield the musk, roebuck, fallow deer, and others of the same class. Every interval between the walls is stocked in this manner. The pastures have abundant vegetation. The roads across them being paved, and raised three feet above their level, no mud collects upon them and no rainwater settles on them, but on the contrary runs off and helps improve the vegetation.

Within these walls, which constitute the boundary of four miles, stands the palace of the Great Khan, the most extensive that has ever yet been known. It reaches from the northern to the southern wall, leaving only a vacant court, where persons of rank and the military guards pass. It has no upper floor, but the roof is very lofty. The paved foundation, or platform, on which it stands is raised ten spans above the level of the ground, and a wall of marble, two paces [about ten feet] wide, rises on all sides. This wall serves as a terrace where those who walk on it are visible from without. Along the exterior edge of the wall is a handsome balustrade with pillars, which the people are allowed to approach. The sides of the great halls and the apartments are ornamented with dragons in carved work and gilt, figures of warriors, birds, and beasts, and with representations of battles. The inside of the roof is contrived so that nothing besides gilding and painting presents itself to the eye. On each of the four sides of the palace there is a grand flight of marble steps by which you ascend from the level of the ground to the wall of marble which surrounds the building, and which constitutes the approach to the palace itself.

The grand hall is extremely long and wide and permits dinners to be served to great multitudes of people. The palace contains a number of separate chambers, all highly beautiful and so admirably located that it seems impossible to suggest any improvement in this respect.

The exterior of the roof is adorned with a variety of colors, red, green, azure, and violet, and the covering is so strong as to last for many years. The glazing of the windows is so well wrought and so delicate as to have the transparency of crystal.

In the rear of the body of the palace there are large buildings containing several apartments, where are kept the private possessions of the monarch, or his treasure in gold and silver bullion, precious stones, and pearls, and also his vessels of gold and silver plate. Here are likewise the apartments of his wives and concubines; and in this privacy he dispatches business at his convenience, free from every kind of interruption.

On the other side of the grand palace, opposite to that in which the emperor resides, is another palace, in every respect similar, which is the residence of Chinghis, his eldest son. At his court are observed all the same ceremonials as at that of his father. Not far from the palace on the northern side, and about a bowshot distance from the surrounding wall, is an artificial hill of earth, the height of which is fully a hundred paces and the circuit at the base about a mile. It is covered with the most beautiful evergreen trees; for whenever his Majesty hears of a handsome tree growing in any place, he causes it to be dug up with all its roots and the earth around it, and however massive it may be, he has it transported by means of elephants to this mound and adds it to the verdant collection. Because the growth on this hill is always green it has acquired the name of the Green Mount.

On its summit is erected an ornamental pavilion, which is likewise entirely green. Altogether, the mound itself, the trees, and the building form a delightful and wonderful scene. In the northern quarter also, and equally within the precincts of the city, there is a large and deep excavation, carefully shaped, the earth from which was used in building the mound. It is furnished with water by a small rivulet and has the appearance of a fishpond, but is used for watering the cattle. The stream, passing along an aqueduct at the foot of the Green Mount, proceeds to fill another great and very deep excavation formed between the private palace of the emperor and that of his son; and the earth from this has also served to increase the height of the mound. In this latter basin there is great variety of fish, from which the table of his Majesty is supplied with any quantity that may be wanted.

The stream discharges at the farther end of the pond, and to prevent the escape of the fish, gratings of copper or iron have been set at the entrance and outlet. It is stocked also with swans and other waterbirds. From the one palace to the other there is a bridge across the water. Such is the great palace. We shall now speak of the city of Taidu [Tatu, or "Great Court," the Tartar City].

CHAPTER 11

Of the New City of Taidu, Built Near That of Khan-balik, and of the City Police

KHAN-BALIK is situated near a large river in the province of Cathay and was in ancient times a great and noble city. The name itself means "the city of the Emperor"; but his Majesty was informed by astrologers that it was destined to become rebellious and he decided to build another capital on the opposite side of the river, where stand the palaces just described. The new and the old cities are separated from each other only by the river between them. The new city received the name of Taidu, and all Cathayans, that is, all inhabitants who were natives of the province of Cathay, were compelled to evacuate the ancient city and settle in the new. Some inhabitants, of whose loyalty he did not entertain any suspicion, were, however, suffered to remain, especially because the new one could not hold all of them.

This new city is perfectly square and is twenty-four miles in circumference. It is enclosed with earthen walls that at the base are about ten paces [fifty feet] thick, but gradually diminish towards the top, which is not more than three paces. All the battlements are white. The whole plan of the city was laid out in lines, and the streets in general are consequently so straight that when a person on the wall over one of the gates looks straight forward, he can see the gate on the opposite side of the city. In the public streets there are, on each side, booths and shops of every description. All building lots throughout the city are square and exactly on a line with each other, each being sufficiently spacious for handsome buildings, with corresponding courts and gardens. Each of these was assigned to the head of a family. In this manner the whole interior of the city is laid out like a chessboard, and planned with a precision and beauty impossible to describe. The wall of the city has twelve gates, three on each side of the square, and over each gate and each angle of the wall there is a handsome building; so that on each side of the square there are five such buildings, containing large rooms, in which are kept the arms of the garrison of the city, every gate being guarded by a thousand men. It should not be thought that such a force is stationed there out of fear of any hostile power whatever, but as a guard suitable to the honor and dignity of the sovereign. Yet it must be admitted that the prophecy of the astrologers excited in him some suspicion with regard to the Cathayans.

In the center of the city there is a great bell suspended in a lofty building, which is sounded every night, and after the third stroke no person dares to be found in the streets, unless upon some urgent occasion, such as to get help for a woman in labor or a man attacked by sickness. In such cases the person is required to carry a light.

Outside each gate is a suburb so wide that it reaches to and joins those of the nearest gates on both sides, and extends a distance of three or four miles, so that the number of inhabitants in these suburbs exceeds that of the city itself. Within each suburb there are at intervals, as far perhaps as a mile from the city, many hotels, or caravansaries, which accommodate merchants arriving from various parts. A separate building is assigned to each nationality, one, as we should say, to the Lombards, another to the Germans, and a third to the French.

The number of public women who prostitute themselves for money, reckoning those in the new city as well as those in the suburbs of the old, is twenty-five thousand. For each hundred and each thousand of these there are superintending officers, who are under a captain-general. The motive for placing them under such command is this:

when ambassadors arrive with any business in which the interests of the Great Khan are concerned, it is customary to maintain them at his Majesty's expense; and in order that they may be treated in the most honorable manner, the captain is ordered to furnish nightly to each individual of the embassy one of these courtesans, who is likewise to be changed every night. As this service is considered in the light of a tribute they owe to the sovereign, they do not receive any remuneration.

Guards, in parties of thirty or forty, continually patrol the streets during the night and look for persons away from their homes at an unseasonable hour, that is, after the third stroke of the great bell. When they meet any under such circumstances, they immediately arrest them and take them in the morning for examination before officers appointed for that purpose. Upon proof of any delinquency, they are sentenced, depending on the offense, to a flogging, which sometimes, however, occasions their death. They adopt this mode of punishment from a disinclination to shedding blood, which their astrologers instruct them to avoid.

Having thus described the city of Taidu, we shall now give an example of the rebellious disposition of its Cathayan inhabitants.

CHAPTER 12

The Oppressions of Achmat and the Plot That Was Formed Against Him

You will hear further on about twelve persons appointed to dispose of lands, offices, and everything else at their discretion. Now one of these was a certain Saracen [a Persian Moslem] named Achmat, a shrewd and able man, who had more power and influence with the Great Khan than any of the others. The fact was, as came out after his death, that Achmat [or Ahmad] had so wrought upon the Khan with his sorcery that the latter had the greatest faith in everything he said, and in this way did everything that Achmat wished him to do.*

*Although it sounds like a tale out of the *Arabian Nights*, the account that follows is completely borne out by Chinese records. Indeed the

This person disposed of all appointments and offices, and passed sentence on all malefactors. Whenever he desired to have anyone whom he hated put to death, whether justly or not, he would go to the Emperor and say: "Such a one deserves death, for he has done this or that against your imperial dignity." Then the Lord would say: "Do as you think right," and so he would have the man executed forthwith.

When people saw how unbounded were his powers and the reliance placed by the Emperor on everything he said, they did not venture to oppose him in anything. No one was so high in rank or power as to be free from dread of him. If any one was accused by him to the Emperor of a capital offense and desired to defend himself, he was unable to present testimony in his own defense, for no one would stand by him, since no one dared to oppose Achmat. And thus the latter caused many to perish unjustly.

Moreover, there was no beautiful woman whom he desired that he did not manage to possess, forcing her to be his wife if she was unmarried, or otherwise compelling her to yield to his desires. Whenever he learned of anyone who had a pretty daughter, certain ruffians of his would go to the father and say: "What do you say? Here is this pretty daughter of yours; give her in marriage to the Bailo [that is, Lord Lieutenant] Achmat and we will arrange for him to give you such a post or office for three years." Thus tempted, the man would surrender his daughter. And Achmat would go to the Emperor and say: "Such an office is vacant, or will be vacant, on such a day. So-and-so is a good man for the post." And the Emperor would reply: "Do as you think best"; and the father of the girl was immediately appointed to the government. Thus either through the ambition of the parents, or through fear of the Minister, all the beautiful women were at his beck, either as wives or mistresses. Also he had some twenty-five sons who held offices of importance, and some of these, under the protection of

Chinese Annals declare, with respect, that when Kublai returned to Shangtu, Marco spoke out boldly in condemnation of Ahmad's crimes and opened the Emperor's eyes to what had been happening. In this chapter I have followed the Yule version.

their father's name, committed crimes like his own, and did many other evil deeds. This Achmat also had amassed a great fortune, for everybody who wanted office sent him a heavy bribe.

In such authority did this man continue for twenty-two years. At last the people of the country—that is, the Cathayans—utterly wearied with the endless outrages and crimes he committed against either their wives or their own persons, conspired to slay him and revolt against the government. Among the rest there was a certain Cathayan named Ch'ienhu, a commander of a thousand, whose mother, daughter, and wife had all been violated by the Minister. Now this man, full of bitter resentment, began to plot the destruction of the Minister with another Cathayan whose name was Wanhu, a commander of ten thousand. They came to the conclusion that the time to do the deed would be during the Great Khan's absence from Khan-balik. For after stopping there three months he used to go to Shangtu and stay three months; and at the same time his son Chinkim used to go away to his usual haunts, leaving Achmat in charge of the city and in a position to obtain the Khan's orders from Shangtu when any emergency arose.

Having come to this conclusion, the two plotters imparted it to some leading Cathayans, and then by common consent sent word to their friends in many other cities that they had determined on such a day, at the signal given by a beacon, to massacre all men with beards, and that the other cities should stand ready to do the same. The reason they spoke of massacring bearded men was that the Cathayans naturally have no beards, while beards are worn by the Tartars, Saracens, and Christians. And it should be known that all the Cathayans detested the Great Khan's rule because he set over them governors who were Tartars, or more frequently, Saracens, and these they could not endure, for they were treated by them just like slaves. You see, the Great Khan had not succeeded to the dominion of Cathay by hereditary right, but held it by conquest, and thus having no confidence in the natives, he put all authority into the hands of Tartars, Saracens, or Christians who were attached to his household and devoted to his service, and were foreigners in Cathay.

Therefore, on the day appointed, the aforesaid Wanhu and Ch'ienhu having entered the palace at night, Wanhu sat down and caused a number of lights to be kindled before him. He then sent a messenger to Achmat, who lived in the Old City, as if to summon him to the presence of Chinkim, the Great Khan's son, who it was pretended had arrived unexpectedly. When Achmat heard this he was much surprised, but made haste to go, for he feared the Prince greatly. When he arrived at the gate, he met a Tartar called Kogatai, who was Captain of the twelve thousand that formed the standing garrison of the city. The latter asked him whither he was bound so late. "To Chinkim, who has just arrived." Said Kogatai, "How can that be? How could he come so secretly that I was not aware of it?" So he followed the Minister with a number of his soldiers. Now the plan of the Cathayans was that if they could make an end of Achmat, they would have nought else to be afraid of. So as soon as Achmat got inside the palace and saw all the lights, he bowed down before Wanhu, supposing him to be Chinkim, and Ch'ienhu who was standing ready with a sword straightaway cut his head off.

As soon as Kogatai, the Tartar captain who had halted at the entrance, saw this, he shouted "Treason!" and instantly let fly an arrow at Wanhu and shot him dead as he sat. At the same time he called his people to seize Ch'ienhu, and sent out a proclamation that anyone found in the streets would be instantly put to death. The Cathayans saw that the Tartars had discovered the plot and that they had no longer any leader, since one was killed and the other seized. So they kept to their houses, and were unable to pass the signal for the rising of the other cities as had been agreed.

Kogatai immediately dispatched messengers to the Great Khan giving a full report of the whole affair, and the Khan sent back orders for him to make a careful investigation and to punish the guilty as they deserved. In the morning Kogatai examined the Cathayans and put to death a number whom he found to be ringleaders in the plot. The same was done in the other cities, when it was found that they too had been in the plot.

After the Great Khan had returned to Khan-balik he was very anxious to discover what had led to this affair. He then learned all about the endless outrages of the abominable Achmat and his sons. He found that he and seven of his sons had forced no end of women to be their wives, besides those whom they had ravished. The Great Khan then ordered all the treasure that Achmat had accumulated in the Old City to be transferred to his own treasury in the New City, and it was found to be an enormous amount. He also ordered the body of Achmat to be dug up and cast into the streets for the dogs to tear; and commanded those of his sons who had followed the father's evil example to be flayed alive.

These circumstances called the Khan's attention to the accursed doctrines of the Saracens, which excuse every crime, yea, even murder itself, when committed against any who are not of their religion. Seeing that this doctrine had led the vile Achmat and his sons to act as they did without any sense of guilt, the Khan was led to entertain the greatest disgust and abhorrence for it. So he summoned the Saracens and prohibited their doing many things which their religion enjoined. Thus, he ordered them to regulate their marriages by the Tartar law, and prohibited their cutting the throats of animals that are killed for food, commanding them to slit the stomach in the Tartar way.

Now when all this happened Messer Marco was on the scene.

CHAPTER 13

Of the Personal Guard of the Great Khan

THE bodyguard of the Great Khan consists of twelve thousand horsemen, who are termed Keshikten, which signifies "Soldiers devoted to their lord." It is not, however, out of fear that he is surrounded by this guard, but as a matter of state.

These twelve thousand men are commanded by four superior officers, each of whom is at the head of three thousand; and each three thousand does constant duty in the palace during three successive days and nights, at the end of which they are relieved by another division. When all the four have completed their period of duty, the first group takes its turn again.

During the day, the nine thousand who are off guard do not quit the palace, unless when employed in the service of his Majesty, or when individuals are called away on urgent private business, in which case they must obtain leave.

CHAPTER 14

Of the Style in Which the Great Khan Holds Court

WHEN his Majesty holds public court, those who attend it are seated in the following order. The table of the sovereign is placed above the others, and he takes his seat on the northern side, with his face turned toward the south; and next to him, on his left hand, sits the Empress. On his right hand, upon seats somewhat lower, are placed his sons, grandsons, and other persons connected with him by blood, so that their heads are on a level with the Emperor's feet. The other princes and the nobility have their places at still lower tables; and the same rules are observed with respect to the females, the wives of the sons, grandsons, and other relatives of the Great Khan being seated on the left hand, each lower than the preceding. Then follow the wives of the nobility and military officers: so that all are seated according to their respective ranks and dignities. The tables are arranged in such a manner that the Great Khan on his elevated throne can overlook the whole. However, not all who assemble on such occasions can be accommodated at tables. The greater part of the officers, and even of the nobles, eat while sitting upon carpets; and on the outside stand a great multitude of persons, some of them petitioners who come from different countries and bring with them many rare and curious articles.

In the middle of the hall, where the Great Khan sits at table, there is a magnificent piece of furniture in the form

of a square coffer, each side of which is three paces in
length, exquisitely carved with figures of animals, and
gilded. It is hollow and holds a golden vase of great capac-
ity. On each of its four sides stands a smaller vessel, containing about a hogshead, one of which is filled with
mare's milk, another with milk of the camel, and the others with the other kinds of beverage in use. Within this
buffet are also all the vessels for serving the liquors to his
Majesty. Some of them are of beautiful gilt plate. Their
size is such that when filled with wine or other liquor the
quantity would be sufficient for eight or ten men.

Before every two persons at the tables,* one of these
flagons is placed, together with a kind of ladle in the
form of a cup with a handle, also of plate; this is to be
used not only for taking the wine out of the flagon, but
for lifting it to the mouth. It is also done this way for
the women. The quantity and richness of the plate belonging to his Majesty is quite incredible.

Officers of rank are likewise appointed to see that all
strangers who happen to arrive at the time of the festival, and are unacquainted with the etiquette of the court,
are suitably accommodated with places. These stewards
are continually moving about the hall, inquiring of the
guests if there is anything they lack, or whether they
want wine, milk, meat, or anything else, in which case it
is immediately brought to them by the attendants.

At each door of the grand hall, or of whatever part
the Great Khan happens to be in, stand two gigantic
men, one on each side, armed with staves to prevent
persons from stepping on the threshold. If by chance
anyone is guilty of this offense, these guards take his
garment, which he must redeem by paying a fine; or if
they do not take the garment, they inflict on him a
certain number of blows. But, as strangers may be unacquainted with the prohibition, officers are appointed to
inform and warn them. All this is done because touch-
ing the threshold is regarded as a bad omen. As some
of the company may be affected by the liquor, it is
impossible to guard against the accident when they are

*Probably the traditional small Chinese tables, each accommodating
only two persons.

leaving the hall, and the order is then not strictly enforced.

The numerous persons who attend at the sideboard of his Majesty, and who serve him, are all obliged to cover their noses and mouths with elegant veils or cloths of silk in order that his food or wine may not be affected by their breath. When drink is called for by him, and the page has presented it, he retires three paces and kneels down, whereupon all who are present also kneel down. At the same moment all the musical instruments, of which there are a great many, begin to play, and continue to do so until he has ceased drinking, when all the company rise again. This salutation is made as often as his Majesty drinks. It is unnecessary to say anything of the victuals, because it may well be imagined how abundant they are.

When the repast is finished and the tables have been removed, various entertainers enter the hall, including comedians, performers on different instruments, tumblers, and jugglers, who exhibit their skill in the presence of the Great Khan, to the amusement and gratification of all the spectators. When these amusements are ended, the guests depart.

CHAPTER 15

Of the Feast Held on the
Great Khan's Birthday

ALL the Tartar and other subjects of the Great Khan celebrate as a festival the day of his Majesty's birth, which took place on the twenty-eighth day of September. This is their greatest festival, excepting the one kept on the first day of the year, which shall be hereafter described. Upon this anniversary the Great Khan appears in a superb dress of cloth of gold, and full twenty thousand nobles and military officers are clad by him in similar dresses, but made of less costly materials. They are, however, of silk and of the color of gold; and along with the vest they receive a girdle of chamois leather, curiously worked with gold and silver thread, and also a pair of boots. Some of the dresses are ornamented with precious stones and pearls to the value of ten thousand bezants of gold,* and are given to those nobles who, from their confidential employments, are nearest to his Majesty's person. These dresses are worn on the thirteen solemn festivals in the year, and those clad in them make an appearance that is truly royal. When his Majesty assumes any particular dress, the nobles of his court wear corresponding but less costly garments, which they always have in readiness. They are not renewed annually, but are made to last about ten years. From this pageant an idea may be formed of the magnificence of the Great Khan, which is unequaled by that of any monarch in the world.

On the occasion of the Great Khan's birthday festival, all his Tartar subjects and the people of every kingdom and province throughout his dominions send him valuable presents, according to established custom. Many persons who come to court to solicit principalities to which they have pretensions also bring presents, and his Majesty accordingly directs the tribunal of twelve, who have charge of such matters, to assign to them such territories and governments as may be proper.

Upon this day likewise all the Christians, idolaters, and Saracens, together with every other description of people, offer up devout prayers to their respective gods and idols that they may bless and preserve the sovereign and bestow upon him long life, health, and prosperity. Such, and so extensive, are the rejoicings on his Majesty's birthday.

We shall now speak of another festival, the White Feast, celebrated at the New Year.

CHAPTER 16

Of the White Feast Held on New Year's Day

IT IS a known fact that the Tartars date the commencement of their year from the month of February, and on that occasion it is customary for the Great Khan, as well as all who are subject to him, in their several countries,

---

*Since a bezant is supposed to have been worth about $250, this would be about $25,000. Whether accurate or not, such figures may account for the story that after Marco's return to Venice he was called "Marco Milione."

to clothe themselves in white, which, according to their ideas, is the emblem of good fortune. This is done in the hope that during the course of the year only what is fortunate may befall them, and that they may enjoy pleasure and comfort.

Upon this day the inhabitants of all the provinces and kingdoms under the Great Khan send him valuable presents of gold, silver, and precious stones, together with many pieces of white cloth, so that his Majesty may enjoy prosperity and happiness throughout the year. With the same view the nobles, princes, and all ranks of the community exchange presents of white articles at their respective houses, embrace each other joyously, and say, "May good fortune attend you through the coming year, and may everything you undertake succeed." On this occasion beautiful white horses (or if not perfectly white, at least the prevailing color) are presented to the Great Khan. In this country white horses are not uncommon.

In making presents to the Great Khan it is moreover the custom, for those who can, to furnish nine* times nine of their gift. Thus, for instance, if a province sends a present of horses, it sends nine times nine, or eighty-one, head. And so also of gold or of cloth. His Majesty receives at this festival no fewer than a hundred thousand horses.

On this day all elephants, amounting to five thousand, are paraded, each draped with cloth fancifully and richly worked with gold and silk in figures of birds and beasts. Each of these supports two coffers filled with vessels of plate and other furnishings for the court. Then follows a train of camels, laden in like manner. When the whole are properly arranged, they pass in review before his Majesty and form a pleasing spectacle.

On the morning of the festival, before the tables are spread, all the princes, nobility, cavaliers, astrologers, physicians, and falconers, and many others holding public offices, the governors of the people and the lands, together with officers of the army, make their entry into the grand hall in front of the Emperor. Those who cannot find room within stand outside the building in such a location as to be within sight of their sovereign.

*Among the Mongols nine was a mystic number.

The assemblage is marshaled in the following order. The first places are assigned to the sons and grandsons of his Majesty and all the imperial family. Next to these are the provincial kings and the nobility of the empire, according to their several degrees, in regular succession. When all have taken the places appointed for them, a great dignitary rises and says with a loud voice, "Bow down and adore!"; and instantly all bend their bodies until their foreheads touch the floor [the ceremonial Chinese bow known as the "kowtow," or, literally, "knock head"]. The dignitary again says, "God bless our lord and grant him joy and happiness." And all reply, "God grant it." And this adoration they repeat four times. This being done, the dignitary advances to a richly adorned altar, upon which is placed a red tablet inscribed with the name of the Great Khan. Near to this stands a censer of burning incense, with which the dignitary, on the behalf of all who are assembled, perfumes the tablet and the altar with great reverence; whereupon everyone present prostrates himself before the tablet.

This ceremony being concluded, they return to their places and then make the presentation of their gifts. When a display has been made of these, and the Great Khan has cast his eyes upon them, the tables are prepared for the feast; and the company, women as well as men, arrange themselves there in the manner described. After dinner the musicians and theatrical performers entertain the court, as has been already related. But on this occasion a lion is led into the presence of his Majesty, one so tame that it is taught to lay itself down at his feet. The sports being finished, everyone departs.

CHAPTER 17*

Concerning the Twelve Thousand Barons Who Receive Robes of Cloth Garnished with Gems

Now you must know that the Great Khan has set apart twelve thousand of his men who are distinguished by the name of Keshikten; and on these twelve thousand

*This chapter is added from the Yule version.

barons he bestows thirteen changes of raiment, all different from one another. In one set twelve thousand are all of one color and there are thirteen different sets of colors. These robes are garnished with gems and pearls and other precious things. And with each change he gives each baron a fine golden girdle of great value.

The Emperor himself has thirteen suits corresponding in color to those of his barons, though his are grander, richer, and costlier. And you may see that what all this costs is incalculable.

CHAPTER 18

Of the Quantity of Game Sent to the Court During the Winter Months

AT THE season when the Great Khan resides in the capital of Cathay, that is, during December, January, and February, at which time the cold is excessive, he gives orders for hunting parties to take place in all the areas within forty days' journey of the court.

The governors of districts are then required to send him all sorts of larger game, such as wild boars, stags, fallow deer, roebucks, and bears, which are taken in the following manner. All persons owning land in the province go to the places where the animals are found and proceed to encircle and kill them, partly with dogs, but chiefly by shooting them with arrows. Such of them as are intended for his Majesty's use are gutted and then sent on carts, in large quantities, by those who live within thirty stages of the capital. Those who are forty stages away do not, on account of the length of the journey, send the carcasses, but only the skins, some dressed and others raw, to be made use of for the army as his Majesty may judge proper.

CHAPTER 19

Of Leopards, Lions, and Eagles That the Khan Uses in Hunting

THE GREAT KHAN uses many leopards [actually cheetah, used from ancient times in hunting] and lynxes for the purpose of chasing deer. He also uses many lions—larger animals than the Egyptian kind, with beautifully colored coats striped white, black, and red [these are evidently tigers]—to catch boars, wild oxen and asses, bears, stags, roebucks, and other beasts that huntsmen prefer. It is a rare sight, when the lion is let loose in pursuit of the animal, to see the savage eagerness and speed with which he overtakes it. His Majesty has them carried in cages on carts, along with a little dog, with which they become familiar. The reason for thus shutting them up is that they would otherwise become so ferocious at the sight of the game that it would be impossible to restrain them. It is necessary to lead them against the wind so that they may not be scented by the game, which would immediately run off.

His Majesty also has eagles that are trained to catch wolves, and such is their size and strength that none, however large, can escape from their talons.*

CHAPTER 20

Of Two Brothers Who Are Keepers of the Khan's Hounds

HIS MAJESTY has in his service two barons, brothers, one named Bayan and the other Mingan, who are, in the language of the Tartars, Kuyukchi, that is to say, "keepers of the mastiffs." They have charge of the hounds, both fleet and slow, and of the mastiffs. Each has ten men, those under one brother wearing a red uniform, and those under the other, a blue, whenever they accompany the Khan to the chase.

The dogs of different kinds which accompany them are not fewer than five thousand. One brother with his division advances on the right hand of the Emperor, and the other on the left; and each advances in regular order until they have enclosed a tract to the extent of a day's march. By this means no beast can escape them. What a beautiful sight it is to see the maneuvers of the hunts-

---

*Apparently the golden eagle. It is said to be still in use in eastern Turkestan. In attacking a wolf or deer it strikes one claw into the neck, another into the back, and then tears out the liver with its beak.

men and the working of the dogs when the Emperor is between them and they are pursuing the stags, bears, and other animals in every direction.

The two brothers are bound to furnish the court daily, from the commencement of October to the end of March, with a thousand pieces of game, quails being excepted, and also with as large a quantity of fish as possible, estimating the fish that three men can eat at a meal as one piece of game.

CHAPTER 21

How the Great Khan Goes Hunting

WHEN his Majesty has made his usual stay in the city, and leaves it in the month of March, he proceeds in a northeasterly direction to within two days' journey of the ocean, attended by full ten thousand falconers, who carry with them a vast number of gerfalcons, peregrine falcons, and sakers, as well as many vultures, for pursuing the game along the banks of the river. It must be understood that he does not keep all these men together, but divides them into several parties of one or two hundred or more, and they follow the sport in various directions. The greater part of the quarry is brought to his Majesty. He has likewise with him ten thousand men called *toscaor,* meaning "lookouts," who are assigned in parties of two or three to stations not far from each other, in such a manner as to cover a considerable tract of country. Each of them has a whistle and a hood, with which they can call in and secure the hawk. Upon the command being given for flying the hawks, those who let them loose do not need to follow them, because the others, whose duty it is, keep careful watch and if need be assist the birds.

Every bird belonging to his Majesty or to any of his nobles has a small silver label fastened to its leg on which is engraved the name of the owner and of the keeper. Thus, when the hawk is secured, it is immediately known to whom it belongs, and restored accordingly. If it happens that the owner is not personally known to the finder, the bird is carried to an officer termed *Bularguchi,* meaning "guardian of unclaimed property." If a horse, sword, bird, or any other article is found, and its owner is not plain, the finder carries it directly to this officer. If, on the other hand, a person finds an article and fails to carry it to the officer, he is punished as a thief. The officer is always on the highest ground, and is distinguished by a particular flag in order that he may be readily found by such as have occasion to apply to him. The effect of this is that no articles are ultimately lost.

When his Majesty travels in this manner toward the ocean, many interesting sights result from the sport, and it may truly be said that it is unrivaled by any other amusement in the world. On account of the narrowness of the passes in some parts of the country where the Great Khan follows the chase, he is borne upon only two elephants, or even one. Otherwise he makes use of four, on the backs of which is placed a pavilion of wood, handsomely carved, the inside lined with cloth of gold and the outside covered with the skins of lions, a kind of conveyance made necessary by the fact that he is troubled by gout.

In the pavilion he always carries with him twelve of his best gerfalcons, with twelve favorite officers to keep him company and amuse him. Those who are on horseback by his side give him notice of the approach of cranes or other birds, whereupon he raises the curtain of the pavilion and gives directions for letting fly the gerfalcons, which seize the cranes and overpower them after a long struggle. Watching this sport as he lies upon his couch gives great pleasure to his Majesty, as well as to the officers and horsemen by whom he is surrounded. After having thus enjoyed the amusement for some hours, he repairs to a place named Cachar Modun, where are pitched the pavilions and tents of his sons and also of the nobles, ladies, and falconers, the number of them exceeding ten thousand and making a handsome appearance. The tent of his Majesty, in which he gives his audiences, is so long and wide that under it ten thousand soldiers might be drawn up, with room for the superior officers and other persons of rank. Its entrance faces the south, and on the eastern side it has another tent

connected with it, forming a capacious reception hall.
This is the tent the Emperor usually occupies with a few
of his nobility, and when he wishes to speak to any other
persons, they are brought here. In the rear of this there
is a large and handsome chamber where he sleeps; and
there are many other tents and apartments for the different
branches of the household, but these are not immediately connected with the great tent.

These halls and chambers are all constructed and furnished in the following manner. Each of them is supported by three pillars of wood, richly carved and gilt.
The tents are covered on the outside with the skins of
lions, striped white, black, and red, and so well joined
that neither wind nor rain can penetrate. Inside they are
lined with the skins of ermines and sables, which are the
most costly of all furs. A sable, if of a size to trim a
dress, is valued at two thousand bezants of gold, provided it be perfect, but if otherwise, only one thousand.
It is esteemed by Tartars the queen of furs. The animal,
which in their language is named *rondes,* is about the
size of a polecat. With these two kinds of skins, the halls
as well as the sleeping-rooms are handsomely fitted up
in compartments, arranged with much taste and skill.
The ropes or cords by which they stretch the tents are
all of silk.

Near to the grand tent of his Majesty are situated
those of his ladies, also very handsome and splendid.
They have in like manner their gerfalcons, their hawks,
and other birds and beasts, with which they take part in
the amusement. The number of persons in these en-
campments is quite incredible, and a spectator might
conceive himself to be in the midst of a populous city
so great is the assemblage from every part of the empire.
The Great Khan is attended by the whole of his family
and household; that is to say, his physicians, astrono-
mers, falconers, and every other kind of officer.

In these parts he remains until the spring, during
which period he never ceases to frequent the lakes and
rivers, where he takes storks, swans, herons, and a variety of other birds. His people are also sent out in various
directions and bring back a large quantity of game. In
this manner, during this season he enjoys himself to a

degree that no person who has not seen it can conceive, the excellence and variety of the sport being beyond description.

It is strictly forbidden to every tradesman, mechanic, or peasant throughout his Majesty's dominions to keep a vulture, hawk, or any other bird for the pursuit of game, or any sporting dog. Nor may a nobleman or cavalier presume to chase beast or bird in the neighborhood where his Majesty takes up residence, the ban being five miles, for example, on one side, ten on another, and perhaps fifteen in a third direction, unless his name be on a list kept by the grand falconer, or he has a special privilege to that effect. Beyond those limits it is permitted. There is an order, however, which prohibits every person throughout all countries subject to the Great Khan from daring to kill hares, roebucks, fallow deer, stags, or other animals of that kind, or any large birds, between the months of March and October. This is to insure that they may increase and multiply; and since any breach of this order is punished, game of every description increases prodigiously.

When the usual time has elapsed, his Majesty returns to the capital by the same route he came, continuing his sport all the way.

CHAPTER 22

The Way the Great Khan's Year Is Divided

UPON the return of the Great Khan to his capital, he holds a grand court, which lasts three days, in the course of which he gives feasts and otherwise entertains those by whom he is surrounded. The amusements of these three days are indeed remarkable. He then quits his palace and proceeds to that city which he has built, as I told you before, and which is called Shangtu, where he has that grand park and palace of cane. To escape the heat he spends his summer there, for the location is a cool one. Here he remains from May until the end of August, when he returns again to his capital and remains until

February and the time of the grand feast of the New
Year.

The hunting expedition toward the sea takes place in
March, April and May. Thus is his year spent: six months
at the capital, three months in hunting, and three months
at the Cane Palace. In this manner he passes his time
with the greatest enjoyment—not to speak of many little
journeys in this or that direction at his pleasure.

CHAPTER 23

Concerning the City of Khan-balik, Its Vast Population and Commerce

THE multitude of inhabitants and the number of
houses in the city of Khan-balik, as also in the twelve
suburbs outside the city (corresponding to the twelve
gates), is greater than the mind can comprehend. The
suburbs are even more populous than the city, and it is
there that the merchants, and others whose business
brings them to the capital, stay. Wherever, indeed, his
Majesty holds court, there these people flock from all
quarters in pursuit of their several objects.

In the suburbs there are also as handsome houses and
stately buildings as in the city, with the exception only
of the palace of the Great Khan. No corpse is suffered
to be buried within the city; and those of the Idolaters
whose custom it is to burn their dead are carried to the
usual spot beyond the suburbs. There likewise all public
executions take place. Women who live by prostituting
themselves for money dare not, unless secretly, exercise
their profession in the city, but must confine themselves
to the suburbs, where, as has already been stated, there
reside above 25,000; nor is this number greater than is
necessary for the vast throngs of merchants and other
strangers who are continually arriving and departing.

To this city everything that is most rare and valuable
in the world finds its way; and more especially does this
apply to India, which furnishes precious stones, pearls,
and various drugs and spices. From the provinces of Cathay itself, as well as from other provinces of the empire,
whatever is of value is brought here to supply the de-

mands of those multitudes who establish their residence
in the vicinity of the court. The quantity of merchandise
sold exceeds also that of any other place; for no fewer
than a thousand carriages and packhorses loaded with
raw silk come here daily; and an immense quantity of
gold tissues and silks of various kinds is manufactured
here.

In the vicinity of the capital are many walled and
other towns, whose inhabitants live chiefly by the court,
selling the articles they produce in return for whatever
they need.

CHAPTER 24

Of the Paper Money Issued by the Great Khan

IN THIS city of Khan-balik is the mint of the Great
Khan, who may truly be said to possess the secret of the
alchemists, since he has the art of making money.

He causes the bark to be stripped from mulberry trees
(the leaves of which are used for feeding silkworms),
and takes from it that thin layer that lies between the
coarser bark and the wood of the tree. This being
steeped, and afterwards pounded in a mortar until reduced to a pulp, is made into paper, resembling that
which is manufactured from cotton, but quite black.
When ready for use, he has it cut into pieces of different
sizes, nearly square, but somewhat longer than they are
wide. Of these, the smallest pass for a half tornesel; the
next size for a Venetian silver groat; others for two, five,
and ten groats; others for one, two, three, and as much
as ten bezants of gold. The coinage of this paper money
is authorized with as much form and ceremony as if it
were actually pure gold or silver: to each note a number
of officers, specially appointed, not only subscribe their
names but also affix their seals. When this has been done
by all of them, the principal officer, having dipped into
vermilion the royal seal committed to his custody,
stamps the piece of paper, so that the form of the seal,
tinged with the vermilion, is impressed upon it.* In this

*The use of paper currency in China is said to go as far back as the
beginning of the 9th century.

way it receives full authority as current money, and the act of counterfeiting it is punished as a capital offense.

When thus coined in large quantities, this paper currency is circulated in every part of the Great Khan's dominions; nor dares any person, at the peril of his life, refuse to accept it. All his subjects receive it without hesitation, because, wherever their business may call them, they can dispose of it in the purchase of any merchandise they may require, such as pearls, jewels, gold, or silver. With it, in short, every article may be procured.

Several times in the course of the year large caravans of merchants arrive with such articles as have just been mentioned, together with gold tissues, which they lay before the Great Khan. He thereupon calls together twelve experienced and skillful persons, who examine the articles with great care and fix their value. Upon the sum at which they have been thus conscientiously appraised he allows a reasonable profit, and immediately pays for them with this paper. To this the owners can have no objection, because, as has been observed, they can use it for their own purchases; and even though they may have come from a country where this kind of money is not current, they can invest it in any merchandise suited to their own markets.

When any persons have paper money which has become worn out, they carry it to the mint, where, upon the payment of only three percent, they receive fresh notes in exchange. Should anyone need gold or silver for the purpose of manufacturing drinking cups, girdles, or other articles made from these metals, they also apply to the mint, and for their paper obtain the bullion they require.*

All his Majesty's armies are paid with this currency, which is to them as good as if it were gold or silver. Upon these grounds, it may certainly be affirmed that the Great Khan has a greater command of treasure than any other sovereign in the universe.

---

*In his enthusiasm, Marco fails to mention the fact that the paper could obtain bullion equal only to half its nominal amount. Like all excessive issues of paper currency, this one eventually led to serious inflation.

CHAPTER 25

*Of the Twelve Barons Appointed for the
Affairs of the Army and the Twelve
Others for the Affairs of the Empire*

THE Great Khan selects twelve noblemen of high rank
whose duty it is to pass on every decision respecting the
army. This includes movement of troops from one area
to another, changes in command, the employment of a
force where it may be judged necessary, and the numbers to be used in any particular service. Besides these,
it is their business to promote officers who have given
proofs of valor in combat and to degrade those who
have shown themselves base and cowardly. All this, however, is done subject to the approval of his Majesty, to
whom they report their opinion of the officer, and who,
upon confirming their decision, grants to him who is pro-
moted the tablet or warrant belonging to his rank, as
before described. He also confers on him large presents,
in order to excite others to merit the same rewards. The
tribunal composed of these twelve nobles is named Thai,
denoting a supreme court, as being responsible to no
other than the sovereign.

Besides this, there is another tribunal, likewise of
twelve nobles, appointed to supervise the government of
the thirty-four provinces of the Empire. These have in
Khan-balik a large and handsome palace or court, containing many chambers and halls. For the business of
each province there is a presiding legal officer, together
with several clerks, who have apartments in the court
and there transact business for the province to which
they belong, under the direction of the tribunal of
twelve. These choose persons for the governments of the
several provinces, whose names are presented to the Great
Khan for confirmation. They also supervise the collection of revenue, both from land and customs, together
with its disbursement, and have control of every other
department of the state, with the exception only of what
relates to the army. This tribunal is named Shieng, signifying that it is a second high court, and, like the other,
responsible only to the Great Khan. But the Thai is regarded as superior in rank and dignity to the latter.

CHAPTER 26

Of the Stations for Post Horses and Couriers

FROM the city of Khan-balik there are many roads leading to the different provinces, and on each of these, that is to say, on every great high road, every twenty-five or thirty miles there are stations with accommodations for travelers. These are called *yamb,* or posthouses. They are large and handsome buildings, with well-furnished apartments hung with silk and provided with everything suitable to persons of rank. Even kings may be lodged at these stations in a becoming manner, as everything that may be required may be obtained from the towns in the vicinity; and for some of them the court makes regular provision.

At each station four hundred good horses are kept in constant readiness in order that all messengers going and coming upon the business of the Great Khan and all ambassadors may have relays, and leaving their jaded horses, be supplied with fresh ones.* Even in mountainous districts remote from the great roads, where there are no villages and the towns are distant from each other, his Majesty has caused buildings of the same kind to be erected, furnished with everything necessary, and provided with the usual supply of horses.

He sends people to dwell in these places in order to cultivate the land and take care of the post; by this means villages are formed. In consequence of these regulations, ambassadors to the court and royal messengers go and return through every province and kingdom of the empire with the greatest convenience and speed. In the management of all this the Great Khan exhibits a superiority over every other emperor or king on earth.

In his dominions no fewer than two hundred thousand horses are thus employed and ten thousand buildings with suitable furniture, are kept up. It is indeed so wonderful a system, and so effective in its operation, as it is scarcely possible to describe. If it be asked how the population of the country can supply sufficient men for these duties, and by what means they can be supported,

*This "pony express" had been in use in China for at least 500 years.

we may answer that all the Idolaters and likewise the Saracens keep six, eight, or ten women, according to their circumstances, by whom they have a prodigious number of children. Some of them have as many as thirty sons capable of following their fathers in arms; whereas with us a man has only one wife, and even although she should prove barren, he is obliged to pass his life with her, and is thus deprived of the chance of raising a family. Hence it is that our population is so much smaller than theirs.

With regard to food, there is no shortage of it, for these people, especially the Tartars, Cathayans, and inhabitants of the province of Manzi (Southern China), subsist for the most part upon rice, panicum, and millet, and these grains yield in their soil a hundred measures for one. Wheat, indeed, does not yield a similar increase, and since they do not use bread, it is eaten only in the form of noodles or farinas. The former grains they boil in milk or stew with their meat. No spot on earth that can possibly be cultivated is suffered to lie idle; and their cattle multiply exceedingly, insomuch that when they take to arms, there is scarcely an individual that does not carry with him six, eight, or more horses for his own personal use. All this will explain why they have so large a population and such abundance to support it.

In between the posthouses there are small villages, at a distance of every three miles, which may contain about forty cottages. In these are stationed the foot messengers in the service of his Majesty. They wear girdles round their waists, to which several small bells are attached, and as they run only three miles from one station to the next, the ringing gives notice of their approach and preparation is accordingly made by a fresh courier to continue with the packet. It is thus carried so swiftly that in the course of two days and nights his Majesty receives news that normally could not be obtained in less than ten days. It often happens that in the fruit season fruit gathered in the morning at Khan-balik is conveyed to the Great Khan at Shangtu by the evening of the following day, although the distance is generally considered as ten days' journey.

At each of these three-mile stations there is a clerk

whose business it is to note the time at which one courier
arrives and the other departs; this is also done at all the
posthouses. Besides this, officers pay monthly visits to
every station to check the management of them and to
punish those couriers who have not been diligent
enough. All couriers are not only exempt from tax, but
also receive good allowances from his Majesty.

The horses in this service do not incur any direct expense, the cities, towns, and villages in the neighborhood
being obliged to furnish and maintain them. By his Majesty's command the governors of the cities have experts
determine the number of horses the inhabitants can supply, those on each side of the station contributing their
due share. The cost of the maintenance of the horses is
afterward deducted by the cities out of the revenue pay-
able to the Great Khan.

It must be understood, however, that all of the four
hundred horses are not constantly on service at the station, but only two hundred, which are kept there for the
space of a month. During this period the other half are
at pasture; and at the beginning of the month, these take
their turn again, each alternately relieving the other.

Wherever there is a river or a lake which the couriers
on foot, or the horsemen, must cross, the neighboring
cities are obliged to keep three or four boats in continual
readiness for that purpose; and where there is an uninhabited desert of several days' journey, the city on its
borders is obliged to furnish horses to such persons and
also to supply provisions to them and their escort. But
cities so situated get a special remuneration from his
Majesty. Where the post stations lie at a distance from
the great road, the horses are partly those of his Majesty
and only partly furnished by the cities and towns of
the district.

When messengers must proceed with extraordinary
dispatch, as in giving word of a disturbance in any part
of the country, the rebellion of a chief, or other important matter, they ride two hundred, or sometimes two
hundred and fifty, miles in the course of a day. On such
occasions they carry with them the tablet of the gerfalcon as a signal of the urgency of their business and
the need for speed. When there are two messengers,

they depart together from the same place, mounted upon good fleet horses; and they gird their bodies tight, bind a cloth round their heads, and push their horses to the utmost. They continue thus till they come to the next posthouse twenty-five miles distant, where they find two other horses, fresh and ready to go. They spring upon them without pausing, and changing in the same manner at every stage, until evening, they can cover two hundred and fifty miles.

In cases of great emergency they continue on their way during the night, and if there is no moon, they are accompanied to the next station by persons who run before them with torches; they do not then make the same speed as in the daytime, the light-bearers not being able to exceed a certain pace. Messengers able to endure such extreme fatigue are held in high esteem.

Now we leave this subject, and I will go on to tell you of a great act of benevolence which the Great Khan performs twice a year.

CHAPTER 27

Of the Help Given by the Emperor to All Provinces in Times of Dearth

EVERY year the Great Khan sends his commissioners to find out whether the crops of any of his subjects have suffered from unfavorable weather, windstorms, violent rains, locusts, worms, or any other plague; and in such cases he not only does not exact the usual tribute, but furnishes them from his granaries with as much corn as they need for subsistence, as well as for sowing their land.

With this in view, in times of great plenty he has large purchases made of the most useful kinds of grain, which is stored in granaries provided for the purpose in the several provinces, and managed with such care as to ensure its keeping for three or four years. He commands that these granaries always be kept full in order to provide against times of scarcity; and when at such a time he sells the grain, he asks no more for four measures than the purchaser would pay for one measure in the market. Similarly, where there has been a loss of cattle in any district, he makes good the loss out of his own, which he has received as his tenth in other provinces. All his thoughts, indeed, are directed toward assisting the people whom he governs, that they may be able to make a living and improve their substance. We must not omit to notice as a peculiarity of the Great Khan that where lightning has struck any herd of cattle, flock of sheep, or other domestic animals, whether the property of one or more persons and however large the herd may be, he does not demand the tenth of the increase of such cattle during three years. So also if a ship laden with merchandise has been struck by lightning, he does not collect from her any custom or share of her cargo, considering the accident an ill omen. God, he says, has shown himself to be displeased with the owner of the goods, and he is unwilling that property bearing the mark of divine wrath should find its way into his treasury.

CHAPTER 28

Of the Trees He Causes to Be
Planted at the Roadsides

THERE is another regulation by the Great Khan that is both ornamental and useful. On both sides of the public roads he has men plant trees of a kind that become large and tall. Besides giving shade in summer, they mark the road when the ground is covered with snow. And this is of great assistance and comfort to travelers.* This is done along the high roads wherever the soil allows; but when the road lies through sandy deserts or over rocky mountains, where it is impossible to have trees, he orders stones to be placed and columns erected as landmarks.

He also appoints officers, whose duty it is to see that all these are properly cared for and the roads kept in good order. Besides the reasons already mentioned, it may be added that the Great Khan is the more inclined

---

*It is said that the remains of the fine avenues of Kublai and his successors can still be seen in North China.

to plant trees because astrologers tell him that those who plant trees are rewarded with long life.

CHAPTER 29

Of the Rice Wine of Cathay

MOST of the inhabitants of the province of Cathay drink a sort of wine made from rice mixed with a variety of spices and drugs. This beverage, or wine as it may be termed, is so good and well flavored that they do not wish for better. It is clear, bright, and pleasant to taste, and being taken very hot, can make one drunk sooner than any other wine.

CHAPTER 30

Concerning the Black Stones Dug in Cathay and Used for Fuel

THROUGHOUT this province there is found a sort of black stone,* which they dig out of the mountains, where it runs in veins. When lighted, it burns like charcoal, and retains the fire much better than wood; it may, indeed, be kept going during the night and in the morning be found still glowing. These stones do not flame, except a little when first lighted, but while burning give out a considerable heat.

There is no scarcity of wood in the country, but the population is so immense, and their stoves and baths, which they are continually heating, so numerous, that the quantity could not supply the demand. There is no person who does not frequent a warm bath at least three times a week, and during the winter daily, if he possibly can. Every man of rank or wealth has one in his house for his own use; so the stock of wood would soon prove inadequate, whereas these stones are wonderfully abundant and cheap.

---

*It is said that coal has been in use in China since before the time of Christ; it is very plentiful in every province.

CHAPTER 31

Of the Khan's Magnanimity Toward the Poor

IT HAS already been pointed out that the Emperor distributes large quantities of grain to his subjects. We shall now speak of his great charity to and care of the poor in the city of Khan-balik. Upon being told of members of a respectable family reduced to poverty by misfortune or unable because of illness to earn a living or raise a supply of any kind of grain, he gives them enough for a year's consumption. At the proper time they present themselves before the officers who supervise such expenditures. Here they declare the amount they received the preceding year and receive the same for the current year.

In a similar way the Emperor provides clothing for the poor, which he does from his tenths [tithes] of wool, silk, and hemp. He has these materials woven into various sorts of cloth in a building erected for that purpose, where every artisan is obliged to work one day a week for his Majesty. Garments thus manufactured he orders to be given to the poor families above described, as they are needed for their winter and summer clothes. He also has clothing provided for his armies, and in every city has woolen cloth woven and has it paid for from the tenths levied at that place.

CHAPTER 32

Of the Emperor's Charity

IT SHOULD be realized that when the Tartars followed their original customs and had not yet adopted the religion of the idolaters, they never gave alms. When a poor man applied to them, they drove him away saying, "Take yourself off along with the troubles God has sent you. Had He loved you as He loves me He would have provided for you."

But since the wise men of the idolaters, and especially the Bakshis already mentioned, have taught his Majesty that providing for the poor is a good work and highly acceptable to their deities, he has helped them in the manner stated, and at his court no one is denied food. Not a day passes in which twenty thousand bowls of rice, millet, and panicum are not distributed by the regular officers. By reason of this immense and astonishing liberality towards the poor, the people all adore the Great Khan.

CHAPTER 33

Of the Astrologers of the City of Khan-balik

THERE are in the city of Khan-balik, including Christians, Saracens, and Cathayans, about five thousand astrologers and soothsayers, for whom the Emperor provides just as he does for the poor and who constantly practice their art.

They have their astrolabes,* upon which are indicated the planetary signs, timetables and aspects for the whole year. The astrologers of each sect annually study their respective tables in order to ascertain the course of the heavenly bodies and their relative positions in each moon. From the paths of the planets in the different signs they predict the weather and foretell the peculiar phenomena each month will produce. For instance, they predict that there will be thunder and storms in one month, earthquakes in another, lightning and violent rains in another, and pestilence, war, discord, and conspiracies in still another.

As they find the signs in their astrolabes, so they declare what will come to pass, adding, however, that God according to his good pleasure may do more or less than they have set down. They write their predictions for the year on small squares in booklets called *tacuin,*† and these they sell for a groat apiece to all persons who wish to peep into the future. Those whose predictions are found to be most often correct are esteemed the greatest

---

*Astronomical instruments. Astronomy is said to have flourished in Kublai's reign but was not so advanced as that practiced by such medieval European scientists as Tyco Brahe.
†This is an Arabic, not a Chinese, word, and is part of the evidence that has led scholars to suspect that Marco Polo did not know Chinese.

masters of their art and are consequently the most honored.

When any person planning some major enterprise, or a distant journey for business purposes, or any other undertaking, wants to know what success it is likely to have, he has recourse to one of these astrologers, and inquires in what disposition the heavens will be at the time. The latter thereupon tells him that before he can answer, he must know the year, the month, and the hour in which he was born. Having learned these, he determines how the person's horoscope corresponds with the aspect of the heavens at the time the inquiry is made. Upon this he grounds his prediction of the outcome of the undertaking.

It should be observed that the Tartars divide time into a cycle of twelve years. To the first they give the name of the Lion; to the second, the Ox; to the third, the Dragon; the fourth, the Dog; and so to the rest of the twelve. When a person is therefore asked in what year he was born, he replies that it was, for example, in the year of the Lion, upon such a day, at such an hour and minute—all of which has been carefully recorded by his parents. At the end of the twelve years of the cycle, they repeat it.

CHAPTER 34

Of the Religion of the Cathayans and Some of Their Customs

As HAS already been observed, these people are idolaters, and for deities, each person has a tablet fixed on the wall of his chamber, upon which is written a name that denotes the most high and heavenly God. To this they pay daily adoration, including the burning of incense. Lifting up their hands and then striking their faces against the floor three times, they beg him to grant them the blessings of a sound mind and a healthy body. But this is all they ask of him. Below this, on the floor, they have another image called Natigay, which they consider the god of all earthly things or whatever issues from the earth. They set beside him images of a wife and children, and worship him in a similar manner, burning incense, lifting up their hands, and bending to the floor. To him they pray for seasonable weather, abundant crops, children, and the like.

They believe the soul to be immortal in the following sense. They hold that immediately upon the death of a man, his soul enters into another body, and, depending on whether he has acted virtuously or wickedly during his life, his future state will become progressively better or worse. If he is a poor man and has conducted himself worthily and decently, he will first be reborn as the son of a gentlewoman, and will himself become a gentleman; then as the son of a lady of rank, and become a nobleman, thus continually ascending in the scale of existence until he is united to the divinity. But if, on the contrary, being the son of a gentleman, he has behaved unworthily, he will in his next state be a clown, and at length a dog, continually descending lower and lower.

Their style of conversation is most courteous; they greet each other politely and cheerfully, have an air of good breeding, and eat their food with meticulous cleanliness. To their parents they show the utmost reverence. If a child acts disrespectfully or neglects to assist his parents when necessary, there is a tribunal whose especial duty it is to punish such filial ingratitude severely.

Criminals who are apprehended and thrown into prison are either executed by strangling, or, if they are still in prison at the end of the three-year periods appointed by his Majesty for a general amnesty, are liberated; but they then have a mark branded upon one of their cheeks so that they may be recognized.

The present Great Khan has prohibited all gambling and other modes of cheating, to which these people are addicted more than any others upon earth. To discourage these habits he said, "I conquered you by the power of my sword, and consequently whatever you possess belongs to me: if you, therefore, gamble, you are gambling with my property." He does not, however, use this as an excuse to take anything arbitrarily from them.

The behavior of all ranks of people when they present themselves before his Majesty ought not to pass unnoticed. When they approach within half a mile of any place where he happens to be, they show their respect for him by assuming a humble and subdued demeanor, insomuch that not the least noise, or any loud voice is heard. Every man of rank carries with him a small vessel into which he spits, no one daring to spit on the floor; this being done, he covers it and makes a salutation. They are likewise accustomed to take with them handsome slippers made of white leather; before they enter the hall they put these on, meanwhile handing over their shoes to the servants. This is done so that they may not soil the beautiful carpets, which are woven with silk and gold and in a variety of colors.

PART 2

A JOURNEY TO THE WEST AND
SOUTHWEST OF CATHAY

CHAPTER 35

Of the Interior of Cathay and
the River Pulisangan

HAVING thus given an account of the government of the province of Cathay and the city of Khan-balik as well as the magnificence of the Great Khan, we shall now proceed to speak of other parts of the empire. You must know then that the Great Khan sent Marco as his emissary on a journey to the west that lasted four months. We shall tell you all he saw both going and returning.

Upon leaving the capital and traveling ten miles, you come to a river named Pulisangan [the Hun-ho, or Muddy River, just below Peiping], which empties into the ocean and is used by many vessels carrying much merchandise. Over this river there is a very impressive stone bridge, perhaps unequaled by any other in the world. Its length is three hundred paces, and its width eight paces; so that ten mounted men can, without inconvenience, ride abreast on it. It has twenty-four arches all

of marble, supported by twenty-five piers, all built with
great skill.

On each side, from one end to the other, there is a
handsome parapet of marble slabs and pillars arranged
in a masterly style. As the bridge ascends, it narrows,
but then the sides run in straight and parallel lines. On
the upper level there is a massive and lofty column rest-
ing upon a tortoise of marble and having near its base
a large figure of a lion and another at the top. At a
distance of a pace and a half there is another handsome
column, with its lion; and so on.

All the spaces between the pillars are filled with slabs
of marble, curiously sculptured and mortised into the
next pillar, forming altogether a beautiful spectacle.
These parapets serve to prevent accidents.

CHAPTER 36

Of the City of Gouza

HAVING crossed this bridge and proceeded thirty miles
in a westerly direction through an area of fine buildings,
vineyards, and fertile fields, one arrives at a large and
handsome city named Gouza [Chochau]. Here there are
many convents of idolaters. The inhabitants in general
live by commerce and handicrafts. They manufacture
gold tissue and the finest taffetas. There are many inns
for travelers.

A mile beyond this place, the roads divide, one going
in a westerly direction through the province of Cathay,
and the other southeasterly toward the province of
Manzi [Southern China]. From the city of Gouza it is a
journey of ten days through Cathay to the kingdom of
Ta-in-fu [Shansi]. In the course of this one passes
through many fine cities, in which manufactures and
commerce flourish and where there are many vineyards
and much cultivated land. From there grapes are carried
into the interior of Cathay, where the vine does not
grow. Mulberry trees also abound, which enable the inhabitants to produce large quantities of silk. All the people of this country are quite civilized as a result of
frequent contact with the towns, which are numerous

and near each other. To these the merchants continually come, carrying their goods from one city to another, as the fairs are held at each.

CHAPTER 37

The Kingdom of Ta-in-fu

AT THE end of ten days' journey, it is said, there is another city, one that is unusually large and handsome, named Ach-baluch. His Majesty's hunting grounds extend to this city, but no one dares hunt here except the princes of his own family and those whose names are on the Grand Falconer's list. Beyond these limits, all persons qualified by rank may pursue game.

It happens, however, that the Great Khan scarcely ever indulges in a chase on this side of the country; and the consequence is that the wild animals, especially hares, multiply to such a degree as to destroy all the crops of the province. When this came to the knowledge of the Great Khan, he came here with the whole of his court, and a vast number of these animals were taken.

A considerable trade is carried on here, and a variety of articles are manufactured, particularly arms and other military equipment, which are here conveniently situated for the use of the Emperor's armies. Vineyards are numerous, and a vast number of grapes are gathered. Other fruits also grow here in plenty, as does the mulberry tree, together with the worms that yield the silk.

Leaving Ta-in-fu and traveling westward, one passes for seven days through a fine country with many cities where commerce and manufacturers dominate, and whose merchants travel profitably in various parts of the country. After this, one reaches the large and very important city of Painfu [P'ing-yang fu]. It likewise contains numerous merchants and artisans, and silk is produced here in great quantity. We shall not say anything further of these places, but proceed to speak of the outstanding city of Kachanfu, first noticing, however, a noble castle named Thaigin.

CHAPTER 38

Of the Castle of Thaigin

IN A westerly direction from Painfu there is a large and handsome fortress named Thaigin which is said to have been built at a remote period by a ruler called the Golden King.* Within the walls of the fort stands a spacious and highly ornamented palace, the hall of which contains paintings of all the renowned princes who, from ancient times, have reigned in this place. Taken together they form a fine sight.

The following is a remarkable circumstance in the history of this king. He was a powerful prince and was always waited upon by young women of great beauty, a vast number of whom he kept at his court. When, for recreation, he rode around his fortress, these damsels drew him in a carriage, which they could do with ease since it was small. They were devoted to him and did anything for him that might contribute to his convenience or amusement. He was a vigorous governor and ruled with dignity and justice.

The situation of the castle, according to the report of the people of the country, was tremendously strong. The king was, however, a vassal of Ung Khan who, as we have said, was known as Prester John [see Book I, Chapter 46], but goaded by pride, he rebelled against him. When this came to the knowledge of Prester John, he was greatly angered, but because of the strong situation of the castle, found it impossible to attack it. Matters had remained some time in this state when seventeen cavaliers belonging to his retinue came before him and declared their intention to seize the Golden King and bring him alive to his Majesty. In this they were encouraged by the promise of a large reward.

They accordingly went to the Golden King and, saying that they had come from a distant country, offered him their services. They so ably and diligently performed their duties in his employ that they gained the esteem and favor of their new master. One day when the king was

---

*The emperor of the so-called Golden Tartars who ruled North China until Genghis Khan overthrew them.

engaged in the chase and a river separated him from the rest of his party, these cavaliers saw their chance to carry out their design. They drew their swords, surrounded the king, and led him away towards the territory of Prester John before he could get any assistance from his own people.

CHAPTER 39

How Prester John Treated
the Golden King

WHEN they reached the court of Prester John, he ordered his prisoner clothed in the meanest apparel and to humiliate him further, set him to looking after his cattle.

In this wretched condition he remained for two years, strict care being taken that he should not escape. At the end of that period, the Golden King was brought before Prester John again, trembling from fear that they would put him to death. But, on the contrary, Prester John, after a severe rebuke and a warning against pride and arrogance, pardoned him. He then directed that he should be dressed in royal apparel and sent back to his principality with an escort of honor. From that time forward he remained loyal and lived on friendly terms with Prester John. The foregoing is what I was told about the Golden King.

Chapter 40

Of a Large and Noble River,
the Kara-moran

UPON leaving the fortress of Thaigin and going about twenty miles, the traveler comes to a river called the Kara-moran [a Mongol name for the Yellow River], which is of such width and depth that no solid bridge can be built across it. Its waters flow into the ocean. On its banks are many cities and castles inhabited by people who carry on an extensive commerce. The country bordering upon it produces ginger, and also silk in large quantities.

The multitude of birds is incredible, especially of

pheasants, which are sold at the rate of three for the value of a Venetian groat. Here too grows a species of large cane in infinite abundance, some of it a foot, and others a foot and a half in circumference; these are employed by the inhabitants for a variety of useful purposes.

Having crossed this river and traveled three days' journey, you arrive at a city named Ka-chan-fu [Puchow], whose inhabitants are idolaters. They carry on a considerable trade and make a variety of articles. The country produces much silk, ginger, and many drugs that are nearly unknown in our part of the world. They also weave gold tissues, as well as every other kind of silken cloth. We shall speak next of the noble and celebrated city of Ken-zan-fu [Sian], in the kingdom of the same name [Shensi].

CHAPTER 41

Of the City of Ken-zan-fu

DEPARTING from Ka-chan-fu and proceeding eight days' journey in a westerly direction,* you continually meet with cities and commercial centers, and pass many gardens and cultivated grounds with an abundance of the mulberry tree which produces silk. The inhabitants in general worship idols, but there are also found here Nestorian Christians, Turkomans, and Saracens. The wild beasts of the country afford excellent sport, and a variety of birds also are taken.

At the end of eight days you arrive at the city of Ken-zan-fu, which was anciently the capital of an extensive, noble, and powerful kingdom, the seat of many nobly descended kings. At present it is governed by Mangalai,† a son of the Great Khan.

It is a center of commerce and famous for its manufactures. Raw silk is produced in large quantities, and tissues of gold and every other kind of silk are woven there. They also prepare every article necessary for the

---

*This is the richly cultivated basin of the Wei River, the most important agricultural region of northwest China.
†Kublai's third son. He died in 1280.

equipment of an army. All provisions are abundant and moderately priced. The inhabitants in general worship idols, but there are some Christians, Turkomans, and Saracens.

In a plain about five miles from the city stands a beautiful palace belonging to King Mangalai, embellished with many fountains and rivulets, both inside and outside the buildings. There is also a fine park surrounded by a high wall, with battlements enclosing an area of five miles where all kinds of wild animals, both beasts and birds, are kept for sport. In its center is this spacious palace, which cannot be surpassed for symmetry and beauty. It contains many marble halls and chambers, ornamented with paintings, beaten gold, and the finest azure. Mangalai, pursuing the footsteps of his father, governs his principality with strict justice and is beloved by his people. He also takes much delight in hunting and hawking.

CHAPTER 42

Of the Boundaries of Cathay and Manzi

TRAVELING westward three days from the residence of Mangalai, you still find towns and castles whose inhabitants subsist by commerce and manufactures, and where there is an abundance of silk. At the end of these three days you enter a region of mountains* and valleys which lie within the province of Han-chung.

The inhabitants of this tract are worshipers of idols, and cultivate the earth. They live also by the chase, the land being covered with woods that harbor many wild beasts, such as tigers, bears, lynxes, fallow deer, antelopes, and stags, which the people turn to good account. This region extends for a distance of twenty days' journey, the way lying entirely over mountains† and through

---

*The Tsin Ling Shan, one of the lofty east-west ranges of western China.
†These immensely rugged mountains could be crossed only by a narrow military road that was often carved into cliffs overhanging great gorges and held up on its outer edge by wooden supports.

valleys and woods, but with towns where travelers may find convenient accommodations.

CHAPTER 43

Concerning the Province of Manzi

AFTER this journey of twenty days toward the west [actually southwest], you arrive at a place called Achbaluch Manzi, which signifies, "the white city on the Manzi border," where the country becomes level and is very populous. The inhabitants live by trade and handicrafts. Large quantities of ginger are produced here, and this is conveyed through all the province of Cathay with great profit to the merchants. The country yields wheat, rice, and other grain plentifully and at little cost.

This plain, thickly covered with villages, continues for two stages, after which you again come to high mountains, valleys, and forests. Traveling twenty days still farther to the west, you continue to find the country inhabited by people who worship idols and subsist upon the fruits of the soil as well as of the chase. Here also, besides the wild animals already enumerated, there are great numbers of that species of animal which produces musk [musk deer].

CHAPTER 44

Of the Province of Sin-din-fu

HAVING traveled those twenty stages through a mountainous country, you reach a plain on the borders of Manzi. Here there is a district named Sin-din-fu [Chengtu], which is also the name of its capital,* a large and noble city, formerly the seat of many rich and powerful kings. The circumference of the city is twenty miles; but at present it is divided in the following manner. The late king had three sons, and it being his wish that each of them should reign after his death, he divided the city among them, separating the parts by walls, although the

*Now the capital of Szechwan province, adjoining Tibet. It is still a large city.

whole continued to be surrounded by one general enclosure.

These three brothers accordingly became kings, and each had a considerable tract of country for his portion, the territory of their father having been extensive and rich. But the Great Khan conquered these three princes and took their inheritance for himself.

The city is watered by many large streams, which, descending from distant mountains, flow around and pass through it in a variety of directions. These rivers range from half a mile in width to two hundred paces [about 1,000 feet], and are very deep. A great bridge crosses one of these rivers within the city. It has on each side a row of marble pillars which support a roof constructed of wood, ornamented with paintings of a red color, and covered with tiles. Throughout the whole length also there are neat compartments and shops, where all sorts of trades are carried on. One of the buildings, larger than the rest, is occupied by the officers who collect duties and a toll from those who pass over the bridge. From this bridge, it is said, his Majesty receives daily the sum of a hundred bezants of gold.

These rivers, uniting below the city, contribute to form the mighty river called the Kiang [Yangtze Kiang, the great central river of China], whose course, before it empties into the ocean, amounts to a hundred days' journey. On these rivers and in the vicinity are many towns and fortified places, and numerous vessels in which large quantities of merchandise are transported to and from the city. The people of the province are idolaters. Departing thence you travel five days, partly along a plain and partly through valleys, where you see many fine mansions, castles, and small towns. The inhabitants live by agriculture. In the city there are factories, particularly of very fine cloths and crapes or gauzes. This county, like the districts already mentioned, is infested with lions [tigers], bears, and other wild animals. At the end of these five days' journey, you reach the desolate country of Thebeth.

CHAPTER 45

Of the Province of Thebeth

THE province named Thebeth [Tibet]* was laid entirely waste at the time that Mangu Khan carried his wars into that country. For a distance of twenty days' journey you see numberless towns and castles in a state of ruin; and because of the absence of inhabitants, wild beasts, and especially tigers, have multiplied to such a degree that merchants and other travelers are exposed to great danger during the night. They must not only carry their provisions along with them, but are obliged upon arriving at halting places to take the following precautions that their horses may not be devoured. In this region, and particularly near rivers, are found bamboos of the length of ten paces, three palms in circumference,† and three palms also in the space between each knot or joint. Several of these, in their green state, the travelers tie together, and when evening approaches, place them at a certain distance from their quarters, with a fire lighted around them. The action of the heat upon the green wood causes the joints to burst with loud explosions. The noise is so loud as to be heard at the distance of two miles, and this terrifies the wild beasts, causing them to flee.

The merchants also provide themselves with iron shackles in order to fasten the legs of their horses, which would otherwise when alarmed by the noise break their halters and run away. From neglect of this precaution, many owners have lost their cattle. Thus you travel for twenty days through a desolate country, finding neither inns nor provisions, unless perhaps once in three or four days, when you take the opportunity of replenishing your stock of necessities. At the end of that period you come upon a few castles and strong points on rocky heights or on the summits of mountains, and gradually enter an inhabited and cultivated district, where there is no longer any danger from beasts of prey.

*The area here described is now in the eastern China provinces of Szechwan and Yunnan. In Polo's time Tibet extended farther east and was under the domination of the Mongol emperors.
†Very large indeed: about 50 feet long and almost 30 inches in girth.

A scandalous custom, which could only arise from the blindness of idolatry, prevails among the people of these parts: they are disinclined to marry young women so long as they are virgins, but require, on the contrary, that they should have had previous relations with many of the other sex. This, they assert, is pleasing to their deities, and they believe that a woman who has not had the company of men is worthless.* Accordingly, upon the arrival of a caravan of merchants, and as soon as they have set up their tents for the night, those mothers who have marriageable daughters conduct them to the place, and entreat the strangers to accept their daughters and enjoy their society so long as they remain in the neighborhood. Such as are most attractive are of course chosen, and the others return home disappointed and chagrined. Those chosen remain with the travelers until their departure. The travelers then return them to their mothers and never attempt to carry them away. It is expected, however, that the merchants will make the young women presents of trinkets, rings, or other tokens of their regard, which the young women take home with them. They wear all these ornaments about the neck or other parts of the body, and she who shows the greatest number of them is considered to have attracted the greatest number of men, and is therefore in higher esteem with the young men who are looking for wives. At her wedding ceremony, she accordingly makes a display of them to the assembly, and the man regards them as a proof that their idols have rendered her lovely in the eyes of men. Once she is married, no one dares to meddle with her, and this rule is never infringed.†

These idolatrous people are treacherous and cruel, and holding it no crime to rob, are the greatest brigands in the world. They subsist by the chase and by fowling, as well as upon the fruits of the earth.

Here are found the animals that produce musk, and

---

*This attitude was until recently not uncommon, especially among primitive peoples, the attractiveness of a girl being judged by the number of lovers she had had.

†In other versions of his manuscript Marco adds: "Now I have related to you this marriage custom . . . to show what a fine country that is for young fellows to go to!"

there are so many that the scent of it is diffused over
the whole country. Once in every month the secretion
takes place, and it forms itself, as has already been said,
into a sort of bag, or boil, full of blood, near the navel.
Throughout every part of this region the animal
abounds, and the odor generally prevails. They are
called *gudderi* in the language of the natives, and are
taken with dogs.

These people have no coined money, nor even the
paper money of the Great Khan, but use salt for currency. Their dress is homely, being of leather, undressed
skins, or canvas.* They have a language peculiar to the
province of Thebeth, which borders on Manzi.

CHAPTER 46

Further Concerning Thebeth

THEBETH was formerly a country of so much importance as to be divided into eight kingdoms, containing
many cities and castles. Its rivers, lakes, and mountains
are numerous. In the rivers gold dust is found in very
large quantities. Not only is coral used for money, but
the women wear it about their necks and adorn their
idols with it. They manufacture camlet [a fine fabric] and
gold cloth, and produce many drugs that have not been
brought to our country.

Among these people you find the most skilled wizards,
who by their diabolic art perform the most extraordinary
marvels that were ever seen or heard. They cause tempests to arise, accompanied with flashes of lightning and
thunderbolts, and many other miraculous effects.

They are altogether an ill-conditioned race. They have
dogs the size of asses, strong enough to hunt all sorts of
wild beasts, particularly the wild oxen called *beyamini*
[probably the gaur], which are extremely large and
fierce. Some of the best lanner falcons are bred here,
and also sakers, very swift of flight, and the natives have
good sport with them. This province of Thebeth is sub-

*This is thought to apply only to the primitive people known as the
Lolos.

ject to the Great Khan, as well as all the other kingdoms
and provinces that have been mentioned. Next to this is
the province of Kaindu.

CHAPTER 47

Of Kaindu and Men Who Turn Over Their
Women to Travelers

KAINDU is a western province which was formerly
subject to its own princes; but it has been brought
under the dominion of the Great Khan and is now ruled
by governors whom he appoints. We are not to understand, however, that it is situated in the western part
of Asia, but only that it lies westward with respect to
our course from the northeastern quarter. It contains
many cities and castles, and the capital city, standing at
the entrance to the province, is likewise named Kaindu.
Near to it there is a large salt lake that abounds in
pearls of a white color, but not round. So great indeed
is the quantity that if his Majesty permitted every individual to search for them, their value would become
trifling; but fishing for them is prohibited to all who do
not obtain his license.

A mountain in the neighborhood yields the turquoise
stone, the mines of which cannot be worked without the
same permission.

The inhabitants of this district have the shameful and
odious habit of considering it no mark of disgrace that
those who travel through the country should have relations with their wives, daughters, or sisters; but, on the
contrary, when strangers arrive, each householder en-
deavors to bring one of them home with him. There he
turns over all the women of the family to him, leaves
him in the position of master of the house, and goes off.
While the stranger is in the house, he places a signal at
the window, such as his hat or some other thing; and as
long as this signal is visible, the husband remains away.
And this custom prevails throughout the province. This
they do in honor of their idols, believing that by such
acts of kindness and hospitality to travelers a blessing is

obtained and that they shall be rewarded with a plentiful supply of the fruits of the earth.*

The money or currency they use is made thus: Their gold is formed into small rods, and is valued according to its weight, without any stamp. This is their greater money; the smaller is made thus: In this country there are salt springs, from which they manufacture salt by boiling it in small pans. When the water has boiled for an hour, it becomes a kind of paste, which is formed into cakes of the value of twopence each. These cakes, which are flat on the lower and convex on the upper side, are placed upon hot tiles near a fire to dry and harden. The stamp of the Great Khan is pressed into them, and it cannot be prepared by any other than his own officers. Eighty of the cakes pass for a saggio of gold. But when these are carried by the traders among the inhabitants of the mountains and other parts that are rarely visited, they obtain a saggio of gold for sixty, fifty, or even forty of the salt cakes, in proportion as they find the natives less civilized, further removed from the towns, and more accustomed to remain where they are.

The same merchants travel in like manner through the mountainous and other parts of the province of Thebeth, where the money of salt has equal currency. Their profits are considerable, because these country people consume the salt with their food and regard it as an indispensable necessity; whereas the inhabitants of the cities use only fragments of the cakes, putting the remainder into circulation as money.

Here also the animals that yield musk are taken in great numbers, and the article is accordingly abundant. Many kinds of good fish are caught in the lake. In the country are found tigers, bears, deer, stags, and antelopes, as well as numerous birds of various sorts. The wine is not made from grapes, but from wheat and rice with a mixture of spices, and is an excellent beverage.

This province also produces cloves. The tree is small; the branches and leaves resemble those of the laurel,

---

*Polo has already told much the same story of the people of Kamul in Book I, Chapter 41. Yule gives a long list of peoples to whom such practices have been ascribed.

but are somethat longer and narrower. Its flowers are white and small, as are the cloves themselves, but as they ripen they become dark. Ginger grows there and also much cassia, besides many other drugs, of which very little is ever brought to Europe.

Upon leaving the city of Kaindu, the journey is ten days to the opposite boundary of the province, in the course of which you come to sizable villages, many fortified posts, and also places good for hunting and fowling. The inhabitants follow the customs and manners already described. At the end of these ten days, you reach the great river Brius [the Kin-sha Kiang, or River of Golden Sands, the upper course of the Yangtze], which bounds the province, and in which are found large quantities of gold dust. It flows into the ocean. We shall now leave this river and shall speak of the province of Karajan [now Yunnan, in western China].

CHAPTER 48

Of the Great Province of Karajan and of Yachi, Its Principal City

HAVING passed the river above mentioned, you enter the province of Karajan, which is so large as to include seven kingdoms. It is situated toward the west; and the inhabitants are idolaters. It is subject to the dominion of the Great Khan, who has appointed as its king his son [actually grandson] Essen-Temur, a rich, magnificent, and powerful prince, who is endowed with much wisdom and virtue and rules with great justice. In traveling from this river five days' journey in a westerly direction, you pass through a country fully inhabited and see many castles. The inhabitants live upon flesh meat and upon the fruits of the earth. Their language is peculiar to them, and is difficult to master. The best horses are bred in this province.

At the end of these five days you arrive at its capital city, which is named Yachi [Kunming, on the Burma Road] and is large and noble. In it are found merchants and artisans, with a mixed population consisting of idolaters, Nestorian Christians, and Saracens or Mahometans;

but the first is the most numerous class. The land is fertile in rice and wheat. The people, however, do not use wheaten bread, which they think unwholesome, but eat rice. Of other grain, with the addition of spices, they make wine, which is clear, light-colored, and most pleasant to the taste. For money they employ the white porcelain shells [cowrie shells] found in the sea, and these they also wear as ornaments about their necks. Eighty of the shells are equal in value to a saggio of silver or two Venetian groats, and eight saggi of good silver to one of pure gold. In this country also there are salt springs, from which all the salt used by the inhabitants is derived. The duty levied on this salt produces a large revenue for the Emperor.

The natives do not consider it as an injury when others have relations with their wives, provided the woman be willing. Here there is a lake nearly a hundred miles in circuit, in which great quantities of various kinds of fish are caught, some of them quite large.

The people are accustomed to eat the undressed flesh of fowl, sheep, oxen, and buffaloes, but cured in the following manner: They cut the meat into very small particles and then put it into pickling salt, along with several of their spices. It is prepared thus for persons of the upper class, but the poorer sort only steep it, after mincing, in a sauce of garlic, and then eat it as if it were dressed.

CHAPTER 49

Of a Further Part of the Province Named Karajan

LEAVING the city of Yachi and traveling ten days in a westerly direction, you reach the chief city of the province of Karajan, which is also called Karajan [the city of Ta-li, located on a great lake]. The country is in the dominion of the Great Khan, and the royal functions are exercised by his son, named Kogatin. Gold is found in the rivers, both in small particles and in lumps; and there are also veins of it in the mountains. Because of the large quantity available, they give a saggio of gold for six saggi of silver. They likewise use cowrie shells in currency, although these are not found in this part of the world, but are brought from India. As I have said before, these people never take virgins for their wives.

Here are found snakes and huge serpents [crocodiles], ten paces in length and ten spans in girth [that is, 50 feet long and 100 inches in girth]. At the fore part, near the head, they have two short legs,* each with three claws, as well as eyes larger than a loaf and very glaring. The jaws are wide enough to swallow a man, the teeth are large and sharp, and their whole appearance is so formidable that neither man, nor any kind of animal, can approach them without terror. Others are of a smaller size, being eight, six, or five paces long.

The following method is used for capturing them. In the daytime, by reason of the great heat, they lurk in caverns, but at night they come out to seek their food, and whatever beast they can lay hold of, they devour. After eating they drag themselves toward some lake, spring, or river in order to drink. As they move along the shore, their vast weight makes a deep impression, as if a heavy beam had been drawn along the sands. Those who hunt them note the path they most frequently use, and drive into the ground several wooden stakes tipped with sharp iron spikes, which they cover with sand. Whenever therefore the animals make their way towards the places they usually haunt, they are wounded by the spikes and speedily killed.

As soon as they see that they are dead, the crows begin to scream; and this serves as a signal to the hunters, who come up to the spot and skin the beast, immediately taking care to secure the gall, which is a highly valued medicine. In cases of a bite by a mad dog, a pennyweight of it, dissolved in wine, is administered. It is also useful in hastening delivery when the labor pains of women come on. When a small quantity of it is applied to carbuncles, pustules, or other eruptions on the body, they are soon cured; and it is efficacious in many other complaints.

---

*Strangely, Polo seems not to have noted the other two legs possessed by all fully equipped crocodiles.

The flesh of the animal is also sold at a high price, because it is thought to have a higher flavor than other kinds of meat, and it is esteemed a delicacy by everyone. In this province the horses are of a large size, and while young, are carried to India for sale. It is the practice to cut off one joint of the tail in order to prevent them from lashing it from side to side, as the swishing about, in riding, appears to them a vile habit. These people ride with long stirrups, as the French do in our part of the world; whereas the Tartars, and almost all other people, wear them short, so that they may rise in their stirrups when they shoot their arrows. They have a complete armor of buffalo hide and carry lances, shields and crossbows. All their arrows are poisoned.

I was assured as a certain fact that many persons, and especially those who harbor evil designs, always carry poison with the intention of swallowing it in case they are captured and face torture. But their rulers, who are aware of this practice, always have dog dung which they make the accused swallow, causing him to vomit the poison. Thus an antidote is ready against the tricks of these wretches.

Before they came under the rule of the Great Khan, these people were addicted to the following brutal custom. When any stranger of fine quality and personal appearance happened to lodge at the house of one of them, he was murdered during the night—not for the sake of his money, but in order that the spirit of the dead person, endowed with his talents and intelligence, might remain with the family, and all their affairs might thus prosper. Many lost their lives in consequence. But as soon as his Majesty began to rule the country, he took measures for suppressing the horrid practice, and as severe punishments have been inflicted, it has ceased to exist.

CHAPTER 50

Of the Province of Zardandan and the City of Vochang

PROCEEDING five days' journey in a westerly direction from Karajan, you enter the province of Zardandan, belonging to the dominion of the Great Khan and of which the principal city is Vochang. The currency of this country is gold by weight, and also cowrie shells. An ounce of gold is exchanged for five ounces of silver and a saggio of gold for five saggi of silver. There being no silver mines in this country, but much gold, the merchants who import silver make a large profit.

Both the men and women of this province have the custom of putting a thin casing of gold on their teeth; these are fitted with great care to the shape of the teeth and remain on them continually.* The men also make dark stripes or bands round their arms and legs by puncturing them in the following manner. They have five needles joined together, which they press into the flesh until blood is drawn; they then rub the punctures with a black coloring matter which leaves an indelible mark.† Such stripes are considered an ornament and a distinction. The men pay little attention to anything but horsemanship, the sports of the chase, and the use of arms and a military life, leaving the entire management of their domestic affairs to their wives, who are assisted by slaves, either purchased or made prisoners in war.

These people have the following singular usage. As soon as a woman has been delivered of a child, and rising from her bed, has washed and swaddled the infant, her husband immediately takes the place she has left, has the child laid beside him, and cares for it for forty days. In the meantime, friends and relations pay him their visits of congratulation, while the woman attends to the business of the house, carries food and drink to the husband in his bed, and suckles the infant at his side.‡

---

*The name Zardandan is itself a Persian word meaning "Gold Teeth." Furthermore, the Chinese name for the people of this area, Kin-Chi, also means "Gold-Teeth."

†The reader will doubtless recognize this as tattooing.

‡The quaint practice that ethnologists call "couvade," which consists of the father taking to his bed with the newborn child while the mother gets up and waits on him hand and foot, has been noted in Africa, Borneo, India, and especially among the aborigines of North and South America. It is taken very seriously by those who practice it and appears to be some kind of expression of the father's kinship with the child and a belief that by "sympathetic magic" his behavior will influence the child's life.

These people eat their meat raw, or prepared in the manner that has been described, and along with it eat rice. Their wine is manufactured from rice with a mixture of spices, and is a good beverage.

In this district they have neither temples nor idols, but worship the elder or ancestor of the family, from whom, they say, they derive their existence and therefore owe him all they possess. They have no knowledge of any kind of writing, nor is this to be wondered at, considering the rude nature of the country, which is a mountainous tract covered with the thickest forests. During the summer season, the atmosphere is so gloomy and unwholesome that merchants and other strangers are obliged to leave the district in order to escape death.

When the natives have business dealings involving payment at some future date, their chief takes a square piece of wood, divides it in two, with notches to indicate the amount due. Each party receives one of the corresponding pieces, as we do with our tallies. When payment is made by the debtor, the creditor delivers up his matching piece, and both remain satisfied.

Neither in this province, nor in the cities of Kain-du, Vochang, or Yachi are there any physicians. When a person of consequence falls ill, his family sends for those sorcerers who offer sacrifices to the idols, and the sick person tells them what ails him.

The sorcerers immediately begin playing on instruments and singing and dancing until one of them, possessed by the evil spirit, falls to the ground like a dead man. The others then ask the person possessed by the devil what the cause is of the man's sickness and how it can be cured. Thereupon the evil spirit, speaking through the mouth of the possessed person, may answer that the sick man has insulted a certain spirit. The sorcerers then beseech the spirit to pardon the sick man on condition that when he recovers he offer up a sacrifice of his own blood. If the demon sees no prospect of a recovery, he will declare that the spirit is so offended that no sacrifice can appease him. If, however, he sees that a cure is likely, he asks that an offering of a certain number of sheep with heads of such and such a color be made, and that certain sorcerers and their wives perform the sacrifice. In this way, he says, the spirit may be appeased. The relatives immediately comply, the sheep are slaughtered, their blood is sprinkled about, and the sorcerers, both men and women, light incense and then perfume the whole house of the sick person, making a smoke with wood of aloes. They pour out, as a libation, the broth from the meat together with some of the spiced liquor; and then they laugh, sing, and revel, all in honor of the deity they are appeasing. Then they feast merrily on the meat that had been offered in sacrifice, and they drink the spiced liquor.

Having finished their meal and received their fees, they return to their homes; and if through God's providence the patient recovers, they attribute his cure to the idol for whom the sacrifice was performed; but if he happens to die, they say that the rites were spoiled because those who prepared the sacrifices presumed to taste them before they gave the spirit his portion.

It should be understood that ceremonies of this kind are not performed for everyone, but only perhaps once or twice a month for noble or wealthy personages. They are common, however, to all the idolatrous inhabitants of the provinces of Cathay and Manzi, among whom a physician is rare.* And thus do the demons sport with the blindness of these deluded and wretched people.

CHAPTER 51

How the Great Khan Conquered the Kingdom of Mien and of Bangala

AT THIS point we should tell of a memorable battle that was fought in this kingdom. It happened that in the year 1272 the Great Khan sent an army into the countries of Vochang and Karazan to protect them against any attack by foreigners. At this period he had not as yet appointed his own sons as rulers.

When the King of Mien [the Chinese name for Burma] and Bangala [Bengal], in India, who was power-

---

*The use of shamans or devil-dancers to exorcise evil spirits has been reported from almost every part of the world, especially among primitive peoples.

ful in terms of subjects, territory, and wealth, heard that an army of Tartars had arrived at Vochang, he immediately advanced to attack it, hoping to deter the Great Khan from again attempting to station a force upon the borders of his dominions. For this purpose he assembled a very large army, including many elephants upon whose backs were placed wooden battlements, or towers, capable of holding twelve or sixteen men. With these, and a large army of horsemen and foot soldiers, he took the road to Vochang, where the Great Khan's army lay, and encamped near it, intending to give his troops a few days of rest.

CHAPTER 52

Of the Battle Fought by the Great Khan's Army

THE approach of the King of Mien with so great a force soon became known to Nasruddin, who commanded the troops of the Great Khan. Although a brave and able officer, he felt much alarmed, not having more than twelve thousand men under him, whereas the enemy had sixty thousand, besides the elephants. He did not, however, betray any apprehension, but descending into the plain of Vochang, took a position in which his flank was covered by a thick wood. In case of a furious charge by the elephants, his troops might be able to retire into this wood and harass them with their arrows.

Calling together his officers, he exhorted them to be as brave as ever, saying that victory did not depend upon the number of men, but upon courage and discipline. He told them that the troops of the King of Mien and Bangala were raw and inexperienced, and their own name was a subject of terror, not merely to the enemy, but to the whole world.

When the enemy learned that the Tartars had descended into the plain, they immediately advanced toward them. The Tartars remained firm, but allowed them to approach their entrenchments. They then charged with great spirit and the utmost eagerness to engage; but it was soon found that the Tartar horses,

unused to the sight of the huge elephants and their
towers, were terrified, and wheeling about, sought to
flee. Nor could their riders restrain them. Meanwhile the
King's forces gained ground with every passing moment.
As soon as the commander saw this, he wisely ordered
his men to dismount, lead their horses into the wood,
and tie them to the trees there. Then without delay they
advanced on the elephants, firing arrows as they went.
The King's forces returned their volleys furiously, but
the Tartars, drawing their bows more powerfully, did
more damage. So heavy were the Tartar volleys that the
elephants were soon covered with arrows and suddenly
gave way, throwing the troops behind them into confu-
sion. Smarting under their wounds and terrified by the
shouts of the enemy, the elephants ran out of control
and at length rushed into some woods not occupied by
the Tartars. There the branches of large trees swept
away the battlements on the elephants and killed the
men in them. Encouraged by the rout of the elephants,
the Tartars remounted their horses, formed their divisions again, and fiercely renewed the battle.

The King's troops also fought bravely and the King
encouraged them to stand firm, but the Tartars, with
their great skill as archers and because of their excellent
armor, were too much for them. Having shot all their
arrows, the men resorted to their swords and iron maces,
and in a moment the field was littered with severed
limbs, bloody corpses, and dying men. So great was the
tumult and the shrieking that it seemed to fill the very
heavens.

The King of Mien himself turned up wherever the
fray was thickest, urging his men on and calling up fresh
reserves. But when he saw that his forces could no
longer hold back the Tartars, he and his men took to
flight, the Tartars pursuing and slaying many of them.
The losses on both sides were severe. A point to be
noted is that the King should have drawn the Tartars
out into the open instead of attacking them where they
could make use of the woods on their flank. In an open
area they could not have withstood the elephants and
could have been surrounded.

After the slaughter of the enemy, the Tartars returned

to the wood into which the elephants had fled, and with the help of captives who knew how to manage the elephants, they captured two hundred or more of them.

Thereafter the Great Khan always used elephants in his armies. The result of the victory was that he took over the whole territory of the King of Bangala and Mien.

CHAPTER 53

Of an Uninhabited Region and of the Kingdom of Mien

LEAVING the province of Zardandan you begin a long descent [the famous Burma Road] which lasts for two and a half days and in which there are no habitations. You then reach a broad plain where three days in every week people come to trade with each other. Many of them come down from nearby mountains to exchange their gold for the silver brought by merchants from distant countries. They get one saggio of gold for five of silver. The inhabitants cannot export their gold themselves but must trade it with the merchants, who supply them with whatever goods they need. Only the natives have access to the gold because it is located in remote areas that no one else can reach.

Beyond this, in a southerly direction, toward the borders of India, lies the province of Mien. The journey occupies fifteen days, through an unpopulated country and forests abounding with elephants, rhinoceroses, and other wild beasts.

CHAPTER 54

Of the City of Mien and of the Towers of Silver and Gold

AFTER the journey of fifteen days you reach the city of Mien, which is large, magnificent, and the capital of the kingdom [Burma]. The inhabitants are idolaters and have a language of their own.

It is related that there formerly reigned in this country a rich and powerful monarch who, when his death was drawing near, gave orders for erecting two pyramidal towers at the head and foot of his tomb, each of marble, ten paces [50 feet] in height, and topped with a ball. One of these pyramids was covered with a plate of gold an inch thick and the other with a plate of silver of the same thickness. Around the balls at the top were suspended small bells of gold and of silver, which tinkled when set in motion by the wind. The whole formed a splendid spectacle. The tomb was in like manner covered with a plate, partly of gold and partly of silver. This the king commanded to be prepared for the honor of his soul and that his memory might not perish.

The Great Khan having resolved to seize this city, sent a valiant officer to do this. The army, at its own desire, was accompanied by some of the jugglers or sorcerers, of whom there were always a great number about the court. When these entered the city, they observed the two richly ornamented pyramids, but would not meddle with them until they could learn his Majesty's pleasure respecting them. The Great Khan, upon being informed that they had been erected in pious memory of a former king, would not suffer them to be violated nor damaged in the smallest degree, the Tartars being accustomed to respect any article connected with the dead. In this country were found many elephants, large and handsome wild oxen, stags, fallow deer, and other animals in great abundance.

CHAPTER 55

Of the Province of Bangala

THE province of Bangala [Bengal] is situated to the south and was not yet brought under the dominion of the Great Khan at the time of Marco Polo's residence at his court.* Operations against it occupied his army for a considerable period, the country, as has been related, being strong and its king powerful.

It has its own peculiar language, and the people are

---

*Some scholars doubt that Polo actually visited Bengal, especially since he is so hazy about its location. He may have confused it with Pegu, in the delta of the Irriwaddy River.

worshipers of idols. The oxen found here are almost as tall as elephants, but not so big. The inhabitants live upon flesh, milk, and rice, of which they have an abundance. Much cotton is grown in the country, and trade flourishes. Spikenard, galingale, ginger, sugar, and many sorts of drugs are among the products of the soil. Merchants come from various parts of India to purchase these.

They likewise purchase eunuchs (of whom there are many in the country, for all prisoners of war are at once castrated) for use as slaves; and as every prince and person of rank wants them for guarding their women, the merchants make a large profit by carrying these slaves to other kingdoms and there selling them. This province is thirty days' journey in extent, and at the eastern extremity of it lies a country named Kangigu.

CHAPTER 56

Of the Province of Kangigu

KANGIGU is a province* situated toward the east [in Indo-China], and is governed by a king. The people are idol worshipers, have their own peculiar language, and have voluntarily submitted to the Great Khan, to whom they pay an annual tribute. The king is so devoted to sensual pleasures that he has about three hundred wives, and when he hears of any handsome woman, he sends for and marries her.

Gold is found here in large quantities, and also many kinds of drugs; but being an inland country and distant from the sea, these products are of little value to them. There are elephants in abundance, and other beasts.

The inhabitants live upon flesh, rice, and milk. They have no wine made from grapes, but prepare it from rice and a mixture of spices. Both men and women have their bodies entirely decorated with needle markings, in figures of beasts and birds; and there are among them specialists whose sole employment is to execute these ornaments upon the hands, legs, and breast. When a

---

*This seems to carry us into Laos and has led such scholars as Yule to suggest that Polo is no longer tracing a route he had covered in person.

black coloring stuff has been rubbed into these punctures, it is impossible to efface the marks by water or otherwise. The man or woman who exhibits the greatest profusion of these figures is esteemed the most attractive.

CHAPTER 57

Of the Province of Amu

AMU is also situated toward the east,* and its inhabitants are subjects of the Great Khan. They live on the flesh of their cattle and the fruits of the earth, and have their own peculiar language. The country produces many horses and oxen, which are sold to merchants and conveyed to India. Buffaloes as well as oxen are numerous as a result of the extent and excellence of the pastures. Both men and women wear rings of gold and silver upon their wrists, arms, and legs; but the ornaments of the women are the more costly.

The distance between this province and that of Kangigu is twenty-five days' journey, and thence to Bangala is twenty days' journey. We shall now speak of a province named Tholoman, situated eight days' journey from the former.

CHAPTER 58

Of Tholoman

THE province of Tholoman lies toward the east, and its inhabitants are idolaters. They have their own peculiar language, and are also subjects of the Great Khan. The people are tall and good looking, their complexion inclining rather to brown than fair. They are just in their dealings and brave in war.

Many of their towns and castles are situated upon lofty mountains. They burn the bodies of their dead; and the bones that are not reduced to ashes, they put into wooden boxes and carry to the mountains, where they

*Since this is taken to be in southeastern Yunnan province, Polo is evidently back in China again.

conceal them in caverns in order that no wild animal may disturb them.

Abundance of gold is found here. For the ordinary small currency they use the cowrie shells that come from India; and this sort of money prevails also in the two provinces of Kangigu and Amu, already mentioned. Their food and drink are flesh, rice, and milk.

CHAPTER 59

Of the City of Chintigui

You then travel for twelve days by a river, on each side of which lie many towns and castles, and at length you reach the large and handsome city of Chintigui. The inhabitants are traders and artisans. They make cloth of the bark of certain trees, which looks well and is the ordinary summer clothing of both sexes. The men are brave warriors. They have no other kind of money than the stamped paper of the Great Khan.

In this province the tigers are so numerous that the inhabitants do not dare to sleep outside of their towns at night; and those who sail the river dare not go to rest with their boats moored near the banks, for these animals have been known to plunge into the water, swim to the vessel, and drag the men out.

In this country are also found the largest and fiercest dogs that can be met with. So courageous and powerful are they that a man with two of them may be a match for a tiger. Should he meet a tiger, he sets on his bold dogs, who instantly advance to the attack. The animal instinctively seeks to back itself against a tree so that he may keep his enemies in front of him. As soon as he sees the dogs, he makes toward the tree, but very slowly, showing no signs of fear, which his pride would not allow. During this deliberate movement, the dogs fasten upon him, and the man shoots at him with his arrows. He in turn tries to seize the dogs, but they are too nimble for him. By this time he has been wounded by so many arrows and so often bitten by the dogs that he falls through weakness and from loss of blood. By these means is he captured.

There is here an extensive manufacture of silks, which are exported in large quantities by the river, which flows through towns and villages. The people subsist entirely by trade. At the end of twelve days you arrive at the city of Sin-din-fu, of which an account has been already given. From there in twenty days you reach Gin-gui, in which we were; and in four days more, the city of Pazan-fu, which belongs to Cathay and lies toward the south. The inhabitants worship idols and burn the bodies of their dead. They are subjects of the Great Khan and his paper money is current among them. They gain their living by trade and manufacture, having silk in abundance, of which they weave tissues mixed with gold and also very fine scarfs. This city has many towns and villages under its jurisdiction: a great river flows beside it and by means of this large quantities of merchandise are conveyed to the city of Khan-balik; for many canals enable them to communicate with the capital. But we shall take our leave of this, and proceeding three days' journey, speak of another city named Chan-glu [Tsangchow].

PART 3

A JOURNEY SOUTHWARD THROUGH THE EASTERN
PROVINCES OF CATHAY AND MANZI

CHAPTER 60

Of the City of Chan-glu

WE WILL now set forth again and travel three days until we come to Chan-glu, which is a large city in the province of Cathay. It is under the dominion of the Great Khan. The inhabitants worship idols and burn the bodies of their dead. The stamped paper of the Emperor is current among them.

In this city and the district surrounding it they make great quantities of salt, using the following process. In the country is found a salty earth; they heap this up and filter water through it, which is then conveyed to very wide pans, not more than four inches in depth. In these it is well boiled, and then left to crystallize. The salt that results is white and good, and is exported to various parts. Great profits are made by those who manufacture it, and the Great Khan derives a considerable revenue from it.

This district produces an abundance of good-tasting peaches of such a size that one of them will weigh two pounds troy weight. We shall now speak of another city, named Chan-gli.

CHAPTER 61

Of the Cities of Chan-gli and Tandinfu

CHAN-GLI [apparently Tsinan-fu, the chief city of Shantung province] is also a city of Cathay, situated toward the south and belonging to the Great Khan; the inhabitants also make use of the Khan's paper currency. Its distance from Chan-glu is five days' journey, in the course of which you pass many cities and castles that are also in the dominions of the Great Khan. They are thriving centers of commerce, and the customs levied at them amount to a large sum.

Through this city passes a wide and deep river on which vast quantities of merchandise, consisting of silk, drugs, and other valuable articles, are shipped. We shall leave this place and give an account of another city, Tandinfu.

When you depart from Chan-gli and travel southwards six days' journey, you pass many towns and castles of great importance and size, whose inhabitants worship idols and burn the bodies of their dead. They subsist by trade and manufactures and have provisions in abundance. At the end of these six days you arrive at a city named Tandinfu, which was formerly a magnificent capital, but which the Great Khan annexed by force of arms. The gardens which surround it, filled with handsome shrubs and excellent fruits, make it a delightful place to live. Silk is produced here in wonderfully large quantities. It has under its jurisdiction eleven cities and considerable towns, all centers of trade and having an abundance of silk.* Before its reduction by the Great Khan, it was the seat of government of its own kind.

In 1273 the Emperor appointed one of his officers of the highest rank, named Litan Sangon,† to the government of this city, with seventy thousand horsemen to protect this province. Upon finding himself master of a rich and highly productive district and at the head of so powerful a force, this man became intoxicated with pride, and schemed rebellion against his sovereign. With this in view he induced leading citizens to join in his plot, and succeeded in stirring up a revolt throughout all the towns and fortified places of the province.

As soon as the Great Khan heard of this plotting, he dispatched against them an army of a hundred thousand men under two other nobles, Ajul and Mongatai. When the approach of this force became known to Litan, he lost no time in assembling an equally large army, and brought it as speedily as possible to action. There was much slaughter on both sides, but at length Litan was killed, and his troops took to flight. Many were slain in the pursuit, and many were made prisoners. These were brought before the Great Khan, who caused the principals to be put to death, and pardoning the others, took them into his own service, to which they ever afterwards remained loyal.‡

CHAPTER 62

Of the City of Singui-matu

TRAVELING from Tandinfu three days in a southerly direction, you pass many considerable towns and strong places where commerce and manufactures flourish. The country is filled with game, both beasts and birds, and produces an ample supply of the necessities of life.

*More than 2000 years B.C. the Chinese Annals speak of silk as an article of tribute from Shantung province.
†Sangon is a Chinese term meaning "Military Governor." Historically, Litan came out in support of the Sung Emperor of Southern China in 1262.
‡The Zelada manuscript here introduces a long description of the extraordinary modesty of the young ladies of Cathay and the elaborate physical tests of virginity that each must undergo before her betrothal.

At the end of three days you arrive at the city of Singui-matu [Tsining], which is noble, large, and handsome, and rich in merchandise and manufactures. All the inhabitants of this city are idolaters, are subjects of the Great Khan, and use paper money. Within it, but on the southern side, flows a large, deep river, which the inhabitants divided into two branches, one of which, flowing east, runs through Cathay, while the other, taking a westerly course, runs towards the province of Manzi. This river joins both provinces. It is astonishing to observe the number and size of the vessels continually passing to-and-fro on it, laden with merchandise of the greatest value.

CHAPTER 63

Concerning the Cities of Lingui and Pingui

ON LEAVING Singui-matu and traveling toward the south for sixteen days, you constantly meet with commercial towns and with castles. At the end of eight days' journey you find a city named Lingui. It is a very splendid and great city; the men are warlike; and it has manufactures and commerce. There are plenty of animals, and an abundance of everything for eating and drinking. After leaving Lingui you proceed three days' journey to the south, passing many cities and castles, all under the Great Khan. All the inhabitants are idolaters and burn their dead. At the end of these three days you find a fine city called Pingui, where there are all the necessities of life, and this city furnishes a great revenue to the Great Khan. You go thence two days' journey to the south, through fair and rich countries, to a city called Cingui [Siju], which is very large and abounds in commerce and manufactures. All its inhabitants are idolaters and burn their dead; they use paper money and are subjects also of the Great Khan. They have much wheat and other grain. In the country through which you then pass, you find cities, towns, and castles, as well as very handsome and useful dogs, and abundance of wheat. The people resemble those just described.

CHAPTER 64

Of the Great River Called the Kara-moran
and of the Cities of Koi-gan-zu and Kuanzu

AT THE end of two days' journey you reach once more the great river Kara-moran [the great Hwang-Ho, or Yellow River], which has its source in the territories that belonged to Prester John. It is a mile wide and of vast depth, and upon its waters great ships sail freely with full loads. Large fish in considerable quantities are caught there.

At a place in this river about a mile distant from the sea there is a station for fifteen thousand vessels, each of them capable of carrying fifteen horses and twenty men, besides the crews to navigate them, and the necessary stores and provisions. These the Great Khan keeps in constant readiness for carrying an army to any of the Indian Isles that may happen to be in rebellion, or for expeditions to any more distant region. These vessels are moored close to the bank of the river, not far from a city named Koi-gan-zu [Hwai-ngan-chow], on the opposite side to which is another named Kuanzu [Kaiju], but the former is a large place and the latter a small one.

Upon crossing this river you enter the great province of Manzi; but it must not be understood that a complete account has been given of the province of Cathay. Not the twentieth part have I described. Marco Polo in traveling through the province has only noted such cities as lay in his route, omitting those on either side, as well as many intervening places, because an account of all of them would prove too tedious for the reader. Leaving these parts we shall therefore proceed to speak first of the way the province of Manzi was acquired, and then of its cities, including their magnificence and riches.

CHAPTER 65

*Of the Noble Province of Manzi and the Way
It Was Conquered by the Great Khan*

THE province of Manzi* is the most magnificent and
the richest known in the eastern world. It was subject to
a prince styled Facfur,† who surpassed in power and
wealth any other except the Great Khan himself. His
disposition was pacific, and his actions benevolent. So
much was he beloved by his people, and such the
strength of his kingdom, enclosed by rivers of the largest
size, that his being molested by any power upon earth
was regarded as impossible. The effect of this opinion
was that he neither paid any attention himself to military
affairs, nor encouraged his people to military training.

The cities of his dominions were remarkably well fortified, being surrounded by deep ditches, a bowshot in
width, and full of water. He did not keep up any cavalry
force, because he was not apprehensive of attack. His
thoughts were directed chiefly to increasing his enjoyments and multiplying his pleasures. He maintained at
his court, and kept near his person, about a thousand
beautiful women, in whose society he took delight. He
was a friend to peace and to justice, which he administered strictly. The smallest act of oppression, or injury
of any kind, committed by one man against another was
appropriately punished. Such indeed was the deep impression made by his justice that when shops filled with
goods happened, through negligence, to be left open, no
person dared enter them or rob them of the smallest
article.

Travelers of all kinds might pass through every part
of the kingdom, by night as well as day, freely and without fear of danger. He was religious and also charitable
to the poor and needy. He annually arranged to save
and take care of 20,000 children whom their wretched

---

*Man-tse, meaning "Barbarians," was the name for Southern China or
the dominion of the Sung Dynasty when the Mongols conquered Cathay or Northern China.
†Faghfur, meaning "Son of Heaven," was a title applied by Persian and
Arabic writers to the Emperor of China.

mothers exposed because of their inability to rear them. When the boys were old enough he had them taught some handicraft, and afterwards married them to young women who were brought up in the same manner.

Very different from the temper and habits of Facfur were those of Kublai Khan, Emperor of the Tartars, whose whole delight consisted in thoughts of war, conquest, and renown. Having annexed a number of provinces and kingdoms, he now directed his attention to the subduing of Manzi, and for this purpose assembled a large army of horse and foot, the command of which he gave to a general named Chinsan Bayan,* which signifies the "Hundred-eyed." This occurred in the year 1268.

A number of vessels were put under the General's command, and he proceeded to the invasion of Manzi. Upon landing there, he immediately summoned the inhabitants of the city of Koi-gan-zu to surrender to his sovereign. Upon their refusal, instead of giving orders for an assault, he advanced to the next city; and when he there received a similar answer, proceeded to a third and a fourth, always getting the same answer. Deeming it no longer prudent to leave so many cities in his rear, even though he expected to be soon joined by another army which the Great Khan was sending him, he resolved to attack one of these cities. By great exertion and skill he succeeded in carrying the place, and put every individual in it to the sword.

As soon as the news of this reached the other cities, it struck their inhabitants with such terror that they hastened to submit. This being done, he advanced with his two armies against Kinsai [the medieval name for the great city of Hangchow], the royal city of King Facfur, who felt all the agitation and dread of a person who has never seen a battle or engaged in any sort of warfare. Alarmed for the safety of his person, he fled to a fleet of vessels that lay in readiness for the purpose, and left the charge of the city to his queen with directions for its being defended to the utmost. He felt sure that her

*Kublai's most famous lieutenant, Chinsan, or Ch'ing hsiang, is a title meaning "Minister of State."

sex would protect her in case she fell into the hands of the enemy. Putting out to sea, and reaching certain strongly fortified islands, he remained there till his death.

After the queen had been left as related, it is said that she learned that the king had been told by his astrologers that he could never be deprived of his sovereignty by any but a chief with a hundred eyes. On the strength of this she felt confident, notwithstanding that the city was daily more and more endangered, that it could not be lost, because it seemed impossible that any mortal could have that many eyes. Inquiring, however, the name of the general who commanded the enemy's troops, and being told it was Chinsan Bayan, which means "a hundred eyes," she was horrified, as she felt certain that this would be the person who, according to the astrologers, would drive her husband from his throne. Overcome by womanish fear, she immediately surrendered.

Once in possession of the capital, the Tartars soon captured the remainder of the province. The queen was brought before Kublai Khan, where she was honorably received by him and given an allowance that enabled her to maintain the dignity of her rank. Having described the conquest of Manzi, we shall now speak of the other cities of that province, and first of Koi-gan-zu [Hwai-ngan-chow].

CHAPTER 66

Of the City of Koi-gan-zu

KOI-GAN-ZU is a very handsome and wealthy city, lying in a direction between southeast and east, at the entrance of the province of Manzi. A prodigious number of vessels are continually passing it, since it is located near the bank of the river Kara-moran.

Large consignments of merchandise are forwarded to this city in order that they may be transported by means of this river to various other places. Salt is manufactured here in great quantities, not only for the city itself, but for export to other parts; and from this salt the Great Khan derives a large revenue.

CHAPTER 67

Of the Town of Pau-ghin and the City of Kain

UPON leaving Koi-gan-zu, you travel one day's journey toward the southeast by a handsome stone causeway into the province of Manzi. On both sides of the causeway there are very extensive marshy lakes, the waters of which are deep enough for shipping. There is no other road by which the province can be entered. It is, however, accessible by water, and it was in this way that the commander of the Great Khan's armies invaded it.

At the end of the day's journey, you reach a good-sized town named Pau-ghin [Pao-ying]. The inhabitants worship idols, burn their dead, use paper money, and are the subjects of the Great Khan. They gain their living by trade and manufacture; they have much silk and weave gold tissues. The necessities of life are there in abundance.

At a distance of a day's journey from Pau-ghin, toward the southeast, stands the large and well-built city of Kain [Kao-yu]. Trade and manufactures flourish here. They have fish in great quantities, and also game, both beasts and birds. Pheasants in particular are so plentiful that for a bit of silver equal to a Venetian groat you may purchase three of these birds, each the size of a peafowl.

CHAPTER 68

Of the Cities of Tin-gui and Chin-gui and of the City of Yan-gui, Which Marco Polo Governed

AT THE end of a day's journey from the last-mentioned place, in the course of which you meet many villages and much tilled land, you reach a city named Tin-gui [Tai-chau], not of any great size, but plentifully furnished with all the necessities of life. The people are merchants, and have many trading vessels. Both beasts and birds are here plentiful. The city is located toward the southeast, and on the left hand—that is, on the eastern side of it, at a distance of three days' journey—is the sea. In the intervening area there are many saltworks where large quantities of salt are manufactured.

You next come to the large and well-built town of Chin-gui [Tung-chou, near the northern shore of the estuary of the Yangtze], whence enough salt is exported for all the neighboring provinces. On this article the Great Khan raises a revenue so large that the amount would scarcely be credited. Here also the inhabitants worship idols, use paper money, and are subjects of his Majesty.

Proceeding in a southeasterly direction from Chin-gui, you come to the important city of Yan-gui [Yang-chow],* which, having twenty-four towns under its jurisdiction, must be considered a place of great consequence. It belongs to the dominion of the Great Khan. The people are idolaters, and live by trade and handicrafts. They manufacture arms and all sorts of military equipment, in consequence of which many troops are stationed in this part of the country.

The city is the residence of one of the twelve nobles (already mentioned) appointed by his Majesty to govern the provinces; and in the place of one of these, Marco Polo, by special order of the Great Khan, acted as governor of this city for three years.†

CHAPTER 69

Of the Province of Nan-ghin

NAN-GHIN [Nan-king] is the name of a large and important province of Manzi, situated toward the west. The people are idolaters, use paper money in currency, are subjects of the Great Khan, and are largely engaged in commerce. They have raw silk, and weave tissues of silver and gold in great quantities and of various patterns. The country produces a great deal of corn. It is

---

*One of the oldest and most celebrated of Chinese cities until its destruction during a rebellion in 1860.

†Since Polo is not included in Chinese lists of the governors of this city, some scholars doubt that his position was quite as exalted as he indicates here. Even so, it is most surprising—and again characteristic of his curiously impersonal approach—that he tells us no more about this city than any other, and nothing about his experiences there.

also rich in domestic cattle as well as beasts and birds that hunters pursue, and has plenty of tigers. It supplies the sovereign with an ample revenue, chiefly from the duties levied upon the rich articles in which the merchants trade. We shall now speak of the splendid city of Sa-yan-fu.

CHAPTER 70

Of the City of Sa-yan-fu and How Nicolo and Maffeo Polo Helped Capture It

SA-YAN-FU [Sian-yang-fu] is a large city of the province of Manzi, having under its jurisdiction twelve large and wealthy towns. It is a great center of commerce and extensive manufactures. The inhabitants burn the bodies of their dead, and are idolaters. They are the subjects of the Great Khan and use his paper currency. Raw silk is there produced in great quantity, and the finest silk cloths, intermixed with gold, are woven. Game of all kinds abounds. The place is amply furnished with everything proper to a great city, and by its uncommon strength it was able to stand a siege of three years, refusing to surrender to the Great Khan even after he had taken over the province of Manzi.

The difficulties that arose in the siege were chiefly the result of the army's being able to approach it only on the northern side, the other sides being surrounded with water, by which it continued to receive supplies. When the situation was reported to his Majesty, he was much vexed that this place alone should obstinately hold out after all the rest of the country had bowed to him.

The above facts having come to the knowledge of the brothers Nicolo and Maffeo, who were then resident at the imperial court, they immediately presented themselves to the Emperor and proposed that they should be allowed to construct machines such as were used in the West, capable of throwing stones three hundred pounds in weight. With these machines the buildings of the city could be destroyed and the inhabitants killed. Their request was granted by the Great Khan, who, warmly approving of the scheme, gave orders that the ablest smiths and carpenters should be placed under their direction; among these were some Nestorian Christians, who proved to be able mechanics.

In a few days they completed their mangonels,* according to instructions furnished by the two brothers; and a trial being made of them in the presence of the Great Khan and his court, they saw them cast stones, each weighing three hundred pounds. The machines were then put on board vessels and brought to the army.

After being set up in front of the city of Sa-yan-fu the first stone hurled by one of them fell with such weight and force upon a building that a great part of it was crushed. So terrified were the inhabitants by this disaster, which to them seemed to be like a thunderbolt from heaven, that they immediately surrendered.† Their submission was accepted on the same terms and conditions as had been granted the rest of the province. The prompt success of their ingenuity increased the reputation and credit of the two Venetian brothers in the opinion of the Great Khan and all his courtiers.

CHAPTER 71

Of the City of Sinju and the
Very Great River Kiang

LEAVING the city of Sa-yan-fu and proceeding fifteen days' journey toward the southeast,‡ you reach the city of Sinju, which, although not large, is a great center of commerce. The number of vessels under its jurisdiction is prodigious in consequence of its being situated near the Kiang [Yangtze Kiang], which is the largest river in the world, its width being in some places ten, in others

---

*Operating on the principle of a giant sling, this machine was used to hurl huge weights, pots of fire, or even dead animals.
†Dates raise a question here because Chinese historians say that Kublai conquered Sian-yang-fu in 1273, whereas Marco did not arrive at Kublai's court before the end of 1274. Yule nevertheless believes that Marco's story had some basis in fact.
‡Actually southwest, since Sinju has been identified as the city of Iching. Marsden uses the name Sin-gui both for this city and for Soochow (see Chapter 75). We follow Yule in calling this city Sinju and referring to Soochow as Suju.

eight, and in others six miles. Its length to the place where it discharges into the sea is upwards of one hundred days' journey. It owes its great size to the vast number of other navigable rivers that empty into it.

A great number of cities and large towns are situated upon its banks, and more than two hundred, in sixteen provinces, make use of it, resulting in a traffic that would seem incredible to anyone who had not seen it. But considering its length and the number of its tributaries, it is not surprising that the cargo transported on it is incalculable. The principal commodity here is salt, which is conveyed by means of the Kiang, and the rivers connected with it, to the towns upon their banks, and afterwards from there to all places in the interior of the country.

On one occasion when Marco Polo was at the city of Sinju, he saw there no less than fifteen thousand vessels; and yet there are other towns along the river where the number is still greater. All these vessels are covered with a kind of deck and have a mast with one sail. Their burden is in general from 4,000 cantari, or quintals, of Venice, to 12,000 cantari [i.e., 200 to 500 tons], which some of them are capable of loading. They do not use hempen rope excepting for the masts and sails. They have canes fifteen paces long, as have been already described, which they split lengthwise into very thin pieces, and these they twist into ropes 300 paces [1,500 feet] long. So skillfully are they made that they are equal in strength to rope made of hemp.

With these ropes each vessel is tracked [towed] along the rivers by means of ten or twelve horses. At many places near the banks there are hills and rocky heights upon which stand temples of idols and other buildings, and there is a continual succession of villages and inhabited places.

CHAPTER 72

Of the City of Kayn-gui

KAYN-GUI [Kwa-chow] is a small town on the southern bank of the aforementioned river, where annually a very large quantity of corn and rice is collected, the greatest part of which is carried to Khan-balik to supply the Emperor. This place communicates with the province of Cathay by means of rivers, lakes, and a wide, deep canal which the Great Khan has had dug in order that vessels may pass from one great river to the other, and from the province of Manzi, by water, as far as Khan-balik, without making any part of the voyage by sea.

This magnificent work is most admirable, not so much from the way it is conducted through the country, or its vast extent, as from its usefulness and benefit to those cities which lie in its course. Wide, solid roads have, moreover, been constructed on its embankments, which makes travel by land very convenient, too.

In the middle of the river, opposite the city of Kwachow, is an island entirely of rock, upon which stand a great temple and monastery, where two hundred monks, as they may be termed, dwell, and perform service to idols. This is the supreme head of many other temples and monasteries.* We shall now speak of the city of Chan-ghian-fu.

CHAPTER 73

Of the City of Chan-ghian-fu

CHAN-GHIAN-FU [Chin-kiang] is a city of the province of Manzi, the inhabitants of which are idolaters, subjects of the Great Khan, and use his paper money. They gain their living by trade and manufacture, and are wealthy. They weave tissues of silk and gold. The hunting there is excellent in every species of game, and provisions are abundant.

There are in this city three Nestorian Christian churches; these were built in the year 1278, when his Majesty appointed a Nestorian, named Mar-Sachis, to govern it for three years. These churches were established by him; and they still stand. Leaving this place, we shall now speak of Tin-gui-gui.

---

*This Buddhist monastery, which is said to have been founded as early as the 3rd or 4th century, was destroyed in the rebellion of 1860.

CHAPTER 74

Of the City of Tin-gui-gui

DEPARTING from Chan-ghian-fu and traveling four days toward the southeast, you pass many towns and fortified places, the inhabitants of which are idolaters, live by crafts and commerce, are the subjects of the Great Khan, and use his paper money. At the end of these four days, you reach the city of Tin-gui-gui [Chang-chow], which is large and handsome, and produces much raw silk, of which tissues of various qualities and patterns are woven. The necessities of life are plentiful here, and the variety of game affords excellent sport.

The inhabitants, however, are a vile, inhuman race. At the time that Chinsan Bayan, or "the Hundred-eyed," subdued the country of Manzi, he dispatched certain Alans, who are Christians, along with a party of his own people, to take this city. As soon as they appeared before it, they were allowed to enter without resistance. The place being surrounded by a double wall, the Alans occupied the first enclosure, where they found a great deal of wine, and having undergone much fatigue and privation, they proceeded to drink to excess, became intoxicated, and fell asleep.

As soon as the people of the city, who were within the second enclosure, saw that their enemies lay slumbering on the ground, they slew them, allowing not one to escape. When Chinsan Bayan learned the fate of his detachment, his indignation and anger rose to the highest pitch and he sent another army to attack the place. When it was captured, he gave orders for putting to the sword all the inhabitants, great and small, without distinction of sex, as an act of retaliation.

CHAPTER 75

Of the Cities of Suju and Va-giu

SUJU [Soochow] is a large and magnificent city, twenty miles in circumference.* The people have vast quantities of raw silk and manufacture it, not only for their own consumption (all of them being clothed in silk), but also for other markets. There are among them some very rich merchants, and the number of inhabitants is astonishing. They are, however, a mean-spirited race, and solely occupied with trade and manufacture. In these indeed they display considerable ability, and if they were as enterprising, manly, and warlike as they are ingenious, their number is so vast that they might not only subdue the whole of the province, but spread their influence still further.

They have among them many physicians of great skill, who can determine the nature of a disorder and know how to apply the proper remedies. There are also distinguished professors of learning, or, as we should term them, philosophers, and others who may be called magicians or enchanters.

On the mountains near the city, rhubarb of the finest quality grows and from there is distributed throughout the province. Ginger is likewise produced in large quantities and is sold at so cheap a rate that forty pounds of the fresh root may be had for the value (in their money) of a Venetian silver groat.

Under the jurisdiction of Suju there are sixteen reputable and wealthy cities and towns, where trade and arts flourish. The name of Soochow signifies "The City of the Earth," as that of Kinsai, "The City of Heaven." Leaving Suju, we shall now speak of another city, distant from it only a day's journey, named Va-giu [Vuju], where there is likewise a vast abundance of raw silk, and where there are many merchants as well as artisans. Silks of the finest quality are woven here and are afterwards shipped to every part of the province. Nothing else being worthy of remark, we shall now proceed to the description of the principal city and metropolis of the province of Manzi, named Kinsai.

*Soochow is still a flourishing city whose chief industries are silk and cotton weaving.

CHAPTER 76

Of the Splendid and Magnificent City of Kinsai

UPON leaving Va-giu you pass, in the course of three days' journey, many towns, castles and villages, all of them well-inhabited and opulent. The people have an abundance of provisions. At the end of three days you reach the noble and magnificent city of Kinsai [Hangchow],* a name that signifies "The Celestial City." This name it merits from its preeminence, among all others in the world, in point of grandeur and beauty, as well as from its many charms, which might lead an inhabitant to imagine himself in paradise.

This city was frequently visited by Marco Polo, who carefully and diligently observed and inquired into every aspect of it, all of which he recorded in his notes, from which the following particulars are drawn. According to common estimate, this city is a hundred miles around. Its streets and canals are extensive, and there are squares or marketplaces, which are frequented by a prodigious number of people and are exceedingly spacious. It is situated between a fresh, very clear lake and a river of great magnitude, the waters of which run via many canals, both large and small, through every quarter of the city, carrying all sewage into the lake and ultimately to the ocean. This furnishes communication by water, in addition to that by land, to all parts of the town, the canals being of sufficient width for boats and the streets for carriages.

It is commonly said that the number of bridges amounts to twelve thousand. Those which cross the principal canals and are connected with the main streets have arches so high and are built with so much skill that the masts of vessels can pass under them. At the same time, carts and horses can pass over them, so gradual is

*The word *King-sze* means "capital" and was applied to the city as the capital of the Sung Dynasty from 1127 on. Together with Peking, Hangchow long represented for Westerners the opulence of the Orient. Out of the tremendous impression which the city obviously made on Polo comes what amounts to a paean of admiration, the high point of his description of China. All travelers of the 13th and 14th centuries, such as Friar Odoric and Ibn Battuta, agreed fully with him on this.

the upward slope of the arch. If they were not so numerous, there would be no way of crossing from one part to another.

Beyond the city, and enclosing it on that side, there is a moat about forty miles in length, very wide, and issuing from the river mentioned before. This was excavated by the ancient kings of the province so that when the river overflowed its banks, the floodwater might be drawn off into this channel. This also serves for defense. The earth dug from it was thrown to the inner side, and forms a mound around the place.

There are within the city ten principal squares or marketplaces, besides innumerable shops along the streets. Each side of these squares is half a mile in length, and in front of them is the main street, forty paces in width and running in a straight line from one end of the city to the other. It is crossed by many low and convenient bridges. These market squares are four miles from each other. Parallel to the main street, but on the opposite side of the squares, runs a very large canal. On the nearer bank of this stand large stone warehouses provided for merchants who arrive from India and other parts with their goods and effects. They are thus situated conveniently close to the market squares. In each of these, three days in every week, from forty to fifty thousand persons come to the markets and supply them with every article that could be desired.

There is a great deal of game of all kinds, such as roebuck, stags, fallow deer, hares, and rabbits, together with partridges, pheasants, francolins, quail, hens, capon, and ducks and geese beyond number, for so easily are they bred on the lake that, for the value of a Venetian silver groat, you may purchase a pair of geese and two pair of ducks. There, too, are the houses where they slaughter cattle, such as oxen, calves, kids, and lambs, to furnish the tables of the rich and of leading citizens. As to the people of the lower classes, they eat every kind of meat, however unclean, without discrimination.

At all seasons there is in the markets a great variety of herbs and fruits, especially pears of an extraordinary size, weighing ten pounds each, that are white inside and very fragrant.* There are also peaches in season, both the yellow and white kinds, and of a delicious flavor. Grapes are not produced there, but are brought in, dried and very good, from other areas. This applies also to wine, which the natives do not prize, being accustomed to a wine prepared from rice and spices. From the sea, fifteen miles distant, a vast quantity of fish is each day brought up the river to the city. There is also an abundance of fish in the lake, which gives employment at all times to a group of fishermen. They vary according to the season, but they are large and fat because they feed on the refuse. At the sight of such a vast quantity of fish, you would think it impossible that it could be sold; and yet in the course of a few hours it is all cleared out, so great is the number of inhabitants who can afford to indulge in such luxuries, including the eating of fish and meat at the same meal.

Each of the ten market squares is surrounded with high dwelling houses, in the lower part of which are shops where every kind of manufacture is carried on and every article of trade is offered, including spices, drugs, trinkets, and pearls. In certain shops nothing is sold but the wine of the country, which they make continually and serve out fresh to their customers at a moderate price. Many streets connect with the market squares, and in some of them are many cold baths, attended by servants of both sexes. The men and women who frequent them have been accustomed from childhood to wash in cold water, which they consider highly conducive to health. At these baths, however, they have rooms provided with warm water for the use of strangers who cannot bear the shock of the cold. All are in the habit of washing themselves daily, and especially before their meals.

In other streets are the quarters of the courtesans, who are more numerous here than I dare to report. They are found not only near the squares, which is where they usually live, but in every part of the city—richly adorned,

*One scholar (Henri Cordier) has suggested that these were Chinese quinces, which are of enormous size.

highly perfumed, occupying well-furnished houses, and attended by many female servants. These women are highly accomplished, and are masters of the arts of caressing and fondling, and of suiting their words to every kind of person. Strangers who have once tasted their charms are as though bewitched, and become so enchanted by their wanton arts that they never forget them. Thus intoxicated with sensual pleasures, when they return home they report that they have been in Kinsai, the Celestial City, and long for the time when they will be able to revisit this paradise.

In other streets are the dwellings of the physicians and the astrologers, who also teach reading and writing, as well as many other arts. They have apartments also among those surrounding the market squares. On opposite sides of each of these squares there are two large buildings, where officers appointed by the Great Khan are stationed to take immediate notice of any differences that may arise between the foreign merchants, or among the natives. It is their duty likewise to see that the guards are posted on the several bridges and to punish any negligence.

On each side of the principal street mentioned earlier, which runs from one end of the city to the other, there are great houses and mansions with their gardens, and near these, the dwellings of the artisans who work in the shops of the various trades. At all hours you see such multitudes of people passing to and fro on their personal affairs that providing enough food for them might be thought impossible. But one notes that on every market day the squares are crowded with tradespeople and with articles brought by cart and boat—all of which they sell out. From the sale of a single article such as pepper, some notion may be formed of the vast quantity of meat, wine, groceries, and the like, required by the inhabitants of Kinsai. From an officer in the Great Khan's customs, Marco Polo learned that the amount of pepper bought daily was forty-three loads, each load being 243 pounds.

The inhabitants of the city are idolaters. They use paper money as currency. The men as well as the women are fair-skinned and handsome. Most of them always dress themselves in silk, as a result of the vast quantity of that material produced in Kinsai, exclusive of what the merchants import from other provinces.

Among the handicrafts in the city, twelve are considered superior to the rest as being more generally useful. For each of these there are a thousand workshops, and each shop employs ten, fifteen, or twenty workmen, and in a few instances as many as forty, under their respective masters. The rich masters do not labor with their own hands, but on the contrary, put on airs and strut about proudly. The wives also avoid work. They are very beautiful, as has been remarked, and are brought up with delicate and languid habits. The costliness of their dresses, in silks and jewelry, can scarcely be imagined. Although the laws of their ancient kings decreed that each citizen should follow the profession of his father, they were allowed when they acquired wealth to avoid manual labor, provided they kept up the establishment and employed persons to work at the family trades.

Their houses are well-built and richly adorned with carved work. So much do they delight in ornaments of this kind, and paintings and ornate buildings, that they lavish enormous sums on them.

By nature the inhabitants of Kinsai are peaceful, and by the example of their former kings, who were themselves unwarlike, they have become accustomed to tranquility. The handling of arms is unknown to them, nor do they keep any in their houses. They are not quarrelsome and they conduct their business affairs with perfect candor and honesty. They are friendly towards each other, and persons who live on the same street, both men and women, are like part of one family.

In their domestic manners they are free from jealousy or suspicion of their wives, and treat them with great respect; and any man who used indecent language to a married woman would be considered contemptible. To strangers who visit their city on business they are very cordial, inviting them freely to their houses, showing them friendly attention, and furnishing them with advice and assistance in their transactions. On the other hand, they dislike the sight of soldiery, not excepting the guards of the Great Khan, and these remind them of how they were deprived of their native kings and rulers.

On the borders of the lake are many handsome and spacious buildings belonging to men of rank and to great dignitaries. There are likewise many idol temples, together with monasteries occupied by monks in the service of the idols. Near the center are two islands, each having a superb building with an incredible number of apartments and separate pavilions. When any inhabitants of the city celebrate a wedding or give a sumptuous entertainment, they resort to one of these islands, where they find prepared every article that may be required, such as vessels, napkins, table linen, and the like. These are provided and kept there at the expense of the citizens by whom the buildings were erected. It sometimes happens that there are a hundred parties, either weddings or other feasts, at one time, but all of them, notwithstanding, are accommodated with separate rooms or pavilions so judiciously arranged that they do not interfere with each other.

In addition to this, there are on the lake a great number of pleasure vessels or barges that can hold ten, fifteen, or twenty persons. They are from fifteen to twenty paces in length, broad-beamed, and not liable to rock. Men who want to enjoy this pastime in the company either of women friends or other men can hire one of these barges, which are always kept in excellent order, and have suitable seats and tables and every other furnishing needed for a party. The cabins have a flat roof or upper deck, where the boatmen stand; and by means of long poles, which they thrust to the bottom of the lake (which is not more than one or two fathoms in depth), shove the barges along. These cabins are painted inside with various colors and figures; all parts of the vessel are likewise adorned with painting. There are windows on either side, which may be opened to allow the company, as they sit at table, to look out in every direction and feast their eyes on the variety and beauty of the passing scene. The pleasure of this exceeds any that can be derived from amusements on land; for as the lake extends the whole length of the city, you have a distant view, as you stand in the boat, of all its grandeur and beauty, its palaces, temples, large convents, and gardens with great trees growing down to the water's edge, while at the same time you can enjoy the sight of other similar boats continually passing you, filled in like manner with parties in pursuit of amusement. In fact, as soon as the labors of the day have ceased, or their business is finished, the inhabitants of this place think of nothing else but passing the remaining hours in pleasure parties with their wives or mistresses. They ride about either in these barges or in carriages, and since the latter constitutes one of the chief amusements of these people, it will be proper to give some account of it.

CHAPTER 77

Further Particulars Concerning the Great City of Kinsai

IT MUST be observed in the first place that the streets of Kinsai are all paved with stone and brick, and so too are all the principal roads running from there through the province of Manzi. By means of these, travelers can go to every part without muddying their feet. But as his Majesty's couriers go on horseback in great haste and cannot ride on pavement, a strip of road is left unpaved for their benefit.

The main street of the city is paved with stone and brick to the width of ten paces on each side, the center strip being filled with gravel and having curved drains for carrying off rain water into nearby canals so that it remains always dry. On this gravel, carriages continually pass to-and-fro. The carriages are long in shape, covered on top, have curtains and cushions of silk, and can hold six persons. Men and women who like riding are in the daily habit of hiring them for that purpose, and so at every hour you can see vast numbers of them driven along the middle part of the street. Some of the riders visit certain gardens, where they are conducted to shady recesses contrived for that purpose by the gardeners. Here the men enjoy themselves all day in the company of their women, returning home, when it gets late, just as they came.

Upon the birth of a child, it is the custom of the parents here to make note of the day, hour, and minute at which the delivery took place. They then inquire of an astrologer under what sign or aspect of the heavens the child was born; and his answer is likewise carefully noted. When the child grows up and is about to engage in a business venture, voyage, or marriage, this document is taken to the astrologer, who, having examined it and weighed all the circumstances, makes a prediction. These people place great confidence in this and are sometimes justified by the event. Of these astrologers, or rather magicians, great numbers are to be met with in every marketplace, and no marriage takes place until one of them has given an opinion of it.

It is also the custom on the death of any great or rich person for the relations, male and female, to clothe themselves in coarse dresses and accompany the body to the place appointed for burning it. Certain persons in the procession play on various musical instruments; and prayers to their idols are chanted in a loud voice. When they arrive at the fire, they throw into the flame many pieces of cotton paper, covered with paintings of male and female servants, horses, camels, silk woven with gold, as well as of gold and silver money. This is done in the belief that the dead person will thereby have these in the other world, and in the original state. As soon as the pyre has been consumed, they play all the instruments at one time, producing a loud and long-drawn-out noise. They imagine that by these ceremonies their idols will be persuaded to receive the soul of the man whose corpse has been burned.

In every street of this city there are stone buildings or towers. In case a fire breaks out in any quarter, which is by no means unusual since the houses are mostly made of wood, the inhabitants may move their possessions to the safety of these towers.

By a regulation of his Majesty, there is a guard of ten watchmen, stationed under cover on all the principal bridges, five on duty by day and five by night. Each of these guards is provided with a drumlike wooden instrument as well as one of metal, together with a water clock which tells the hours of the day and night. When the first hour of the night has passed, one of the watchmen strikes once on the wooden instrument, and also upon the gong. At the end of the second hour he strikes twice, and so on as the hours advance. The guard is not allowed to sleep and must be always on the alert. In the morning as soon as the sun rises, they strike a single stroke again, as in the evening before, and so on from hour to hour.

Some of these watchmen patrol the streets to see whether any person has a light or fire burning after the curfew hour. If they find one, they mark the door; and in the morning the owner of the house is taken before the magistrates, and if he cannot give a good excuse for his offense, he is punished. If they find any person out at an unlawful hour, they arrest him, and in the morning he is carried before the same tribunal. If they notice any person who is unable to work because of illness, they send him to one of the many hospitals founded by the ancient kings and liberally endowed. Once he is cured, he is obliged to work at some trade.

As soon as a fire breaks out in a house, the guards give the alarm by beating on the wooden drums, whereupon watchmen from all bridges within a certain distance assemble to extinguish it, as well as to save the property of the merchants, or others, by moving them to the above-mentioned stone towers. The goods are also sometimes put into boats and carried to the islands on the lake. When the fire occurs at night, the only inhabitants permitted to be present are those whose goods are actually being removed, together with the assembled watchmen, of whom there are seldom less than from one to two thousand.

In cases of rioting or insurrection among the citizens, this police guard is also utilized; but independently of them, his Majesty always keeps on hand a large body of troops, both infantry and cavalry, under the command of his ablest officers.

For the purposes of the nightly watch, towers of earth have been thrown up at a distance of more than a mile from each other. On top of these is a wooden drum, which, when struck with a mallet by the guard stationed there, can be heard at a great distance. If precautions of this nature were not taken there would be a danger that half the city would be consumed. The usefulness of these guards in case of a popular uprising is obvious.

When the Great Khan subdued the province of Manzi, he divided it into nine parts and appointed a king or viceroy to act as supreme governor and administer justice in each. These make a yearly report to his Majesty of the amount of the revenue, as well as of every other matter under their jurisdiction. They are changed every three years, as are all other public officers.

One of these nine viceroys resides in the city of Kinsai and has authority over more than a hundred and forty cities and towns, all large and rich. Nor is this number to be wondered at, considering that in the province of Manzi there are no fewer than twelve hundred cities, each with a large population of industrious and wealthy inhabitants. In each of these, according to its size and other circumstances, his Majesty keeps a garrison, consisting in some places of a thousand, in others of ten or twenty thousand men. It is not to be thought that all these troops are Tartars. On the contrary, they are chiefly natives of the province of Cathay. The Tartars are horsemen, and cavalry cannot be quartered around cities which stand in low, marshy places, but only those on firm, dry ground, where such troops can be exercised. To the former, he sends Cathayans and such men of Manzi as appear to have a military inclination; for it is his practice to make an annual selection of those best qualified to bear arms. But the soldiers drawn from the province of Manzi he does not put on duty in their native cities. On the contrary, he sends them to places perhaps twenty days distant, where they remain for four or five years. At the end of that time they are allowed to return to their homes, and others are sent to replace them. This regulation applies equally to the Cathayans.

The greater part of the Great Khan's revenues from cities is spent on the maintenance of these garrisons. When it happens that a city is in rebellion (and it is not uncommon for these people when fired by rage, or when intoxicated, to murder their governors), a part of the garrison of a neighboring city is immediately dispatched to crush the city where such excesses have been committed. For such purposes the city of Kinsai constantly supports a garrison of thirty thousand soldiers; and the smallest number stationed at any place is one thousand.

It now remains to speak of a very fine palace that was formerly the residence of King Facfur, whose ancestors enclosed an area ten miles in circumference and divided it into three parts. The center part was entered by a lofty gate, on each side of which was a magnificent pavilion, the roofs of which were supported by rows of pillars ornamented with the most beautiful azure and gold. The pavilion opposite the gate, at the farther side of the court, was even grander than the others, its roof being richly adorned, the pillars gilt, and the walls on the inner side ornamented with exquisite paintings from the history of former kings.

Here annually King Facfur was accustomed to hold court, and to entertain at a feast his principal nobles, the chief magistrates, and the prominent citizens of Kinsai. In these pavilions might be seen at one time ten thousand persons comfortably seated at table. This festival lasted ten or twelve days, and the magnificence of the display of silks, gold, and precious stones exceeded all imagination; for every guest tried to exhibit as much finery as he possibly could.

Behind the pavilion last mentioned (that which faced the grand gate) was a wall with a passage in it. This separated the outside court of the palace from an inner court, which formed a kind of large cloister and led to the various apartments of the King and Queen. From this cloister you entered a covered passage six paces in width and extending all the way to the margin of the lake. On each side of this were entrances to ten courts, in the form of long cloisters, and each cloister or court had fifty apartments with their own gardens, the residence of a thousand young women who served the King.

Accompanied sometimes by his queen, and on other occasions by a party of his damsels, it was his custom to take his pleasure on the lake, in barges covered with silk, and to visit the temples on its banks. The other two parts of the estate were laid out in groves, ponds, beautiful gardens stocked with fruit trees, and also enclosures for all sorts of animals for sport, such an antelopes, deer, stags, hares, and rabbits. Here likewise the King amused himself in company with his damsels, some in carriages and some on horseback. No man was allowed to be present, but on the other hand, the damsels were trained to hunt with dogs. When they grew weary, they would retire to the groves on the shores of the lake, and taking off their clothes, come forth naked and plunge into the water and swim playfully about, while the King watched with delight. Then they would return to the palace.

Sometimes he would have his dinner brought to him in one of these groves, where the lofty trees cast a thick shade, and his young women would wait on him there. Thus he passed his time in constant dalliance, without ever giving the slightest thought to arms. The result was that the Great Khan was able to deprive him of all his splendid possessions and drive him from his throne.*

All these details were told to me when I was in the city by a rich old merchant who had been a confidential servant to King Facfur and knew all the circumstances of his life. Having known the palace in its origin state, he was eager to show it to me. Since they were occupied by the King's viceroy, the pavilions in front are still maintained as they used to be, but the women's apartments have fallen into ruin and only vestiges of them remain. The wall that encircled the park has also fallen down and neither animals nor trees are anywhere to be seen.

At a distance of twenty-five miles from this city, in a northeasterly direction, lies the sea, where there is an extremely fine port named Gan-pu [Ningpo], frequented by all the ships that bring merchandise from India.

Marco Polo happened to be in Kinsai at the time of the annual report to his Majesty's commissioners of the revenue and number of inhabitants, and he learned that there were 160 tomans of fireplaces (that is, of families dwelling under the same roof); and as a toman is ten thousand, it follows that the whole city must have contained 1,600,000 families. In all this multitude there was only one church of Nestorian Christians.

*This description of the King of Manzi corresponds to that which histories of China give of the Emperor Tu-Tsong. He actually died two years before his capital fell to Kublai Khan.

Every father, or head of a household, is required to list on the door of his house the names of each member of his family, as well as the number of his horses. When any person dies, or leaves the dwelling, the name is struck out; similarly, when anyone is born, the name is added to the list. Thus the authorities know at all times the exact number of inhabitants. The same practice is followed throughout the province of Cathay as well as Manzi. In like manner, all the keepers of inns and public hotels inscribe the names of those who stay with them, noting the day and the hour of their arrival and departure. A copy of this record is transmitted daily to the magistrates stationed in the market squares. In Manzi it is a custom of poor people who are unable to support their families to sell their children to the rich in order that they may be fed and brought up in a better way than they themselves could afford.

CHAPTER 78

Of the Revenues of the Great Khan

WE SHALL now speak of the revenue which the Great Khan draws from the city of Kinsai and the places within its jurisdiction, an area constituting a ninth part of Manzi. Upon salt, the most productive article, he levies a yearly duty of eighty tomans of gold (each toman being eighty thousand saggi, and each saggio fully equal to a gold florin or ducat), or 6,400,000 ducats. This vast quantity results from the nearness of the province to the sea, and the number of salt lakes or marshes in which during the heat of summer the salt becomes crystallized. From these, enough salt is taken to supply five other divisions of the province.

There is cultivated and manufactured in Kinsai a large quantity of sugar, which pays, as do all other groceries, three and one-third percent. The same is also levied on the rice wine. The twelve classes of artisans, each of whom has a thousand shops, and also the merchants, both those who import the goods and those who carry them into the interior or export them by sea, also pay a duty. But goods coming by sea from distant countries, such as India, pay ten percent. So likewise all native articles, such as cattle, vegetables, and silk, pay a tax to the King.

The account being made up in the presence of Marco Polo, he had an opportunity to see that the annual revenue to his Majesty, exclusive of that from salt, amounted to 210 tomans, or 16,800,000 ducats.*

CHAPTER 79

Of the City of Ta-pin-zu and Others

LEAVING the city of Kinsai and traveling one day's journey towards the southeast, continually passing houses, villas, and delightful gardens where every kind of vegetable is produced in abundance, you arrive at the city of Ta-pin-zu [Shao-hing], which is very handsome and large, and belongs to the jurisdiction of Kinsai. The inhabitants worship idols, use paper money, burn the bodies of their dead, are subjects of the Great Khan, and gain their subsistence by trade and crafts. This place not demanding any further notice, we shall proceed to speak of the city of Uguiu.

From Ta-pin-zu, traveling three days towards the southeast, you come to the city of Uguiu, and still farther in the same direction, two days' journey, you pass in continual succession so many towns, castles, and other inhabited places, and such is their nearness to each other that to a stranger they have the appearance of one extended city. All of them are dependent upon Kinsai. The people are idolaters, and the country supplies the necessities of life in great abundance. Here are found canes of greater bulk and length than those already noticed, being four spans in girth and fifteen paces long.

Proceeding further, three days' journey in the same direction, you reach the town of Gen-gui, and still advancing to the southeast, you constantly meet with towns full of inhabitants who are employed at their trades, and

---

*This is a total revenue of about $50,000,000, but Yule has suggested that this is based on paper currency and that it was really less than half this amount. Perhaps this was another of the figures that may have given rise to the nickname of "Marco of the Millions."

cultivate the soil. In this part of the province of Manzi there are no sheep, but many oxen, cows, buffaloes, and goats, and a vast number of pigs. At the end of the fourth day you arrive at the city of Chanshan, built upon a hill that stands in the middle of the river, which by dividing into two branches, appears to embrace it. These streams take opposite directions, one to the southeast, and the other to the northwest. The cities last mentioned are likewise under the dominion of the Great Khan, and dependent upon Kinsai. The people worship idols, and live by trade. There is in the country abundance of game, both beasts and birds. Proceeding three days further you reach the large and noble city of Gie-za, which is the last within the jurisdiction of Kinsai. Having passed this city, you enter another kingdom or viceroyalty of Manzi, named Kon-cha.

CHAPTER 80

Of the Kingdom of Kon-cha

UPON leaving the last city of the kingdom of Kinsai, you enter that of Kon-cha [Fukien]. In the course of six days' journey through this country in a southeast direction, over hills and along valleys, you continually pass towns and villages where the necessities of life are in abundance, and there is much field sport, particularly of birds. The people are subjects of the Great Khan and are engaged in commerce and manufactures.

In these parts there are tigers of great size and strength. Ginger and galingale [an aromatic root]* are produced in large quantities, as well as other drugs. For the value of a Venetian silver groat you may have eighty pounds of fresh ginger, so plentiful is it. There is also a vegetable which has all the properties of saffron, including the odor and color, and yet it is not really saffron. It is held in great esteem, and being an ingredient in all their dishes, is expensive.

The people in this part of the country are addicted to eating human flesh, esteeming it more delicate than any

*Since this is one of the great tea-producing areas of China it seems strange that Polo never mentions tea.

other, provided the person has not died from any disease. When they advance to combat they throw loose their hair about their ears, and they paint their faces a bright blue color. They arm themselves with lances and swords, and all march on foot excepting their chief, who rides on horseback. They are such a savage race that when they slay their enemies in battle, they are anxious to drink their blood, and afterwards they devour their flesh.* Leaving this subject, we shall now speak of the city of Kue-lin-fu [Kien-ning].

The journey of six days being accomplished, you arrive at the city of Kue-lin-fu, which is of considerable size and contains three very handsome bridges, upwards of a hundred paces in length, and eight paces in width. The women of the place are very handsome and live in luxurious ease. There is much raw silk produced here, and it is made into silk pieces of various sorts. Cottons woven of colored threads are carried for sale to every part of Manzi. The people are employed in commerce, and export quantities of ginger and galingale.

I have been told, but did not myself see the animal, that there are found at this place a species of domestic fowl which have no feathers; they have instead black hair resembling the fur of cats.† Such a sight must be extraordinary. They lay eggs like other fowls, and they are good to eat. The multitude of tigers makes traveling dangerous unless a number of persons go in company.

CHAPTER 81

Of the City of Un-guen

UPON leaving the city of Kue-lin-fu and traveling three days, during which you are continually passing towns and castles of which the inhabitants are idolaters, have silk in abundance, and export it in considerable quantities, you reach the city of Un-guen.

---

*It is assumed that this refers to some of the aboriginal people still living in the mountains behind Foochow.
†Cordier says that these are known to the Chinese as the "velvet-hair fowls" and are familiar to European poultry-fanciers.

This place is remarkable for its great production of sugar, which is sent from there to the city of Khan-balik for the supply of the court. Before it came under the dominion of the Great Khan, the natives did not know how to manufacture sugar of a fine quality, but boiled it in such a way that when left to cool it turned into dark-brown paste. But at the time this city became subject to his Majesty's government, there happened to be at the court some persons from Babylon [Egypt] who were expert in the process, and who, being sent here, taught the inhabitants how to refine the sugar by means of the ashes in certain woods.

Traveling fifteen miles farther in the same direction, you come to the city of Fuju [Foochow], which belongs to the kingdom, or viceroyalty, of Kon-cha. In this place is stationed a large army to protect the country, and to be always ready to act in the event of rebellion.

Through the middle of it passes a river, a mile in breadth, with large and handsome buildings on both banks.* In front of these lie a great number of ships loaded with merchandise, and especially sugar, of which large quantities are manufactured here too. Many vessels arrive at this port from India, loaded by merchants bringing rich assortments of jewels and pearls, the sale of which is most profitable to them. This river empties into the sea at no great distance from the port named Zaitun. The ships coming from India ascend the river as far up as the city of Fugiu, which abounds in every sort of provision and has delightful gardens producing delicious fruits.

CHAPTER 82

Of the City and Port of Zaitun and the City of Tin-gui

UPON leaving the city of Fuju and crossing the river to proceed in a southeasterly direction, you travel for five days through a well-populated country, passing towns, villages, and substantial dwellings, rich in all

*The Min River, whose scenery has been compared with that of the Hudson.

kinds of products. The road lies over hills, across plains, and through woods full of the shrubs from which camphor comes. The country abounds also with game. The inhabitants are subjects of the Great Khan and within the jurisdiction of Fuju.

At the end of five days' journey, you arrive at the noble and handsome city of Zaitun,* which has a port famous for the vast quantity of shipping, loaded with merchandise, that enters it and is afterwards distributed through every part of the province of Manzi. The quantity of pepper imported there is so great that what is carried to Alexandria to supply the demand of the western parts of the world is trifling in comparison—perhaps not more than a hundredth part. It is indeed impossible to convey any idea of the number of merchants and the accumulation of goods in this place, which is held to be one of the largest ports in the world. The Great Khan derives a vast revenue from this place, as every merchant is obliged to pay a 10 percent duty on his goods. In addition, freight charges cost him 30 percent for small wares, 44 for pepper, and 40 for sandalwood and other drugs, as well as articles of trade in general. It is estimated by the merchants that their costs, including customs and freight, amount to half the value of the cargo; and yet their profit on the other half is so large that they are always happy to return with another stock of merchandise.

The country is delightful. The people are idolaters. They have all the necessities of life in plenty, they are peaceable, and they are fond of ease and indulgence. Many persons come here from the interior of India to have their bodies ornamented by puncturing with needles (in the manner already described), the city being famous for the number of its artists skilled in that practice.

The river that flows through Zaitun is large and rapid, and is a branch of that which passes the city of Kinsai. At the place where it separates from the principal chan-

---

*This may be either Chang-chow on the Bay of Amoy or Chuan-chow on the Formosa Strait about 100 miles south of Foochow (now Minhow).

nel stands the city of Tin-gui [Tinju]. Of this place there is nothing to be observed except that cups or bowls and dishes of porcelain ware are manufactured there. The process was described as follows. They collect a certain kind of earth, as though from a mine, then expose it to the wind, rain, and sun for thirty or forty years. By this treatment it becomes refined and is suitable for being made into the vessels mentioned above. The colors are then laid on and the ware is afterwards baked in ovens or furnaces. Those persons, therefore, who cause the earth to be dug, really do so for their children and grandchildren. Great quantities of the finished product are sold in the city, and you may purchase eight porcelain cups* for a Venetian groat.

We have now described the viceroyalty of Kon-cha, one of the nine divisions of Manzi, from which the Great Khan draws as large a revenue as even from Kinsai. Of the others we shall not attempt to speak, because Marco Polo did not himself visit any of their cities, as he did those of Kinsai and Kon-cha. It should be observed that throughout the province of Manzi one language and one style of writing prevails, yet in the different parts of the country there is a difference in dialect similar to that between the Genoese, Milanese, Florentine, and other Italian states, whose inhabitants, although they each have their peculiar speech, can understand each other.

Not having yet completed the subjects on which Marco Polo purposed to write, he will now bring this Second Book to a close and will begin another dealing with the countries and provinces of India, dividing it up into Greater, Lesser, and Middle India. These areas he visited while in the service of the Great Khan, who sent him there on business, and afterwards when (accompanied by his father and uncle on their homeward journey) he escorted the Queen destined for King Arghun.

He will have an opportunity to relate many extraordinary things observed by himself personally in those

*This is of course what is familiar throughout the world as chinaware, or simply china. Although crude forms of it were long known in China, the kind Polo saw was probably developed not long before he arrived. It was in the century after Polo left China, that is, under the Ming Dynasty, that the making of porcelain reached its peak.

countries, but at the same time will not omit to notice others of which he was told by creditable persons, or which were pointed out to him on the mariners' maps of the coasts of India.

BOOK III

✳

OF THE SEA OF CHIN AND THE GREAT ISLAND
OF ZIPANGU, WHICH LIES TO THE EAST OF
CATHAY, AND OF THE ISLANDS OF JAVA,
ANGAMAN AND ZEILAN, WHICH ARE IN
LESSER INDIA. OF GREATER INDIA, THE RICHEST
AND NOBLEST COUNTRY IN THE WORLD. OF
THE ISLANDS OF THE MALES AND THE FEMALES,
SOCOTRA, MADAGASCAR, AND ZANZIBAR,
AND THE PROVINCES OF ABYSSINIA AND ADEN,
WHICH COMPRISE MIDDLE INDIA

Book III

CHAPTER 1

Of India

HAVING dealt with various regions in the preceding parts of our work we shall now go on to tell you about India.

We shall begin with the ships used by their merchants. These are built with the wood known as fir and have a single deck. Below this the space is divided into about sixty small cabins—depending on the size of the vessel—each accommodating one merchant. Each of the vessels has a good helm for steering. They generally have four masts with four sails, and some have two other masts which can be set up and taken down at will. Some of the larger ships have as many as thirteen bulkheads or compartments in the hold made with stout planks strongly mortised together.* These are intended to serve in case the vessel springs a leak as a result of striking against a rock or receiving a blow from a whale. The latter accident is not uncommon, for the ship's motion through the water at night creates a white foam that attracts the attention of a hungry animal. Expecting to find food it rushes in, rams the vessel, and often staves in some part of the bottom. The water then pours into the breach and makes its way into the bilge, which is always kept clear. On locating the leak, the crew at once removes the cargo from that compartment, whereas the water is held in it because its boards are so well fitted that it is watertight. The crew then repairs the damage and returns the cargo to the hold.

The ships are double-planked, that is, with a course

*The Chinese use watertight compartments in their larger river craft as well as in seagoing junks. This practice was not introduced into European vessels until the 19th century.

of sheathing boards over the planking in every part. They are caulked with oakum both inside and out, and are fastened with iron nails. They are not coated with pitch because the country doesn't produce that, but the bottoms are smeared with an even better preparation. The people take quicklime and hemp chopped into bits, pound them, and then mix them with oil from a certain tree. This forms a kind of paste which is in many ways better than pitch.

Ships of the largest size require a crew of three hundred men; others, two hundred; and some only one hundred and fifty. They carry from five to six thousand baskets or bags of pepper.

In former times they were larger than they are today; but the violence of the sea has in many places broken up or washed away parts of the islands, especially around some of the principal ports, and the water is not deep enough for vessels of such draught.

The vessels are rowed with oars or sweeps, each of which requires four men to work it. The larger ones are accompanied by two or three large barks or tenders, themselves capable of carrying about one thousand baskets of pepper and are manned by sixty, eighty, or one hundred sailors. These small craft often tow the larger, when the latter are using their oars. They can even tow them when they are under sail, provided the wind be abeam, but not when astern, because in that case the sails of the larger vessel would take the wind out of those of the smaller and run it down. The ships also carry with them as many as ten small boats for laying out anchors, fishing, and other services. They are slung over the sides and lowered into the water when they are to be used. The tenders are also provided with smaller boats.

When a ship has been on a voyage for a year or more and stands in need of repair, the practice is to give her a layer of sheathing over the original ones, thus forming a third course, which is caulked and paid in the same manner as the others. When she needs further repairs, this is repeated to the number of six layers, after which she is condemned as unserviceable and not seaworthy.

Having thus described the shipping, we shall proceed

to an account of India itself; but in the first instance we shall speak of certain islands in the part of the ocean where we are at present, and shall begin with the island named Zipangu [Japan].

CHAPTER 2

Of the Island of Zipangu and the Great Khan's Attack Against It

ZIPANGU* is an island in the eastern ocean about fifteen hundred miles from the mainland, or coast of Manzi.

It is of considerable size; its inhabitants have fair complexions, are well made, and are civilized in their manners. Their religion is the worship of idols. They are independent of every foreign power and governed only by their own kings. They have gold in the greatest abundance, its sources being inexhaustible, but as the king does not allow it to be exported, few merchants visit the country. Nor is it frequented by much shipping from other parts.

The extraordinary richness of the sovereign's palace, according to those who have access to it, is a wonderful sight. The entire roof is covered with a plating of gold, just as we cover houses, or more properly churches, with lead. The ceilings of the halls are of the same precious metal; many of the apartments have small tables of pure gold of considerable thickness; and the windows also have golden ornaments. So vast indeed are the riches of the palace that it is impossible to convey an idea of them.

On this island there are large quantities of pearls, pink, round, and huge, and worth as much as, if not more than, the white kind.

It is customary for one group of the inhabitants to bury their dead and for another to burn them. The for-

---

*Zipangu (or Chipangu) was the European name for Japan during the Middle Ages and the Age of Discovery. It represents the Chinese *Jih-pen-kwé*, of which the Japanese term Nippon (or Nihon), meaning "land of the rising sun," is a variation. Our word Japan was probably taken from the Malay form, *Japún*.

mer make a practice of putting one of these pearls into the mouth of the corpse. A number of precious stones are also found there.

So celebrated was the wealth of this island that the Great Khan Kublai, now reigning, conceived a desire to conquer and annex it. To do this, he fitted out a great fleet and sent a large body of troops under the command of two of his principal officers, Abakan and Vonsancin. The expedition sailed from the ports of Zaitun and Kinsai, and crossing the sea, reached the island safely.

However, jealousy developed between the two commanders, as a result of which one of them treated the plans of the other with contempt and resisted his orders. Because of this they were unable to capture any city or fortified place, with one exception which was carried by assault when the garrison refused to surrender. Orders were given to put everyone to the sword. As a result, the heads of all the inhabitants were cut off, excepting eight persons who, by means of a magic charm consisting of a jewel or amulet inserted under the skin of the right arm, were rendered safe from any weapon made of iron. When this was discovered, they were beaten with a heavy wooden club, and soon died.

It happened after a time that a north wind began to blow with great force, and the ships of the Tartars, which lay near the shore of the island, were driven foul of each other. It was decided in a council of the officers that they ought to get away from the land; and accordingly, as soon as the troops were re-embarked, they stood out to sea. The gale, however, increased to such a degree that a number of vessels foundered. By floating on pieces of wreckage, some men reached an island lying about four miles from the coast of Zipangu.

The other ships, which (not being so near the land) did not suffer from the storm, and in which the two chiefs and all the principal officers were, returned home to the Great Khan.

CHAPTER 3

What Came of the Expedition

THE number of Tartars who were left upon the island where they had been wrecked was about thirty thousand. Finding themselves without ships, abandoned by their leaders, and having neither arms nor provisions, they expected nothing less than to be captured or to perish, especially since they could find neither shelter nor food on the island.

As soon as the gale ceased and the sea became calm, the people from the main island of Zipangu came over with a large force in numerous boats in order to seize the shipwrecked Tartars. Having landed, they proceeded in search of them, but in a straggling, disorderly manner. While the enemy was coming after them by one road, the Tartars, being concealed from view by high land in the center of the island, made a circuit of the coast by another. This brought them to the place where the fleet of boats was at anchor. Finding these all unguarded, but with their colors flying, they instantly seized them, and pushing off from the island sailed for the principal city of Zipangu. Because of the colors they flew they were allowed to enter unmolested. Here they found few of the inhabitants except women, whom they retained for their own use, driving out all others.

When the king learned what had taken place he was greatly mortified, and immediately gave directions for a strict blockade of the city. This was so effective that no one was able to enter or leave the place during the six months that the siege continued. At the end of this time the Tartars, despairing of aid, surrendered upon condition that their lives be spared.

These events took place in the course of the year 1279.* The Great Khan, having learned some years later that the unfortunate outcome of the expedition was the result of dissension between the two commanders,

---

*Histories tell us that the expedition took place in 1281 and was scattered by a storm, and that the army, abandoned on an island by the generals, was defeated by the Japanese. Nothing is said of jealous generals or of shipwrecked men invading or even reaching the Japanese mainland.

caused the head of one of them to be cut off. The other he sent to the savage island of Zorza, where it is the custom to execute criminals in the following manner. They are wrapped in the hide of a buffalo fresh from the beast, which is then sewed tight. As this dries, it compresses the body to such a degree that the sufferer is incapable of moving or helping himself, and thus perishes miserably.

CHAPTER 4

Of the Many Idols Worshiped in Zipangu and of People Addicted to Eating Human Flesh

ON THIS island of Zipangu and others in its vicinity, their idols are fashioned in a variety of shapes, some of them having the heads of oxen, some of swine, dogs, goats, and many other animals. Some exhibit a single head with two faces, others three heads, one of them in the proper place, and one upon each shoulder. Some have four arms, others ten, and some a hundred, those which have the greatest number being regarded as the most powerful and therefore entitled to the most reverence.

When they are asked by Christians why they give their deities these different forms, they answer that their fathers did so before them. "Those who preceded us," they say, "left them so, and so shall we leave them to our posterity."

The various ceremonies practiced before these idols are so wicked and diabolical that it would be nothing less than an abomination to give an account of them in this book. The reader should, however, be informed that the idolatrous inhabitants of these islands, when they seize an enemy who cannot raise his ransom, invite to their house all their relations and friends; then putting their prisoner to death, they cook and eat him in a convivial manner, asserting that human flesh surpasses every other in flavor.

It should be understood that the sea in which the island of Zipangu is situated is called the Sea of Chin,*

*This is the closest Marco comes to the name "China."

and so extensive is this eastern sea that according to experienced pilots and mariners, who should know, it contains no fewer than 7,440 islands, mostly inhabited. It is said that every one of the trees which grow in them gives off a fragrant odor. They produce many spices and drugs, particularly aloes, and much pepper, both white and black.

It is impossible to estimate the value of the gold and other articles found in these islands. But their distance from the continent is so great, and the navigation so difficult, that vessels sailing there from the ports of Zaitun and Kinsai do not reap large profits; for they consume a whole year in the voyage, sailing in the winter and returning in the summer.* In these regions, one wind prevails during the winter, and another during the summer, so that they must avail themselves of the one for the outward, and the other for the homeward voyage. These countries are far from the continent of India. In terming this sea the Sea of Chin we must understand it, nevertheless, to be a part of the ocean; for as we speak of "the English Sea" or of "the Aegean Sea," so do the eastern people of "the Sea of Chin" and of "the Indian Sea." We shall here treat no further of these countries and islands, not only because of their lying far out of the way but because of my not having visited them personally, and their not being under the dominion of the Great Khan. We return now to Zaitun.

Departing from the port of Zaitun and steering a westerly course but inclining to the south for fifteen hundred miles, you pass the gulf named Keinan [Hainan], which extends northward for a distance of two months' sail. To the north it bounds the province of Manzi and on its other side the countries of Ania, Toloman, and many others already mentioned. Within this gulf there are a multitude of islands, for the most part well-inhabited. About the coasts much gold dust is collected from the sea at those points where the rivers empty into it. Copper also, and many other articles, are found there, and with these a trade is carried on, one island supplying

---

*Other Polo manuscripts assert that the voyage was very profitable despite this.

what another does not produce. They also trade with the people of the continent, exchanging their gold and copper for such necessities as they require. In most of these islands grain is raised in abundance. This gulf is so extensive and the inhabitants so numerous that it appears to be another world.

CHAPTER 5

Of the Country of Ziamba

WE NOW return to our former subject. Upon leaving Zaitun and navigating fifteen hundred miles across this gulf, as has been mentioned, you arrive at a country named Ziamba [a part of Annam] which is of great extent, and rich. It is governed by its own kings, and has its own peculiar language. The inhabitants are worshipers of idols. An annual tribute, in elephants and aloes wood, and nothing else, is paid to the Great Khan, the circumstances of which shall be related.

About the year 1278, Kublai, having learned of the great wealth of this kingdom, resolved to send a large force of infantry and cavalry to conquer it. The country was accordingly invaded by a powerful army under the command of one of his generals, Sogatu. The king, whose name was Accambale, and who was far advanced in years, feeling himself incapable of resisting the forces of the Great Khan, retired to his strongholds and there defended himself valiantly.

Open towns, however, and villages on the plains, were in the meantime overrun and laid waste, and the king, perceiving that his whole territory would be ruined, sent ambassadors to the Great Khan. They pleaded for the old king, saying that he had always preserved his dominions in a state of peace and was anxious to save his people from destruction. They said he was willing to pay yearly an honorary tribute of elephants and sweet-scented wood.

Upon receiving this proposal, the Great Khan, taking pity on him, immediately sent orders to Sogatu to retire from that country and proceed to the conquest of other countries, which was done without delay. From that time the king has annually presented to the Great Khan a tribute of twenty of the largest and handsomest elephants to be found in his districts. Thus it was that the King of Ziamba became the subject of the Great Khan.

We shall now mention some other circumstances respecting this king and his country. In the first place, it should be noticed that in his dominions no young woman can be given in marriage until she has been first tried by the king. Those who prove agreeable to him he retains for some time and when they are dismissed furnishes them with a sum of money, in order that they may be able to make advantageous matches in accordance with their station. In the year 1285 when Marco Polo visited this place the king had 326 children, male and female. Most of the former had distinguished themselves as valiant soldiers. The country abounds with elephants; there are also many forests of a fine black ebony which is made into various handsome articles of furniture. No other circumstance requires particular mention. Leaving this place, we shall now speak of the island called Java Major.

CHAPTER 6

Of the Island of Java

DEPARTING from Ziamba, and steering between south and southeast fifteen hundred miles, you reach an island of very great size named Java. According to the reports of some well-informed navigators it is the greatest in the world and has a circumference of three thousand miles [actually about half that]. It is under the dominion of only one king, and the inhabitants pay tribute to no other power. They are worshipers of idols.

The country abounds in rich commodities. Pepper, nutmegs, spikenard, galingale, cubebs, cloves and all the other valuable spices and drugs are produced there, and it is therefore visited by many ships laden with merchandise, which yield much profit to the owners.

The quantity of gold collected there exceeds all calculation and belief. From there the merchants of Zaitun and of Manzi in general have imported, and to this day import, a great deal of that metal and from there is also obtained the greatest part of the spices distributed throughout the world. The fact that the Great Khan has not brought the island under subjection to him must be attributed to the length and dangers of the voyage.*

CHAPTER 7

Of the Islands of Sondur and Kondur

UPON leaving Java [Polo means Ziamba] and steering a course between south and southwest for seven hundred miles, you arrive at two islands, the larger of which is named Sondur, and the other Kondur [the islands of Pulo Condore]. Both being uninhabited, it is unnecessary to say more respecting them.

Having gone a distance of fifty miles in a southeasterly direction one reaches an extensive and rich province that forms a part of the mainland and is named Locac [Thailand or Malaya]. Its inhabitants are idolaters. They have a language peculiar to themselves and are governed by their own king, who pays no tribute to any other, the situation of the country protecting it from hostile attack. If he could get at it, the Great Khan would not have delayed bringing it under his dominion.

In this country brazilwood† is produced in large quantities. Gold is abundant to a degree scarcely credible; elephants are also found there; and game is plentiful.

From here are exported all those porcelain shells that are used for money in other countries, as has already been noted. Here they cultivate a fruit called *berchi* which is about as large as a lemon and has a delicious flavor. Besides these circumstances there is nothing further that requires mention, unless it be that the country is wild and mountainous and is rarely visited by strangers. The king discourages such visits in order that his treasures and other secrets of his realm may be as little known to the rest of the world as possible.

---

*Kublai tried to conquer it in 1293, the year after the Polos left China, but he failed.
†A dyewood; it probably gave its name to the South American country where it was sought.

CHAPTER 8

Of the Island of Pentan

DEPARTING from Locac, and keeping a southerly course for five hundred miles, the traveler reaches an island named Pentan [probably Bintan, off Singapore], the coast of which is wild and uncultivated, but the woods of which abound with sweet-scented trees [probably sandalwood]. Between the province of Locac and this island of Pentan the sea, for a distance of sixty miles, is not more than four fathoms in depth, which obliges those who navigate it to lift the rudders of their ships. After sailing these sixty miles in a southeasterly direction, and then thirty miles farther, one arrives at an island, in itself a kingdom, named Malayur [probably off eastern Sumatra], which is also the name of its chief city. The people are governed by a king and have their own peculiar language. The town is large and well-built. A considerable trade is carried on there in spices and drugs, with which the place abounds. Nothing else that requires notice presents itself. Proceeding onwards, we shall now speak of Java Minor.

CHAPTER 9

Of the Island of Java Minor

UPON leaving the island of Pentan and steering southeast for about one hundred miles, you reach the island of Java the Lesser [Sumatra]. Small as it may be by comparison, it is not less than two thousand miles in circuit.

In this island there are eight kingdoms, each governed by its own king, and each with its own language. The people are idolaters. It contains an abundance of riches and all sorts of spices, aloes wood, sapanwood for dyeing, and various other kinds of drugs, which, on account of the length of the voyage and the danger of the navigation, are not imported into our country, but which find their way to the provinces of Manzi and Cathay.

We shall now treat separately of the inhabitants of each of these kingdoms. But in the first place it is important to note that the island lies so far to the south as to render the North Star invisible. Six of its eight kingdoms were visited by Marco Polo and these he will describe, omitting the other two because he did not have an opportunity to see them.

We shall begin with the kingdom of Ferlec [the northeast horn of Sumatra, called by European seamen "Diamond Point"]. Its inhabitants are, for the most part, idolaters, but many of those who dwell in the seaport towns have been converted to the religion of Mahomet by the Saracen merchants who constantly visit them. Those who inhabit the mountains live in a beastly manner. They eat human flesh and all other sorts of flesh, clean and unclean. They worship a variety of objects, for each individual adores throughout the day the first thing that he sees when he rises in the morning.

Upon leaving Ferlec you enter Basman [Passier], which is independent of the others and has its own peculiar language. The people profess obedience to the Great Khan but pay him no tribute, and they are so far away that his troops cannot be sent to them. The whole island, indeed, is nominally subject to him, and when ships pass that way the opportunity is taken to send him rare and curious articles, and especially a particular sort of falcon.

In this country there are many wild elephants and unicorns [rhinoceroses], the latter much smaller than the elephant but with similar feet. Their hide resembles that of the buffalo. In the middle of the forehead they have a single horn, but they do not attack with this weapon—employing instead their tongue, which is armed with long, sharp spines—and their knees or feet. Their method of attack is to trample upon a person and then lacerate him with the tongue. Their head is like that of a wild boar and they carry it low, towards the ground. They take delight in muddy pools and are filthy in their habits. They are not at all those animals [unicorn] which are said to allow themselves to be taken by maidens, but are of a quite contrary nature. Monkeys of various sorts are also found in this district, and vultures as black as crows, large in size, and very good at pursuing a quarry.

It should be known that what is reported respecting the shriveled bodies of diminutive human beings, or pigmies, brought from India, is an idle tale, such so-called men being manufactured on this island in the following manner. There is a medium-sized monkey here which has a face like that of a man. Those who make it their business to catch them shave off the hair, leaving only a little around the chin and those other parts where it naturally grows on the human body. They then dry and preserve them with camphor and other drugs; and having prepared them in such a way that they look exactly like little men, they put them into wooden boxes and sell them to traders, who carry them to all parts of the world. But this is merely an imposition. Neither in India nor in any other country, however wild, have pigmies so diminutive as these been found. Sufficient having been said of this kingdom we shall now speak of another, named Samara [probably Sumatra].

CHAPTER 10

Of the Kingdoms Named Samara and Dagroian

LEAVING Basman, you enter the kingdom of Samara. In this Marco Polo resided five months, during which, much against his will, he was detained by contrary winds [the southwest monsoon]. The North Star is not visible here, nor even the stars that are in the Wain. The people are idolaters; they are governed by a powerful prince, who professes himself the vassal of the Great Khan.

As it was necessary to continue for so long a time at this island Marco Polo established himself on shore with a party of about two thousand men. To guard against trouble from the savage natives who look for opportunities to seize stragglers, kill and eat them, he caused a large and deep ditch to be dug around him on the land side, in such manner that each end terminated in the port, where the shipping lay. He fortified the ditch with several blockhouses or redoubts of wood, the country having a great deal of that material. Thus defended, he kept the party in complete safety during the five months of their stay. Such was the confidence inspired among the natives that they furnished victuals and other necessary things according to an agreement made with them.

Their fish is the finest that can be found anywhere. There is no wheat here, but the people live upon rice. They do not make wine but from a species of tree resembling the date-bearing palm [gomuti palm] they get an excellent beverage in the following manner. They cut off a branch and put a vessel over the stump to catch the juice as it distils from the wound. This fills up in the course of a day and a night. This liquor is very health-giving and provides relief in dropsical complaints, as well as in those of the lungs and the spleen. When these cuts stop yielding juice, the natives contrive to revive the trees by piping water from the river; the juice then runs again as it did at first. Some trees naturally yield liquor of a reddish color; that of others is paler.

Indian nuts [coconuts] also grow here the size of a man's head and contain a pulp that is sweet and pleasant to the taste, and white as milk. The center of this pulp is filled with a liquor clear as water, cool, better flavored and more delicate than wine or any other kind of drink. The inhabitants feed upon flesh of every sort, good or bad, without distinction.

Dagroian is governed by its own prince, and has its peculiar language. Its inhabitants are uncivilized, worship idols, and acknowledge the authority of the Great Khan. When any member of the family becomes ill, they observe this horrible custom: The relations of the sick person send for magicians whom they require, upon examination of the symptoms, to declare whether he will recover. These, according to the opinion suggested to them by the evil spirit, reply that he will or will not recover. If the decision be that he cannot, the relations call in certain men whose peculiar duty it is, and who perform their business with dexterity, to close the mouth of the patient until he is suffocated. This being done, they cut the body in pieces and prepare it for eating. When it has been so dressed, the relations assemble and eat it zestfully, not leaving so much as the marrow in the bones. Should any particle of the body be suffered to remain it would breed worms; and they believe these, for want of further sustenance, would perish, and their death would result in a grievous punishment to the soul of the deceased. They afterwards collect the bones and having put them in a small, neat box, carry them to some cavern in the mountains where they may be safe from disturbance by wild animals. If they have it in their power to seize any stranger who cannot pay for his ransom they put him to death and devour him.

CHAPTER 11

Of the Kingdoms Named Lambri and Fanfur

LAMBRI, in like manner, has its own king and its peculiar language. The people also worship idols and call themselves vassals of the Great Khan. The country produces brazil or sapanwood, and camphor, with a variety of other drugs. They sow a vegetable resembling sapanwood, and when it springs up and begins to throw out shoots they transplant it to another spot where it is allowed to remain for three years. It is then taken up by the roots and used as a dyestuff. Marco Polo brought some of the seeds of this plant with him to Venice and sowed them there, but the climate being too cold, none of them came up.

In this kingdom there are men with tails a span in length, like those of the dog, but these creatures are not covered with hair.* The greater number of them are formed in this manner, but they live in the mountains and not in the towns. The rhinoceros is common in the woods and there is an abundance of all sorts of game, both beasts and birds.

Fanfur [on the west coast] is a kingdom of the same island and is governed by its own prince. In this part of the country a species of camphor, much superior to any other, is produced. It is named the camphor of Fanfur, and is worth its weight in gold.

There is no wheat nor other corn here, the inhabitants eating rice, with milk, and the wine extracted from trees in the manner described in the chapter on Samara. They have also a tree from which, by an unusual process, they obtain a kind of meal [sago]. The stem is lofty and so thick it would take two men to span it. When the outer

*Stories of tailed and hairy men were common from ancient times to well beyond the Middle Ages.

bark is stripped from this, the inner substance is found to be about three inches in thickness and the central part is filled with a pith which yields a meal, or flour, resembling that from the acorn. The pith is put into vessels filled with water and is stirred about with a stick in order that the fibers and other impurities may rise to the top, and the pure part settle to the bottom. When this has been done the water is poured off, and the purified flour which remains is made into cakes and various kinds of *pasta* dishes. Of this, which resembles barley bread in appearance and taste, Marco Polo frequently ate, and some of it he brought home to Venice.

The wood of the tree, about three inches thick, may be compared to iron, in that when thrown into water it immediately sinks. It can be split evenly from one end to the other, like bamboo cane. The natives make short lances of it: were they of any considerable length they would be too heavy to carry or use. They are sharpened at one end and rendered so hard by fire that they can penetrate any sort of armor, and in many respects are preferable to iron.

We have now said enough about this kingdom. Of the other kingdoms composing the remaining part we shall not speak, because Marco Polo did not visit them. We shall next describe a small island named Nocueran [Nicobar].

CHAPTER 12

Of the Island of Nocueran

UPON leaving Java Minor and the kingdom of Lambri and sailing about 150 miles, you arrive at two islands, one of which is named Nocueran, the other Angaman.

Nocueran is not under the government of a king and the people are like beasts. Both men and women go naked, without a covering to any part of the body. They are idolaters. Their woods abound in the noblest and most valuable trees, such as the white and the red sandal, those which bear the Indian coconuts, cloves and sapan. Besides this they have a variety of drugs. Proceeding further, we shall speak of Angaman.

CHAPTER 13

Of the Island of Angaman

ANGAMAN is a very large island [the Andaman Islands], not governed by a king. The inhabitants are idolaters, and are a most brutish and savage race, having heads, eyes, and teeth like those of dogs. They are cruel, and every person not of their own nation whom they can lay their hands on, they kill and eat. They have an abundance and variety of drugs. Their food is rice and milk, and meat of every description. They have Indian nuts [coconuts], apples, and many other fruits different from those which grow in our country.

CHAPTER 14

Of the Island of Zeilan

DEPARTING from the island of Angaman and steering a course something to the southward of west, for a thousand miles, the island of Zeilan [Ceylon] presents itself. This, for its size, is better circumstanced than any other island in the world. It is 2,400 miles in circumference [really less than 700 miles], but in ancient times it was still larger, its circumference then measuring full 3,600 miles, as shown in mariners' maps. But the northern gales, which blow with violence, have corroded the mountains so that they have in some parts fallen and sunk in the sea, and the island, from that cause, is no longer its original size.

It is governed by a king whose name is Sendernaz. The people worship idols and are independent of every other state. Both men and women go nearly nude, only wrapping a cloth round the middle part of their bodies. They have no grain besides rice and sesame, of which latter they make oil. Their food is milk, rice, and flesh, and they drink the wine drawn from trees, which has already been described. There is the best dyewood here that can be met with anywhere.

The island produces more beautiful and valuable rubies than are found in any other part of the world and likewise sapphires, topazes, amethyst, garnets, and many other precious stones. The king is reported to possess the grandest ruby that ever was seen, a span in length, the thickness of a man's arm, brilliant beyond description, and without a single flaw.* It has the appearance of a glowing fire, and is so valuable that no estimate can be made of its worth. The Great Khan, Kublai, sent ambassadors to this monarch, with a request that he should let him have this ruby in return for the value of a city. The king's answer was that he would not sell it for all the treasure of the universe; nor could he, on any terms, allow it to go out of his dominions, since it had been handed down to him by his ancestors. The Great Khan failed therefore to get it.

The people of this island are no soldiers but on the contrary are abject and timid creatures. When they need soldiers they bring in Mahometans from other countries.

CHAPTER 15

The History of Sagamoni Borcan

FURTHERMORE, I must not omit certain matters that I heard when I visited the island on my homeward voyage. In this island of Zeilan there is a very high mountain so rocky and precipitous that the ascent to the top is impracticable excepting by means of iron chains. By means of these some persons attain the summit where the tomb of Adam, our first parent, is reported to be found. Such is the account given by the Saracens. But the idolaters assert that it contains the body of Sagamoni Borcan,† the founder of their religious system whom they revere as a great saint. The son of a king of the island, he devoted himself to a holy life, refusing to accept kingdoms or any other worldly possessions, although his father endeavored, by tempting him with women and every other imaginable gratification, to divert him from his resolve. Every attempt to dissuade him was in vain and the young man fled secretly to this lofty

---

*Ceylon was always reputed to have rubies of fabulous size and value.
† This is Polo's spelling of *Sakya-Muni*, the name of the Buddha, and of *Burkhan*, the Mongolian synonym for Buddha.

mountain where, observing chastity and strict abstinence, he at length died.*

The father, distracted with the most poignant grief, caused an image of his son to be shaped of gold and precious stones, and required that all the inhabitants of the island should honor and worship it as a deity. They say, moreover, that he has died eighty-four times; that he died first as a man and came to life again as an ox, that he then died as an ox and came to life again as a horse, and so on; and every time he became some kind of animal. But when he died the eighty-fourth time they say he became a god. Such was the origin of the worship of idols in that country; but Sagamoni Borcan is still regarded as superior to every other. In this belief, people from far-off parts make pilgrimages to the mountain on which he was buried. Some of his hair, his teeth, and the bowl he made use of are still preserved, and shown with much ceremony. The Saracens, on the other hand, maintain that these belonged to Adam, and are in like manner led by their devotion to visit the mountain.

It happened that in the year 1284 the Great Khan heard of these relics of our first parent from certain Saracens who had been there, and felt so strong a desire to possess them that he was induced to send an embassy to demand them of the King of Zeilan. After a long and tedious journey, his ambassadors at length reached their destination and obtained from the king two large molars, together with some of the hair, and a handsome vessel of green stone. When the Great Khan heard that the messengers were returning with such valuable curiosities, he ordered all the people of Khan-balik to march out of the city to meet them, and they were conducted to his presence with great pomp and solemnity. Having mentioned these particulars respecting the mountain of Zeilan, we shall proceed to the kingdom of Maabar [India].

---

*Except that he places the story in Ceylon instead of northern India, Marco gives a substantially accurate outline of the Buddha's ascetic life.

CHAPTER 16

Of the Province of Maabar

LEAVING the island of Zeilan and sailing in a westerly direction sixty miles you reach the great province of Maabar [the Coromandel or Eastern coast of India] which is not an island, but a part of the continent of the Greater India, as it is termed, being the noblest and richest country in the world.

It is governed by four kings of whom the principal is named Sender-bandi. Within his dominions is a fishery for pearls in the gulf of a bay between Maabar and the island of Zeilan where the water is not more than ten to twelve fathoms in depth, and in some places not more than two fathoms.

This fishery is conducted in the following manner. A number of merchants form companies and employ many vessels and boats of different sizes, equipped to ride safely at anchor. They carry with them persons who are skilled in the art of diving for the oysters in which pearls are enclosed. These they bring up in bags made of netting that are fastened about their bodies, and then repeat the operation—rising to the surface when they can no longer hold their breath. Then, after a short interval, they dive again. The greater proportion of the pearls obtained from the fisheries in this gulf are round and of a good luster. The spot where the oysters are taken in the greatest number is on the shores of the mainland and is called Betala.

The gulf being infested with a kind of large fish which often proves dangerous to the divers, the merchants take the precaution of being accompanied by certain enchanters belonging to a class of Brahmans. By means of their magic, these men have the power of stupefying these fish so as to prevent them from doing mischief. They discontinue the charm in the evening in order that dishonest persons may be discouraged from diving at night and stealing the oysters. The enchanters are likewise skilled in the art of bewitching all kinds of beasts and birds.

The fishery begins in the month of April and lasts till the middle of May. The privilege of engaging in it is farmed out by the king, to whom a tenth part of the produce is allowed. To the magicians they allow a twentieth part and thus reserve, to themselves, a considerable profit. By the time the period is over, the stock of oysters is exhausted and the vessels are then taken to another place, fully three hundred miles from this gulf, where they establish themselves in the month of September and remain till the middle of October. The king insists on a choice of all the large and well-shaped pearls, but as he pays liberally for them the merchants are not disinclined to bring them to him.

CHAPTER 17

More of the Province of Maabar

THE natives of this part of the country always go naked, except that they cover their private parts with a piece of cloth. The king wears no more cloth than the rest except that he has a piece of richer cloth and is distinguished by various kinds of ornaments, such as a collar set with jewels, sapphires, emeralds, and rubies of immense value. He also wears, suspended from the neck and reaching to the breast, a fine silken string containing 104 large, handsome pearls and rubies. The reason for this particular number is that he is required by the rules of his religion to repeat a prayer, or invocation, that many times daily in honor of his gods, and this his ancestors never failed to perform. The daily prayer consists of these words, *pacauta, pacauta, pacauta,** which they repeat 104 times. On each arm he wears three gold bracelets adorned with pearls and jewels; on three different parts of the leg—golden bands ornamented in the same manner; and on the toes of his feet, as well as on his fingers, rings of great value. It is, indeed, a matter of course for him to display such splendid things, as the precious stones and pearls are all found in his own kingdom.

He also has at the least a thousand wives and concubines and when he sees a woman whose beauty pleases

---

*Probably *Bagava,* a form of Bhagavata, the Hindu word for Lord.

him he immediately signifies his desire to possess her. In this manner, he took the wife of his brother who, being a discreet and sensible man, was prevailed upon not to quarrel about it. Repeatedly he was about to make war, when his mother bared her breasts to them and declared, "If you attack each other I will cut off these breasts that fed you." And so they never forced the issue.

The king retains about his person many knights, whose name signifies "the devoted servants of his majesty in this world and the next." These attend him at court, ride by his side in processions, and accompany him on all other occasions. They exercise considerable authority in every part of the realm. Upon the death of the king, and when the ceremony of burning his body takes place, all these devoted servants throw themselves into the same fire and are consumed with the royal corpse, thereby signifying their intention of accompanying him in another life.

The following custom likewise prevails. When a king dies, the son who succeeds him does not meddle with the treasure his father had amassed. His impression is that it would reflect upon his own ability to govern if he did not show himself as capable of enriching the treasury as his father was. It is therefore supposed that immense wealth has been accumulated by successive generations.

No horses being bred in this country, the king and his three brothers spend large sums annually in the purchase of them from merchants who bring them thither for sale and become rich by the traffic. They import as many as five thousand at a time and for each of them pay five hundred saggi of gold, which is equal to one hundred marks of silver [about $1,000]. At the end of the year perhaps not three hundred of these remain alive, and thus they must be replaced. But it is my opinion that the climate is unfavorable to the race of horses, and that from this arises the difficulty in breeding or preserving them. For food they give them meat dressed with rice and other prepared meats, the country not producing any grain besides rice. A mare, although of a large size, and covered by a handsome horse, produces only a small ill-shaped colt with deformed legs and unfit to be trained for riding.

The following extraordinary custom prevails at this place. When a man who has been condemned to death for a crime declares his willingness to sacrifice himself in honor of some particular idol his relations and friends immediately place him in a kind of chair and give him twelve knives of good temper and well sharpened. They then carry him about the city, proclaiming that this is a brave man who is about to sacrifice himself out of devotion to the idol. Upon reaching the place where the sentence is to be executed, he snatches up two of the knives, and crying out "I sacrifice myself in honor of such an idol" hastily thrusts one of them into each thigh, then one into each arm, two into the belly, and two into the breast. Having repeated at every wound the words that have been mentioned, he plunges the last of them into his heart and immediately expires. His relations then proceed, with great triumph and rejoicing, to burn the body; and his wife, out of pious regard for her husband, throws herself upon the pile and is consumed with him. Women who do this are much applauded by the community as, on the other hand, those who shrink from it are despised and reviled.*

Most of the idolatrous inhabitants of this kingdom revere the ox and none can be induced to eat its flesh. But there is a particular class of men termed *gavi* [the so-called pariahs] who dare not to kill the animal, but when they find a carcass, whether it has died a natural death or otherwise, they will eat it.

All the people daub their houses with cow dung. They all sit on carpets on the ground, and when asked why they do so they reply that a seat on the earth is honorable; that as we sprang from the earth, so we shall return to it; that none can do it sufficient honor and none should despise the earth. These *gavi* and all their tribe are descendants of those who slew Saint Thomas the Apostle, and on this account no member of this tribe

---

*The practice of *suttee* is an ancient one in India and was not made illegal until the 19th century.

can possibly enter the building where the body of the blessed apostle rests. Were the strength of ten men employed to bring one of them to the spot, they could not hold him here, so great is the supernatural power of the holy corpse.

The country produces no other grain than rice and sesame.

The people go to battle with lances and shields, but without clothing, and make very poor soldiers. They do not kill cattle nor any kind of animal for food, but when they want to eat the flesh of sheep or other beasts, or of birds, they procure the Saracens, who are not bound by the same laws and customs, to kill the animals.

Both men and women wash their entire bodies in water both morning and evening. Until this ablution has taken place they neither eat nor drink; and anyone who neglected this observance would be regarded as a heretic. It ought to be noticed that in eating they make use of the right hand only and never touch their food with the left, reserving the latter for cleansing the private parts of the body. They drink out of a particular vessel and each individual from his own, never making use of the drinking vessel of another person. When they drink they do not put their lips to the vessel but hold it above the head, and pour the liquor into the mouth, not allowing the vessel to touch the lips. In giving drink to a stranger, they do not hand their vessel to him, but pour the wine or other liquid into his hands, from which he drinks it as from a cup.

Criminals in this country are punished with strict justice. With regard to debtors the following customs prevail. If request for payment has been repeatedly made by a creditor, and the debtor puts him off with false promises, the former may attach his person by drawing a circle round him which he may not leave until he has satisfied his creditor either by payment or by giving adequate security. Should he attempt to escape, he renders himself liable to the punishment of death.

When he was in this country on his return homeward, Messer Marco happened to be an eyewitness of a remarkable example of this. The king owed a sum of money to a certain foreign merchant, and although frequently asked for payment put him off for a long time with promises. One day when the king was riding on horseback the merchant took the opportunity of describing a circle round him and his horse. As soon as the king saw what had been done, he immediately halted and would ride no further until the demand of the merchant was fully satisfied. The bystanders beheld what happened and marveled at the king, saying that he was most just for he himself submitted to the laws of justice.

These people abstain from drinking wine made from grapes, and should a person be detected drinking wine, so shameful would it be thought that his evidence would not be accepted in court. A similar prejudice exists against persons sailing the sea, who, they observe, must be desperate, and whose testimony in court ought not to be admitted. They do not, however, hold fornication to be a crime.

The heat of the country is most excessive, and the inhabitants therefore go naked. There is no rain excepting in the months of June, July, and August,* and if it were not for the cooling effect of the rain during these three months, it would be impossible to stand it.

In this country there are many experts in the science of physiognomy, which teaches understanding of the nature and qualities of men, and whether they tend to good or evil. These qualities are immediately detected on looking at a man or woman. They also know what events are signified by a meeting with certain beasts or birds. More attention is paid by them to the flight of birds than by anyone else, and from these they predict good or bad fortune. There is one hour in every day of the week which they regard as unlucky, and in these hours they do not make purchases or transact any kind of business. They tell time by the length of a man's shadow when he stands erect.

When an infant is born, the father or the mother makes note of the day of the week, the phase of the

*This statement seems to apply more accurately to the western coast of India than to the Coromandel coast.

moon, the name of the month, and the hour. This is done because every future act of their lives is regulated by astrology.

As soon as a son attains the age of thirteen years they set him at liberty, and no longer suffer him to remain in his father's house, giving him twenty to twenty-four groats. Thus provided, he is considered capable of gaining his own livelihood by engaging in some kind of trade. These boys never stop running about all day long, buying an article in one place and selling it in another. At the season when the pearl fishery is going on, they frequent the beach and make purchases from the fishermen or others, of five, six, or more small pearls, according to their means. They then carry these to the merchants (who, on account of the heat of the sun, remain in their houses), and say: "These pearls have cost us so much; allow us such a profit on them as you may judge reasonable." The merchants then give something beyond the cost price. In this manner they deal in many other articles, and become excellent and acute traders. When business is over for the day, they carry to their mothers their food to be cooked and served, but they never eat anything at their father's expense.

Not only in this kingdom, but throughout India in general, all the beasts and birds are unlike ours, excepting the quails, which are exactly like ours. There are bats as large as vultures, and vultures as black as crows, and much larger than ours. Their flight is rapid, and they never fail to seize their prey.

In their temples there are many idols, both of the male and the female sex; and to these, fathers and mothers dedicate their daughters. Having been so dedicated, they are expected to attend whenever the priests of the convent require them to contribute to the gratification of the idol. On such occasions they go there, singing and playing on instruments, and adding to the festivity. These young women are very numerous, and form large bands. Several times a week they carry an offering of food to the idol to whose service they are devoted, and they say the idol partakes of this food. A table for the purpose is placed before it, and upon this the dishes remain for a full hour, during which damsels never cease to sing, play, and make wanton gestures. This lasts as long as a person of high rank would need for making a leisurely meal. They then declare that the spirit of the idol is content with its share of the entertainment provided, and, ranging themselves around it, they proceed to eat. This they do several times every year until they are married.

The reason given for assembling the young women, and performing these ceremonies, is this. The priests declare that the god is out of humor with and angry with the goddess, refusing to have connection or even to converse with her; and that if something is not done to restore peace and harmony between them, all the affairs of the monastery will go to ruin, as the grace and blessing of the divinities will be withheld from them. For this purpose they expect the girls to come nude, with only a cloth round their waists, to chant hymns to the god and goddess. These people believe that the god often solaces himself with the goddess.

The natives make use of a kind of bedstead, or cot, of very light canework, so ingeniously contrived that when they lie on them, and are inclined to sleep, they can draw the curtains about them by pulling a string. This they do in order to keep out tarantulas, which bite severely, as well as to prevent their being annoyed by fleas and other small insects; while at the same time the air, so necessary for reducing the excessive heat, is not kept out. Luxuries of this nature, however, are enjoyed only by persons of rank and wealth; those of the inferior class lie in the open streets.

CHAPTER 18

Of the Place Where the Holy Body of
St. Thomas Lies

IN THIS province of Maabar is the body of the glorious Saint Thomas the Apostle, who there suffered martyrdom. It rests in a small city [south of Madras] not frequented by many merchants. But a vast number of both Christians and Saracens go there. The latter regard him as a great Saint, and call him *Avariun,* signifying a "Holy Man."

The Christians who make this pilgrimage take earth from the spot where he was slain, which is of a red color, and reverently carry it away with them. They often employ it afterwards in the performance of miracles and give it, diluted with water, to the sick, and thus cure many disorders.

In the year of our Lord 1288, a powerful prince of the country who at harvest had gathered a very great quantity of rice and did not have granaries sufficient to accommodate it, thought proper to make use of the religious house belonging to the church of Saint Thomas. This being against the will of those who were in charge of it, they beseeched him not to occupy this building intended for pilgrims who came to visit the body of this glorious saint. But he obstinately refused to remove the grain. On the following night the holy apostle appeared to him in a vision, holding in his hand a small lance which he pointed at the throat of the prince, saying to him: "If thou dost not immediately leave my house which thou hast occupied, I shall put thee to a miserable death." Awaking in violent alarm, the baron instantly gave orders for doing what was required of him, declaring publicly that he had seen the apostle in a vision. A variety of miracles are daily performed there, such as the healing of those who are sick or deformed. The Christians who take care of the church possess groves of those trees which produce Indian nuts, and from these they get their living, paying, as a tax to one of the royal brothers, a groat monthly for each tree.

It is related that the death of this most holy apostle took place in the following manner. Having retired to a hermitage, where he was engaged in prayer, and being surrounded by a number of peacocks with which the country abounds, an idolater of the tribe of the gavi, who happened to be passing that way and did not perceive the holy man, shot an arrow at a peacock, which struck the apostle in the side. Finding himself wounded, he had time only to thank the Lord for all his mercies, and resign his spirit into His hands.

In this province the natives, although black, are not

born of so dark a color as they afterwards attain by artificial means, esteeming blackness the perfection of beauty. For this purpose, they rub the children with oil of sesame three times every day. They make the images of their deities black, but they paint the devil white and assert that all the demons are of that color. Those among them who pay adoration to the ox attach some of the hair of the wild bull to the manes of their horses when they go to battle, believing that everyone who carries it about with him is secure from all danger. On this account the hair of the wild bull sells for a high price in these countries.

CHAPTER 19

Of the Kingdom of Mutfili or Monsul

THE kingdom of Mutfili [Motupalli, now a fishing village 170 miles north of Madras] is that which you enter on leaving Maabar, after proceeding five hundred miles in a northerly direction. Its inhabitants worship idols, and are independent of any other state. They subsist upon rice, flesh, fish, and fruits.

It is in the mountains of this kingdom that diamonds are found.* During the rainy season the water descends in violent torrents among the rocks and caverns, and when it has subsided the people search for diamonds in the riverbeds, where they find many. Messer Marco said that in the summer, when the heat is excessive, and there is no rain, they climb the mountains, which is exhausting, and infested with dangerous snakes. Near the summit, it is said, there are deep valleys full of caverns and surrounded by cliffs, among which the diamonds are found; and here many eagles and white storks, attracted by the snakes on which they feed, make their nests. The persons looking for the diamonds take their stand near the mouths of the caverns and cast down pieces of meat which the eagles and storks pursue into the valley and carry off to the tops of the rocks. The men immediately ascend, drive the birds away, and recovering the pieces

*The famous Golconda field, which has yielded some of the greatest diamonds in the world.

of meat, frequently find diamonds sticking to them. Should the eagles have had time to devour the flesh, the men watch the places of their roosting at night and in the morning find the stones among their droppings.* But you must not suppose that the good diamonds are sent to Christians; for they are carried to the Great Khan, and to the kings and chiefs of that country.

In this country they manufacture the finest cottons that are to be met with in any part of India. They have cattle enough and the largest sheep in the world, and plenty of all kinds of food.

CHAPTER 20

Of the Province of Lar

LEAVING the place, where rests the body of the glorious Saint Thomas, and proceeding westward, you enter the province of Lar [the Mysore area] whence the Brahmans, who are spread over India, originate. These are the best and most honorable merchants that can be found. Nothing can induce them to lie, even though their lives depend upon it. They also abhor robbery or taking the goods of other persons. They are likewise remarkable for continence, being satisfied with one wife. When any foreign merchant unacquainted with the customs of the country commits merchandise into the care of one of these men, the Brahman disposes of it and renders a faithful account of the proceeds, attending scrupulously to the interests of the stranger and not demanding any recompense. The owner, however, may grant him whatever profit he thinks proper.

They eat meat, and drink the wine of the country. They do not, however, kill any animals themselves, but have this done by Mahometans. Brahmans are distinguished by a badge consisting of a thick cotton cord which passes over the shoulder and is tied under the arm in such a manner that the thread appears upon the breast and behind the back.

The king is extremely rich and powerful and delights

---

*The same tale was told by Sinbad the Sailor in the *Arabian Nights* and was widespread in Eastern literatures.

in the possession of pearls and valuable stones. When the traders from Maabar offer him superior ones he trusts their estimate of the value and gives them double the sum that each cost them. Under these circumstances, he is offered many fine jewels.

The people are gross idolaters, and are addicted to sorcery and divination. When they are about to make a purchase of goods, they immediately observe the shadow cast by their own bodies in the sunshine, and if the shadow be as large as it should be, they make the purchase that day. Moreover, when they are in any shop for the purpose of buying anything, if they see a tarantula, of which there are many, they notice from which side it comes and regulate their business accordingly. Again, when they are going out of their houses, if they hear anyone sneeze they turn back into the house and stay at home.

They are very abstemious in regard to eating and live to an advanced age. Their teeth are kept sound by the use of a certain vegetable which they chew. It also promotes digestion, and is generally good for the human body.

Among the natives of this region there is a class peculiarly devoted to a religious life who are named Chughi [Jogi], and who in honor of their divinities lead most austere lives. They go perfectly naked and say there can be no shame in the state of nudity in which they came into the world. With respect to what are called the parts of shame they observe that, since these are not organs of sin for them, they have no reason to blush at their exposure.

They pay adoration to the ox, and carry a small figure of one, made of gilt brass or other metal, attached to their forehead. They also burn the bones of oxen, reducing them to powder, and with this make an ointment with which they mark various parts of the body in a reverential manner. If they meet a person with whom they are upon cordial terms, they smear the center of his forehead with some of these prepared ashes.

They do not deprive any creature of life, not even a fly, a flea, or a louse, believing they have souls; and to feed upon any animals they would consider a heinous sin. They even abstain from eating vegetables, herbs, or roots, until they have become dry, believing that these also have souls. They make no use of spoons or of plates, but spread their food upon the dried leaves of the Adam's apple, called apples of paradise. When they want to relieve themselves, they go to the seashore to do so and then scatter what they have done to prevent it from breeding worms because the death of these creatures for lack of food would weigh on their consciences. They live to a great age, some of them even to 150 years, and enjoy health and vigor, although they sleep on the bare earth. This must be attributed to their temperance and chastity.* And when a novice has to be received among them, they keep him awhile in their convent, making him follow their rule of life. Then to test him they send for some of those girls who are devoted to the idols and let them try the continence of the novice with their blandishments. If he remains unaroused they retain him; but if he shows any emotion, they reject him, for they say they do not want any man of loose desires.

CHAPTER 21

Of the City of Kael

KAEL [once a port in the Tinnevelly district] is a considerable city, governed by Astiar (one of four brothers, kings of the country of Maabar), who is rich in gold and jewels and preserves his country in a state of profound peace. On this account it is a favorite port of call for foreign merchants, who are well received and treated by the king. Accordingly all ships coming from the west— as from Ormus, Kisi, Aden, and various parts of Arabia—laden with merchandise and horses, make this port, which is also well situated for commerce. The prince maintains not fewer than three hundred women in the most splendid manner.

All the people of this city, as well as the natives of India in general, are addicted to having in their mouths the leaf called *tembul* [the Persian word for betel], which

---

*The following passage is added in the French manuscript translated by Yule. It is even more detailed in the Zelada manuscript.

they do partly from habit and partly from the gratification it affords. Upon chewing it, they spit out the saliva which it causes. Persons of rank have the leaf prepared with camphor and other aromatic drugs, and also with a mixture of quicklime. I have been told that it is very beneficial. If any man means to insult another in the grossest and most contemptuous manner, he spits the juice of this leaf in his face. Thus insulted the injured party hastens to the king, states his grievance, and declares his willingness to decide the quarrel by combat. The king thereupon furnishes them with arms, consisting of a sword and small shield; and all the people assemble to be spectators of the conflict, which lasts till one of them remains dead on the field. They are, however, forbidden to wound with the point of the sword.

CHAPTER 22

Of the Kingdom of Koulam

UPON leaving Maabar and proceeding five hundred miles toward the southwest, you arrive at the kingdom of Koulam [Quilan]. It is the residence of many Christians and Jews, who retain their own language. The king is not tributary to any other.

Much good dyewood grows there, and pepper in great abundance, being found both in the wooded and open parts of the country. It is gathered in the months of May, June, and July; and the vines which produce it are cultivated in plantations. Indigo of excellent quality and in large quantities is also made here. They procure it from a certain herb which is taken up by the roots and put into tubs of water, where it remains till it rots; they then press out the juice. Upon being exposed to the sun this evaporates* and leaves a kind of paste, which is cut into small pieces of the form in which we see it.

The heat during some months is so great as to be scarcely endured; yet merchants come here from such various parts of the world as, for instance, the kingdoms of Manzi and Arabia, attracted by the great profits upon

---

*It is the process of fermentation, not the sun, that creates the heat.

the merchandise they import and upon their returning cargoes.

Many of the animals found here are different from those of other parts. There are entirely black tigers; and various birds of the parrot kind—some of them as white as snow—with the feet and the beak red. Other birds have a mixture of red and azure; and still others are of a diminutive size. The peacocks also are handsomer and larger than ours, as well as of a different form, and even the domestic fowls have a peculiar appearance. The same applies to the fruits. The cause of such diversity, it is said, is the intense heat that prevails in these regions.

Wine is made from the sugar yielded by a species of palm. It is extremely good and makes one drunk faster than the wine from grapes. The inhabitants possess an abundance of everything necessary for food excepting grain, of which there is no other kind than rice. But the quantity of this is very great. Among them are many astrologers and physicians, well versed in their art.

All the people, both male and female, are black, and with the exception of a loincloth, go quite naked. They are extremely sensual, and they take as wives their relations by blood, their cousins, and the widows of their deceased brothers. But this, as I have been informed, is the state of morals in every part of India.

CHAPTER 23

Of Komari

KOMARI [Cape Comorin] is a province where a part of the North Star, invisible at Java and to within about thirty miles of this place, may be just seen, and where it appears to be a cubit above the horizon. The country is not much cultivated but is chiefly covered with forests, containing a variety of beasts, especially apes, so formed and of such a size as to have the appearance of men. There are also long-tailed monkeys, much smaller than the former in size. Tigers, leopards, and lynxes abound.

CHAPTER 24

Of the Kingdom of Ely

LEAVING the province of Komari and proceeding westward three hundred miles you reach the kingdom of Ely, which has its own king and peculiar language. It does not pay tribute to any other state. The people worship idols. There is no harbor, but a large river with a safe entrance. The strength of the country does not consist in the multitude of its inhabitants, nor in their bravery, but in the difficulty of the passes by which it must be approached, and which render invasion nearly impossible.

It produces large quantities of pepper and ginger, with many other articles of spicery. Should a vessel be accidentally driven within the mouth of its river, they seize and confiscate all the goods she may have on board, saying: "You intended to go elsewhere, but our gods led you to us so that we may possess your property."

The ships from Manzi arrive here before the end of the fine-weather season and try to get their cargoes shipped in a week or less, because of sandbanks along the coast, which often prove dangerous, however well provided the ships may be with large wooden anchors for holding against strong gales. The country is infested with tigers, and many other ferocious animals.

CHAPTER 25

Of Malabar

MALABAR [the southwest coast, from Quilan to Ely] is an extensive kingdom of the Greater India situated toward the west, and I must not omit to give some details of it. The people are governed by their own king who is independent of every other state, and they have their own language.

In this country, the North Star is seen about two fathoms above the horizon. Here, as in the kingdom of Guzerat, which is not far distant, there are numerous pirates who yearly scour these seas with more than one hundred small vessels, seizing and plundering all the merchant ships that pass that way. They take to sea their wives and children during the whole of the summer's cruise. In order that no ships may escape them, they anchor their vessels at a distance of five miles from each other, twenty ships thus occupying a space of a hundred miles. Upon a trader's coming in sight of one of them they signal by fire or smoke, whereupon they all draw together and capture the vessel as she attempts to pass. No injury is done to the crew; but as soon as they have made prize of the ship, they turn them loose on shore advising them to get another cargo, which, in case it passes that way again, may be captured a second time.

In this kingdom there is a vast abundance of pepper, ginger, cinnamon, and Indian nuts. It manufactures the finest and most beautiful cottons that can be found in any part of the world. The ships from Manzi bring copper as ballast and besides this, gold brocades, silks, gauzes, gold and silver bullion, together with many kinds of drugs not produced in Malabar; and these they barter for the commodities of the province. There are merchants on the spot who ship the former to Aden, whence they are transported to Alexandria.

Having now spoken of the kingdom of Malabar we shall proceed to describe that of Guzerat which borders on it. Should we attempt to treat of all the cities of India the account would be too long, and prove tiresome. We shall therefore touch only on those places concerning which we have particular and interesting information.

CHAPTER 26

Of the Kingdom of Guzerat

THE kingdom of Guzerat [north of Bombay], which is bounded on the western side by the Indian Sea, is governed by its own king, and has its own peculiar language. The North Star appears from here to have an altitude of six fathoms.

This country harbors pirates of the most desperate character. When in their cruises they seize a traveling merchant they immediately make him drink a dose of seawater, which produces a violent purging. In this way they discover whether he has swallowed any pearls or jewels.

Here there is also a great abundance of ginger, pepper, and indigo. Cotton is produced in large quantities from a tree that is about six yards in height,* and bears for a period of twenty years; but the cotton taken from trees of that age is not adapted for spinning, but only for quilting. But that taken from trees twelve years old is suitable for muslins and other fabrics of extraordinary fineness. Great quantities of skins of goats, buffaloes, wild oxen, rhinoceroses, and other beasts are dressed here, and vessels are loaded with them for export to different parts of Arabia. They also make coverlets for beds of red and blue leather, extremely delicate and soft, and stitched with gold and silver thread; the Mahometans are accustomed to sleep upon these. Cushions ornamented with gold wire in the form of birds and beasts are also manufactured here, and in some instances their value is as high as six silver marks. The embroidery here is finer in workmanship than that done in any other part of the world. Proceeding further, we shall now speak of the kingdom named Kanan.

CHAPTER 27

Of the Kingdom of Kanan

KANAN [near Bombay] is a large and noble kingdom, situated toward the west. We say toward the west because Messer Marco's journey was from the eastern side, and he speaks of the countries in accordance with the direction in which he approaches them.

It is governed by a prince who does not pay tribute to any other. The people are idolaters and have their own peculiar language. Neither pepper nor ginger grow here, but the country produces large quantities of a sort of incense which is not white,† but of a dark color. Many ships frequent the place in order to load this drug, as well as a variety of other articles. They likewise take on

*Apparently somewhat exaggerated.
†That is, not frankincense, which came from Arabia.

board a number of horses, to be carried for sale to different parts of India.

CHAPTER 28

Concerning the Kingdom of Kambaia

KAMBAIA [Cambay] is an extensive kingdom, situated toward the west, governed by its own king who pays no tribute to any other and having its own language. The people are idolaters. In this country, the North Star is seen still higher than in any of the preceding in consequence of its lying further to the northwest. The trade carried on is very considerable and a great quantity of indigo is manufactured. There is an abundance of cotton cloth, as well as of cotton in the wool. Many skins, well-dressed, are exported in exchange for gold, silver, copper, and tutty [eye powder, or salve, prepared from zinc]. Nothing else deserving notice, I shall proceed to speak of the kingdom of Somnath.

CHAPTER 29

Of the Kingdom of Somnath

SOMNATH [port on the peninsula west of the Bay of Cambay] is likewise a kingdom lying toward the west, the inhabitants of which are idolaters, are governed by a king who pays no tribute, have their own peculiar language, and are a well-disposed people.

They gain their living by commerce and manufacture, and the place is frequented by a number of merchants who bring their articles of merchandise and take away those of the country in return. I was informed, however, that the priests who serve in the temples of the idols are the most cruel in the world. We shall now proceed to speak of the kingdom named Kesmacoran.

CHAPTER 30

Of the Kingdom of Kesmacoran

THIS is an extensive country [beyond the Indus River in the region of Makran], having its own king and its own peculiar language. Some of the inhabitants are idolaters, but the greater part are Saracens. They subsist by trade and manufacture. Their food is rice and wheat, together with flesh and milk, which they have in abundance. Many merchants come here, both by sea and land.

This is the last province of Greater India as you proceed to the northwest; for, as it begins at Maabar, so it terminates here. In describing it, we have noticed only the provinces and cities that lie upon the seacoast; for were we to deal with those situated in the interior, it would render our work too long.

We shall now speak of some of the Indian Islands. One of them is termed the Island of Males and the other the Island of Females.

CHAPTER 31

Of the Islands of Males and of Females

DISTANT from Kesmacoran about five hundred miles toward the south, in the ocean, there are two islands within about thirty miles of each other.* One of these is inhabited by men, without the company of women, and is called the Island of Males; the other, by women without men, and is called the Island of Females.

The inhabitants of both are of the same race and are baptized Christians, but observing the law of the Old Testament. The men visit the Island of Females and remain there for three months, namely, March, April, and May, each man occupying a separate house along with his wife. They then return to the male island where they live the rest of the year, without the company of any female.

The wives retain their sons until they are of the age of twelve years, when they are sent to join their fathers. The

*No such islands are known; the legend, which is an amplified version of the fable of the Amazons, was widespread.

daughters they keep at home, until they become marriageable, and then bestow them upon some of the men of the other island. This mode of living is occasioned by the peculiar nature of the climate, which does not allow them to remain all the year with their wives, unless at the risk of falling a sacrifice. They have their bishop, who is subordinate to the see of the island of Socotra.

The men provide for their wives by sowing the grain, but the latter till the soil and reap the harvest. The island likewise produces a variety of fruits. The men live upon milk, flesh, rice, and fish, of which they catch an immense quantity, being expert fishermen. Both fresh and salted fish is sold to traders, but the principal object of such traders is to purchase ambergris, which is collected there.

CHAPTER 32

Of the Island of Socotra

UPON leaving these islands, and proceeding five hundred miles in a southerly direction, you reach the island of Socotra,* which is very large, and abounds with the necessities of life. The inhabitants find much ambergris upon their coasts, which is voided from the entrails of whales. Whales being in great demand, they make it a business to take these fish;† and this they do by means of a barbed iron which they thrust into the whale so firmly that it cannot be drawn out. To the iron harpoon a long line is fastened, with a buoy at the end, so that the fish, when dead, can be found. They then drag it to shore and extract the ambergris from its belly while from its head they procure several casks of oil.

All the people, both male and female, go nearly naked, having only a scanty covering before and behind, like the idolaters previously described. They have no other grain than rice upon which, with flesh and milk,

---

*In the Indian Ocean off the Ethiopian coast; it still exports such products as aloes and incense.
†The Zelada manuscript goes on to describe in vivid detail the way pieces of tunny are used to lure the whale in close and how, after the whale has been harpooned and tries to dive, the hunters hamper him by attaching buoys to the line until he is exhausted.

they subsist. Their religion is Christianity and they are duly baptized and are under the government, temporal as well as spiritual, of an archbishop; he is not subject to the Pope of Rome but to a patriarch who resides in the city of Baghdad, by whom he is appointed. Or sometimes he is elected by the people themselves, and their choice is then confirmed.

Many pirates resort to this island with the goods which they have captured, and which the natives purchase without scruple, justifying themselves on the ground of their being plundered from heathens and Saracens. All ships bound for Aden touch here, and make large purchases of fish and ambergris, as well as of various kinds of woven cotton goods manufactured on the island.

The inhabitants deal more in sorcery and witchcraft than any other people, although forbidden to do so by their archbishop, who excommunicates them for the sin. Of this, however, they take little account. If any vessel belonging to a pirate should damage one of theirs they lay him under a spell so that he cannot proceed on his cruise until he has made good the damage. Even should he have had a fair and leading wind they have the power of causing it to change and obliging him, in spite of himself, to return to the island. They can, in like manner, make the sea calm, and at will can raise tempests, cause shipwrecks, and produce many other extraordinary effects that need not be described in detail. We shall now speak of the island of Madagascar.

CHAPTER 33

Of the Great Island of Madagascar

LEAVING the island of Socotra and steering a course between south and southwest for a thousand miles [actually 1,800 miles], you arrive at the great island of Madagascar,* which is one of the largest and most fertile in

*There is no evidence that Marco visited here, or Zanzibar, which is described in the next chapter. There are no camels or elephants on the island, and it is believed that he confused it with some such place on the African mainland as Mogadishu, where camels were constantly slaughtered for food.

the world. In circuit it is three thousand miles. The inhabitants are Saracens, followers of the law of Mahomet. They have four sheiks, which in our language may be expressed by "elders," who divide the government among them. The people live by trade and manufacture, and sell a vast number of elephants' teeth, as those animals abound in the country, as they also do in Zanzibar.

The principal food eaten at all seasons of the year is camels' meat. Flesh of other cattle serves also for food, but the former is preferred, as being both the most wholesome and the most palatable of any found in this part of the world. The woods contain many trees of red sandalwood and the price of it is low. There is also much ambergris from the whales and it is collected for sale as the tide throws it up on the coast.

The natives catch lynxes, tigers, and a variety of other animals such as stags, antelopes, and fallow deer, which afford much sport; as do also birds, which are different from those of our climates.

The island is visited by many ships from various parts of the world, and these bring an assortment of goods consisting of brocades and silks of various patterns, which are sold to the merchants of the island, or bartered for goods in return. They make large profits.

Ships do not visit numerous other islands lying farther south, Madagascar and the island of Zanzibar alone being frequented. This is because the ocean current runs with such velocity toward the south that it renders return impossible. The vessels that sail from the coast of Malabar for this island make the voyage in twenty or twenty-five days, but on their return are obliged to struggle for three months, so strong is the current running southward.

The people of the island report that at a certain season of the year an extraordinary kind of bird, which they call a roc, comes from the southern region. In form it is said to resemble the eagle, but it is incomparably greater in size, being so large and strong as to be able to seize an elephant with its talons and lift it into the air in order to drop it to the ground and in this way kill it. The bird feasts upon the dead carcass. Persons who have seen this bird assert that when the wings are spread they measure sixteen paces [eighty feet] from point to point; and that the feathers are eight paces in length, and thick in proportion.*

Messer Marco Polo, conceiving that these creatures might be griffins, which are represented in paintings as half birds and half lions, closely questioned eyewitnesses on this point; but they maintained that their shape was entirely that of birds, or as it might be said, of the eagle.

Having heard this extraordinary report, the Great Khan sent messengers to the island on the pretext of demanding the release of one of his servants who had been detained there, but in reality to investigate the country, and the truth of the wonderful things told of it. When they returned to his Majesty they brought with them, so I have heard, a feather of the *rukh,* positively affirmed to have measured ninety spans [four hundred fifty feet], and the quill part to have been two palms in circumference. This surprising evidence gave his Majesty extreme pleasure, and he bestowed valuable gifts upon those who presented it.

They were also the bearers of the tusk of a wild boar, an animal that grows to the size of a buffalo, and it was found to weigh fourteen pounds. The island contains likewise camelopards [giraffes, which are, however, not found on Madagascar], asses, and other wild animals, very different from these of our country. Having said all that is necessary on this subject, we shall now proceed to speak of Zanzibar.

CHAPTER 34

Of the Island of Zanzibar

BEYOND the island of Madagascar lies that of Zanzibar, which is reported to be two thousand miles in circuit.† The inhabitants worship idols, have their own peculiar language and do not pay tribute to any foreign

---

*The fable of the *rukh* or some other such gigantic bird is old and is told in many places, including of course the Sinbad the Sailor version in the *Arabian Nights*. The fact is that fossil evidence indicates there were once birds not much smaller than these.
†It is actually a small island, but the name was applied to a long stretch of the East African coast.

power. They are large in stature, but their height is not in proportion to the bulk of their bodies; otherwise, they would be gigantic. They are, however, strongly made, and one of them is capable of carrying what would be a load for four of our people. At the same time, he would require as much food as five of us. They are black, and go naked, covering only their private parts. Their hair is so curly that even when dipped in water it can with difficulty be straightened out. They have large mouths, their noses turn up toward the forehead, their ears are long, and their eyes so large and frightful that they look like demons. Their hands and their heads are also large and out of proportion.

There are in this island the most ill-favored women in the world. They have large mouths and thick noses, and their breasts are ugly and four times as large as those of other women. They feed on flesh, milk, rice, and dates. They have no grapevines, but make a sort of wine from rice and sugar and some spicy drugs. It is very pleasant to the taste, and has the intoxicating quality of other wines.

In this island elephants are found in vast numbers, and their teeth [tusks] form an important article of trade. It should be observed of these animals that their mode of copulating is the opposite of that of animals in general (because of the position of the female organ) and is like that of human beings.*

In this country is also found the giraffe, which is a handsome beast. Its body is well-proportioned, the fore-legs long, the hindlegs short, the neck very long, the head small, and its manners gentle. It is light in color and has circular reddish spots. Its neck, including the head, is three paces long.

The sheep of the country are different from ours, being all white excepting their heads, which are black; and this also is the color of the dogs. The animals in general have a different appearance from ours.

Many trading ships visit the place, which barter their goods for elephants' teeth and ambergris, of which much

---

*Having referred to this as an old and exploded fable, Colonel Yule omits this passage from his translation.

is found on the coasts of the island in consequence of the sea abounding with whales.

The chiefs of the island sometimes go to war with each other, and their people display much bravery in battle and contempt of death. They have no horses, but fight upon elephants and camels. Upon the backs of the former they place towers capable of containing from fifteen to twenty men armed with swords, lances, and stones. Before combat they give drinks of wine to their elephants, supposing that it makes them more spirited and more ferocious in the assault.

I have described only the principal and most celebrated provinces of India; and the same has been done with respect to the islands, the number of which is quite incredible. Indeed, I have heard from mariners and eminent pilots of these countries, and have seen in the writings of those who have navigated the Indian seas, that they amount to no fewer than 12,700, including both the uninhabited and the inhabited islands.

The area termed Greater India extends from Maabar to Kesmacoran, and comprehends thirteen large kingdoms, of which we have enumerated ten. Lesser India commences at Ziampa, and extends to Mutfili, comprehending eight kingdoms, exclusive of those in the islands, which are very numerous. We shall now speak of Second or Middle India,* which is called Abascia [Abyssinia or Ethiopia].

CHAPTER 35

Of the Great Province Named Abascia, or Middle India

ABASCIA is an extensive country termed Middle, or Second India. Its principal king is a Christian. Of the other six, who are tributary to the first, three are Christians and three are Saracens.

I was informed that the Christians of these parts are distinguished by three signs, or marks, one on the fore-

---

*Medieval Europeans thought of India as divided into Greater India (from the Ganges to beyond the Indus), Lesser India (from Indo-China to the east coast of India), and Middle India (Ethiopia).

head and one on each cheek, which are imprinted with a hot iron. This may be considered as a baptism with fire, after the baptism with water. The Saracens have only one mark, which is on the forehead and reaches to the middle of the nose. The Jews, who are likewise numerous here, have two marks, and these upon the cheeks.

The capital of the principal Christian king is in the interior of the country. The dominions of the Saracen princes lie toward the province of Aden [not modern Aden, but Adel on the Ethiopian coast]. The conversion of these people to the Christian faith was the work of the glorious apostle, St. Thomas, who having preached the gospel in the kingdom of Nubia, and converted its inhabitants, afterwards visited Abascia, and there, by the influence of his words and the performance of miracles, produced the same effect. He subsequently went to abide in the province of Maabar, where, after converting an infinite number of persons, he received, as we have already mentioned, the crown of martyrdom, and was buried on the spot.

These people of Abascia are brave and good warriors, being constantly at war with the Soldan [Sultan] of Aden, the people of Nubia, and many others whose countries border upon theirs. In consequence of this unceasing practice in arms, they are accounted the best soldiers in this part of the world.

In the year 1288, as I was informed, this great Abyssinian prince resolved to visit in person the holy sepulcher of Christ in Jerusalem, a pilgrimage that is every year made by vast numbers of his subjects. He was, however, dissuaded from it by the officers of his government, who convinced him of the dangers to which he would be exposed in passing through so many places belonging to the Saracens, his enemies. He then determined to send a bishop as his representative, a man of high reputation for sanctity, who, upon his arrival at Jerusalem, recited the prayers and made the offerings which the king had directed. Returning, however, through the dominions of the Soldan of Aden, the latter caused him to be brought into his presence, and tried to persuade him to become a Mahometan. Upon his refusing to abandon the Christian faith, the Soldan, ignoring the resentment of the Abyssinian monarch, caused the man to be circumcised, and then allowed him to depart. Upon his arrival, and making a report of the indignity and violence to which he had been subjected, the king immediately gave orders for assembling an army, with himself at the head of it, for the purpose of exterminating the Soldan. The Soldan, on his part, called to his assistance two Mahometan princes, his neighbors, by whom he was joined with a very large force. In the conflict that ensued, the Abyssinian king was victorious, and having taken the city of Aden, he gave it up to pillage in revenge for the insult to his bishop.

The inhabitants of this kingdom live upon wheat, rice, flesh, and milk. They extract oil from sesame, and have all sorts of provisions. In the country there are elephants, lions, giraffes, and a variety of other animals, such as wild asses, and monkeys that resemble men, together with many birds, wild and domestic. It is extremely rich in gold, and much frequented by merchants, who obtain large profits. We shall now speak of the province of Aden.

CHAPTER 36

Of the Province of Aden

THE province of Aden is governed by a king who bears the title of Soldan. The inhabitants are all Saracens, and utterly detest the Christians. In this kingdom there are many towns and castles, and it has the advantage of an excellent port, frequented by ships arriving from India with spices and drugs. The merchants who purchase them with the intention of conveying them to Alexandria, unload them from the ships in which they are imported, and distribute the cargoes on board other smaller vessels or barks. With these they navigate a gulf of the sea for twenty days, more or less, according to the weather. Having reached their port, they load their goods on camels and transport them overland, thirty days' journey, to the River Nile. Here they are again put into small vessels, called *jerms,* in which they are conveyed by that river to Kairo,* and from there, by an artificial canal, named Kalizene, at length to Alexandria.

This is the least difficult and the shortest route the merchants can take with their goods, the produce of India, from Aden to that city. In this port of Aden [in Arabia, at the southern end of the Red Sea], likewise, the merchants ship a great number of Arabian horses, which they carry for sale to all the kingdoms and islands of India, obtaining high prices for them and making large profits.

The Soldan of Aden possesses immense treasures, arising from the duties he levies both on the merchandise that comes from India, and that which is shipped through his port as the returning cargo, this being the most considerable mart in all that quarter, and the place to which all trading vessels resort.

I was told that when the Soldan of Babylon led his army for the first time against the city of Acre, and took it [in 1291], this city of Aden assisted him with thirty thousand horses and forty thousand camels, out of hate for the Christians. We shall now speak of the city of Escier.

CHAPTER 37

Of the City of Escier

THE ruler of this city Escier [Shihr, in Arabia] is a Mahometan, who governs it with justice under the superior authority of the Soldan of Aden.

Its distance from there is about forty miles to the southeast [actually to the northeast]. Subordinate to it are many towns and castles. Its port is good, and it is visited by many merchant ships from India, which carry back a number of excellent horses, highly esteemed in that country, and sold there at good prices. This district produces a large quantity of white incense of the first quality [true Arabian frankincense], which distills, drop by drop, from a certain small tree that resembles the fir.

*Because Marco never uses the name Cairo, but always Babylon, Yule surmises that this passage was edited.

The people occasionally tap the tree, or pare away the bark, and from the incision the frankincense gradually oozes, and afterwards becomes hard. Even when no incision is made, a dripping takes place in consequence of the excessive heat of the climate.

There are also many palm trees, which produce good dates in abundance. No grain excepting rice and millet is cultivated in this country, and it is necessary to obtain a supply from other parts. There is no wine made from grapes; but they prepare a liquor from rice, sugar, and dates that is delicious. They have a small breed of sheep, whose ears are not located like those in other species; two small horns grow in place of them, and lower down, toward the nose, there are two openings that serve the purpose of ears.

These people are great fishermen, and catch the tunny in such numbers that two may be purchased for a Venetian groat. They dry them in the sun, and since the country [the Arabian desert] is, as it were, burned up by the sun, and no sort of vegetable is to be seen, they accustom their cattle, cows, sheep, camels, and horses to feed upon dried fish, which they learn to eat without any signs of dislike. The fish used for this purpose are of a small kind which they take in vast quantities during the months of March, April, and May; they dry these and lay them up in their houses as food for their cattle. These will also feed upon the fresh fish, but are more accustomed to eat them in the dried state.

In consequence of the scarcity of grain, the natives make a kind of biscuit of the larger fish, in the following manner: they chop it into very small pieces and moisten it with a liquid made thick by a mixture of flour, which gives it the consistency of paste. This they form into a kind of bread, which they dry and harden by exposure to a burning sun. A stock of this biscuit is laid up to serve for a year's consumption.

The frankincense before mentioned is so cheap in the country as to be purchased by the governor at the rate of ten gold ducats the quintal, and then sold to the merchants at forty bezants. This he does under the direction of the Soldan of Aden, who monopolizes all that is produced in the district at the above price, and derives a large profit from the resale. Nothing further presenting itself at this place, we shall now speak of the city of Dufar.

CHAPTER 38

Of the City of Dufar

DUFAR is a large and respectable city or town at a distance of twenty miles from Escier in a southeasterly direction [actually it is about four hundred miles to the northeast]. Its inhabitants are Mahometans, and its ruler also is a subject of the Soldan of Aden. This place lies near the sea and has a good port, frequented by many ships.

Arabian horses are collected here from the inland country, and these the merchants buy up and carry to India, where they dispose of them at a good profit. Frankincense is likewise produced here, and purchased by the merchants. Dufar has other towns and castles under its jurisdiction. We shall now speak of the gulf at Kalayati.

CHAPTER 39

Of the City of Kalayati

KALAYATI is a large town situated near a gulf named Kalatu about six hundred miles northwest from Dufar.* The people are followers of the law of Mahomet, and are subject to the Melik of Ormus, who, when he is attacked and hard-pressed by another power, retreats to the protection of this city, which is so strong in itself and so advantageously situated that it has never yet been taken by an enemy.

The country around it not yielding any kind of grain, it is imported from other districts. Its harbor is good and many merchant ships arrive there from India; these sell their piece goods and spices to great advantage, there being a big demand from inland towns and castles. These likewise carry away loads of horses which they sell advantageously in India.

*On the Gulf of Oman, south of Muskat.

The fortress is so situated at the entrance of the gulf of Kalatu that no vessel can come in or depart without its permission. Occasionally it happens that the Melik of this city, who has an understanding with, and is tributary to, the King of Kerman, throws off his allegiance when the latter demands an unusual contribution. Upon his refusing to pay the demand, and an army being sent to compel him, he leaves Ormus and makes his stand at Kalayati, where he can prevent any ship from entering or sailing. The King of Kerman, being thus deprived of his revenues, is forced to end the dispute with the Melik.

The strong castle at this place constitutes, as it were, the key not only of the gulf, but also of the sea itself, since passing ships can at all times be seen from there. The inhabitants of this country subsist in general on dates and on fish, either fresh or salted, having constantly a large supply of both; but persons of rank, and those who can afford it, obtain corn for their use from other parts. Upon leaving Kalayati, and proceeding three hundred miles toward the northeast, you reach the island of Ormus.

CHAPTER 40

Of Ormus

UPON the island of Ormus there is a large and handsome city [Hormuz] built close to the sea. It is governed by a *melik*, which is a title equivalent to that of lord. He has many towns and castles under his authority.

The inhabitants are Saracens, all of them professing the faith of Mahomet. The heat here is extreme; but every house is provided with ventilators [wind-catching funnels are still in use here] by means of which they introduce air at will to the different floors, and into every apartment. Without this it would be impossible to live in the place. We shall not say more of this city, as in a former book we have given an account of it, together with Kisi and Kerman.

Having thus treated at sufficient length of those provinces and cities of Greater India situated near the seacoast, as well as some of the countries of Ethiopia, termed Middle India, I shall now, before I bring the work to a close, turn back to notice some regions lying toward the north, which I omitted to speak of in the preceding Books.

BOOK IV

✳

OF THE REGION OF DARKNESS, THE PROVINCE
OF RUSSIA, GREAT TURKEY, AND THE WAR
BETWEEN THE TARTARS OF THE WEST AND
THE TARTARS OF THE EAST

[Note: The following chapters on Mongol history (or as
Yule terms them, "quasihistory") and on Russia and
Siberia do not appear in the first Italian printed edition
or in Marsden's translation, but later editions have generally included them. Like Yule and other editors I feel
they contribute little, except perhaps in the sections on
Russia and Siberia, and I have not hesitated to con-
dense the more repetitious or verbose passages.]

CHAPTER 1

Of Great Turkey

IN GREAT Turkey [Chinese Turkestan] there is a king called Kaidu, who is the nephew of the Great Khan, for he was son of the son of Chagatai, who was brother [actually the uncle, not the brother, of Kublai] to the Great Khan. He possesses many cities and castles, and is a very great lord. He is Tartar, and his men also are Tartar, and they are good warriors, which is no wonder, for they are all brought up to make war; and I tell you that this Kaidu never gave obedience to the Great Khan, without first making great war.

And you must know that this Great Turkey lies to the northwest when we leave Ormus, by the way already mentioned. Great Turkey is beyond the river Ion [the Amu Daria], and stretches northward to the territory of the Great Khan.

This Kaidu has already fought many battles with the people of the Great Khan, and I will relate to you how he came to quarrel with him. You must know that Kaidu sent word one day to the Great Khan that he wanted his share of what they had obtained by conquest, claiming a part of the provinces of Cathay and of Manzi. The Great Khan told him that he was quite willing to give him his share, as he had done to his other sons, if he, on his part, would come to his court and attend his council as often as he sent for him; and the Great Khan demanded further that he should obey him like his other sons and barons. On this condition the Great Khan said that he would give him part of their conquest of China.

Kaidu, who distrusted his uncle the Great Khan, rejected this condition, saying that he was willing to yield him obedience in his own country, but that he would not go to his court as he feared he would be put to death. Thus originated the quarrel between the Great Khan and Kaidu, which led to a great war, and there were many great battles between them. And the Great Khan posted an army round the kingdom of Kaidu to prevent him or his people from doing any injury to his territory or people. But, in spite of all these precautions, Kaidu invaded his territory, and fought many times with the forces sent to oppose him. Now King Kaidu, by exerting himself, could bring into the field a hundred thousand horsemen, all good men, and well trained for war and battle. And, moreover, he had with him many barons of the lineage of the emperor, that is of Genghis Khan, who was the founder of the empire.

We will now tell of certain battles between Kaidu and the Great Khan's people; but first we will describe their mode of fighting. When they go to war, each is obliged to carry with him sixty arrows, thirty of which are of a smaller size intended for shooting at a distance, but the other thirty are larger, and have a broad blade. These they use at close quarters and strike their enemies in the faces and arms and cut the strings of their bows and do great damage with them. And when they have shot all their arrows they take their swords and maces and give one another heavy blows with them.

CHAPTER 2

Of Battles That Were Fought by King Kaidu Against His Uncle, the Great Khan

IN THE year 1266 this King Kaidu with his cousins, one of whom was called Jesudar, assembled a vast number of people and attacked two of the Great Khan's barons who also were cousins of King Kaidu, though they held lands of the Great Khan. One of these was named Tibai or Ciban. They were sons of Chagatai, who had received Christian baptism and was brother to the Emperor Kublai.

Kaidu, with his people, fought with these, his two cousins, who also had a great army, for on both sides there were about a hundred thousand horsemen. They fought very hard together, and many were slain on both sides, but at last King Kaidu gained the victory, and did great damage to the others. But the two brothers, the cousins of King Kaidu, escaped without injury, for they had good horses, which bore them swiftly away.

Having thus gained the victory, Kaidu's pride and arrogance increased and he returned to his own country where he remained full two years in peace, without any hostilities between him and the Great Khan. But at the end of two years Kaidu again assembled a great army. He knew that the Great Khan's son, Nomogan, was at Karakorum, and that with him was George, the grandson of Prester John, and these two barons also had a very great army of horsemen. King Kaidu, having assembled his host, marched from his own country, and without any occurrence worth mentioning arrived in the neighborhood of Karakorum, where the two barons, the son of the Great Khan, and the grandson of Prester John, were with their army.

The latter, instead of being frightened, prepared to meet them with the utmost ardor and courage; and having assembled their whole army, which consisted of no less than sixty thousand horsemen, they marched out and established their camp in good order at a distance of about ten miles from King Kaidu, who was encamped with his men in the same plain. Each party remained in their camp till the third day preparing for battle in the best way they could, for their numbers were about equal—neither exceeding sixty thousand horsemen well armed with bows and arrows, and each with a sword, mace, and shield.

Both armies were divided into six squadrons of ten thousand men each, and each having its commander. And when the two armies were drawn up in the field and waited only for the signal to be given by sounding the *nacars* [kettledrums], they sang and sounded their instruments of music in such a manner that it was wonderful to hear. For the Tartars are not allowed to begin a battle till they hear the *nacars* of their lord begin to sound; and it is their custom, while thus waiting, to sing and sound their two-corded instruments very sweetly. As soon as the sound of the *nacars* was heard the battle began and they put their hands to their bows and placed the arrows to the strings. In an instant the air was filled with arrows like rain, and you might see many a man and many a horse struck down dead, and the shouting and the noise of the battle was so great that one could hardly have heard God's thunder. In truth, they fought like mortal enemies. And as long as they had any arrows left, those who were able never stopped shooting; but so many were slain and mortally wounded that the battle went favorably for neither party.

When they had spent their arrows they placed the bows in their cases and seized swords and maces, and rushing upon each other began to give terrible blows with them. Thus they began a very fierce and dreadful battle, doing such execution upon each other that the ground was soon covered with corpses. Kaidu especially performed great feats of arms, and but for his personal prowess, which fired his followers, they were several times nearly defeated. And on the other side, the son of the Great Khan and the grandson of Prester John also acquitted themselves with great bravery. In a word, this was one of the bloodiest battles that had ever taken place among the Tartars. It lasted till nightfall, and in spite of all their efforts, neither party could drive the other from the field, which was covered with so many corpses that it was a pity to see, and many a lady that day was made a widow, and many a child an orphan. And when the sun set, both parties stopped fighting, and returned to their camps to rest for the night.

Next morning King Kaidu, who had received information that the Great Khan had sent a very powerful army against him, roused his men at daybreak, and all having mounted, he ordered them to proceed homewards. Their opponents were so weary with the previous day's battle that they made no attempt to follow them, but let them go without interference. Kaidu's men continued their retreat until they came to Samarcand, in Great Turkey.

CHAPTER 3

*What the Great Khan Said of the Injuries Done
by His Nephew Kaidu*

Now the Great Khan was greatly enraged against
Kaidu, who was always doing so much injury to his people and his territory, and he said that if he had not been
his nephew, he should not have escaped a dark death.
This feeling of kinship hindered him from destroying
him and his land, and thus Kaidu escaped from the
hands of the Great Khan. We will now leave this matter,
and we will tell you the strange history of King Kaidu's daughter.

CHAPTER 4

*Of the Daughter of King Kaidu and How Strong
and Valiant She Was*

You should know, then, that King Kaidu had a daughter named, in the Tartar language, Aigiarm, which
means "Shining Moon." This damsel was so strong that
there was no young man in the whole kingdom who
could overcome her. She vanquished them all.

Her father the king wished to marry her off; but she
declined, saying that she would never take a husband till
she met with some nobleman who could conquer her by
force. Thereupon the king her father gave her a written
promise that she might marry whom she would. She now
made it known in different parts of the world that if any
young man would come and try his strength with her
and overcome her by force, she would accept him for
her husband.

This proclamation was no sooner made than many
came from all parts to try their fortune. The trial was
made with great solemnity. The king took his place in
the principal hall of the palace with a large company of
men and women; then came the king's daughter, in a
dress of sendal very richly adorned, and next came the
young man, also in a dress of sendal. The agreement
was, that if the young man could throw her to the
ground, he was to have her for wife; but if, on the con-

trary, the king's daughter overcame him, he was to forfeit to her a hundred horses. In this manner the damsel won more than ten thousand horses, for she met with no one able to conquer her, which was no wonder, for she was so tall and strongly built that she might almost be taken for a giantess.

At last, about the year 1280, there came the son of a rich king who was very beautiful and young. He was attended by a very fine company, and brought with him a thousand beautiful horses. Immediately on his arrival he announced that he had come to try his strength with the lady. King Kaidu received him very gladly for he was very desirous to have this youth for his son-in-law, knowing him to be the son of the King of Pamar. Kaidu privately urged his daughter to let herself be vanquished. But she said she would not do so for anything in the world. Thereupon the king and queen took their places in the hall with a great gathering, and the king's daughter presented herself as usual, and also the king's son, who was remarkable no less for his beauty than for his great strength.

When they were brought into the hall, it was agreed that if the young prince were conquered he should forfeit the thousand horses he had brought with him. Then the wrestling began; and all who were there, including the king and queen, wished heartily that the prince might be the victor, and become the husband of the princess. But, contrary to their hopes, after much pulling and tugging, the king's daughter won, and the young prince was thrown on the pavement of the palace and lost his thousand horses. There was no one in the hall who did not lament his defeat.

After this the king took his daughter with him into many battles and not a cavalier in the host displayed so much valor. At last the damsel rushed into the midst of the enemy, and seizing upon a horseman carried him off to her own people.* We will now end this episode and proceed to describe a great battle between Kaidu and Arghun, the son of Abaga, Lord of the East.

---

*Versions of this legend are widespread, the most familiar being those told of the Amazons and of Brunhild in the Nibelungen.

CHAPTER 5

How Abaga Sent His Son with an Army

Now Abaga, the Lord of the East, held many provinces and many lands which bordered on the territory of King Kaidu on the side toward the tree which is called in the book of Alexander, *Arbor Secco*. And Abaga, in consequence of the damage done to his lands by King Kaidu, sent his son Arghun with a very great number of horsemen into the country of the Arbor Secco, as far as the river Ion, where they remained to protect the country against King Kaidu's people, garrisoning many cities and castles thereabouts. Thereupon, King Kaidu assembled a great number of horsemen and gave the command to his brother Barac [not a brother of Kaidu, but the ruler of Great Turkey], a prudent and brave man, with orders to fight Arghun. Barac promised to fulfill his wishes. He set out with his army and proceeded for many days till he reached the river Ion, where he was only ten miles from the army of Arghun. Both sides immediately prepared for battle, and in a very fierce engagement which took place three days afterward the army of Barac was overpowered, and pushed with great slaughter over the river.

CHAPTER 6

How Arghun Succeeded His Father in the Sovereignty

Soon after this victory, Arghun received news that his father Abaga was dead, which grieved him greatly. He set out with his army for his father's court, a distance of forty days' journey, in order to claim the sovereignty.

Now Abaga had a brother named Acomat Soldan [a younger son of Hulaku], who had become a Saracen, and who no sooner heard of his brother's death than he formed the design of seizing the succession himself, believing Arghun was too far away to prevent him. He therefore collected a powerful army, went direct to the court of his brother Abaga, and seized control.

There he found such an immense quantity of treasure as could hardly be believed, and by distributing this very lavishly among Abaga's barons and knights he won their hearts, and they declared they would have no other lord but him. Moreover, Acomat Soldan showed himself a very good lord, and made himself beloved by everybody. But he had not long enjoyed his usurped power, when news came that Arghun was approaching with a very great army. Acomat showed no alarm, but boldly summoned his barons and others, and within a week he had assembled a vast number of cavalry, who all declared that they were ready to march against Arghun, seize him and put him to death.

CHAPTER 7

The Battle Between Acomat and Arghun

WHEN Acomat Soldan had collected sixty thousand horsemen he set out to encounter Arghun, and at the end of ten days' march he learned that the enemy was only five days' march from him, and equal in number to his own army. Then Acomat pitched his camp on a great plain, as a favorable place for giving battle.

As soon as he arranged his camp he called together his people and addressed them as follows: "Lords, you know well that I ought to be lord of all my brother Abaga held, because I was the son of his father and I assisted in the conquest of all the lands and territories we possess. I will say no more, for I know you are wise men and love justice, and that you will act for the honor and good of us all." When he had ended, all the barons and knights and others who were there replied that they would not desert him as long as they had life in their bodies.

To return to Arghun; as soon as he received word of the movements of Acomat and knew that he was encamped with so large an army, he was greatly disturbed, but he thought it wise to show courage and spirit before his men. Having called all his barons and counselors into his tent, he addressed them as follows: "Brothers and friends, you know well how tenderly my father loved you; while alive he treated you as brothers and sons, and you know in how many battles you were with him and how you helped him to conquer the land he possessed. You know, too, that I am the son of him who loved you so much, and I myself love you as though you were my own body. And you know, further, that he has become a Saracen and thus worships Mahomet, and it would ill become us to let Saracens rule over Tartars. And truly everyone ought to reckon on victory, since justice is on our side and our enemies are in the wrong. I will say no more, but again implore every one of you to do his duty."

When the barons and knights had heard Arghun's address, each resolved that he would prefer death in battle to defeat; and one of the great barons arose and spoke thus: "My lord, we know well that what you have said to us is the truth, and therefore I will speak for all your men and tell you openly that we will not fail you as long as we have life in our bodies." Accordingly, early next morning Arghun and his men began their march with resolute hearts, and when they reached the plain in which Acomat was encamped, they established their camp in good order. Then Arghun sent two trusty messengers on a mission to his uncle.

When these two messengers, who were men of ripe years, arrived at the enemy's camp they dismounted at Acomat's tent and having entered it, saluted him courteously. After they had remained seated a short time one of the messengers rose and delivered his message as follows: "Lord Acomat, your nephew wonders much at your conduct in taking from him his sovereignty, and now again in coming to engage him in mortal combat; truly this is not good, nor have you acted as a good uncle ought to act toward his nephew. Wherefore, he begs you gently that you restore him his right, so that there will be no battle between you, and he will show you all honor, and you shall be lord of all his land under him. This is the message your nephew sends you by us."

When Acomat Soldan had heard the message, he replied as follows: "Sir messenger, what my nephew says means nothing, for the land is mine and not his. I conquered it as much as his father did; and therefore tell my nephew that if he wishes, I will make him a great lord, and I will give him land enough, and he shall be

as my son, and the highest in rank after me. And if he
does not, you may assure him that I will do all in my
power to put him to death. Now this is what I will do
for my nephew, and no other thing or other arrangement
shall you ever have from me."

The messengers immediately departed, and riding as
fast as they could to Arghun's camp, told him all that
had happened. When Arghun heard his uncle's message,
he was so enraged that he exclaimed in the hearing of
all who were near him, "Since I have received such injury and insult from my uncle, may I not live if I do not
take such revenge that all the world shall talk of it!"

After these words, he addressed his barons and
knights: "Now nothing remains but to go forth as quickly
as we can and put these faithless traitors to death, and
it is my desire that we attack them tomorrow morning,
and do our utmost to destroy them."

Next morning Arghun, having called his men to arms,
advanced toward the enemy. Acomat had done the
same, and the two armies engaged without further par-
ley. The battle began with a shower of arrows like rain
from heaven, and you might see everywhere the riders
thrown from the horses, and the cries and groans of
those who lay mortally wounded were dreadful to hear.
The slaughter was very great on both sides; but at last,
though Arghun himself displayed extraordinary valor
and set an example to all his men, it was in vain, for
fortune turned against him and his men were compelled
to fly, closely pursued by Acomat and his men, who
worked havoc upon them.

Arghun himself was captured, after which the pursuit
was abandoned, and the victors returned to their camp
and tents. Acomat caused his nephew to be confined,
and, being a man given to his pleasures, he returned to
his court to enjoy the society of the fair ladies who
served him, leaving command of the army to a chief,
with strict orders to keep Arghun closely guarded, and
to return to court by short marches so as not to tire
his men.

CHAPTER 8

How Arghun Was Liberated and Slew Acomat

Now it happened that a great Tartar baron, who was well along in years, took pity on Arghun, and said that it was a great wickedness and disloyalty to hold their lord a prisoner, and that he would do his best to set him free. He began by bringing many other barons around to the same view, and his personal influence was so great that he easily won them over to the enterprise. The name of the leader of the enterprise was Boga and his chief fellow conspirators were Elcidai, Togan, Tegana, Taga, Tiar Oulatai, and Samagar.

With these, Boga went to the tent where Arghun was confined and told him that they repented the part they had taken against him, and that as reparation they had come to set him free and take him for their lord.

When Arghun heard Boga's words, he thought at first that they came to mock him, and was very angry. "Sirs, you sin greatly in making me an object of mockery, and ought to be satisfied with the wrong you have already done me in imprisoning your rightful lord. Therefore, I pray, go your way and mock me no more."

"My lord," said Boga, "be assured that we are not mocking you at all, but what we say is quite true, and we swear to it upon our faith." Then all the barons took an oath that they would consider him their lord.

Arghun, on his side, swore that he would never trouble them for what was past, but that he would hold them all as dear as his father Abaga had done. And as soon as these mutual oaths had been taken, they let Arghun out of prison and received him as their lord. Then Arghun told them to shoot their arrows at the tent in which the chief who had the command of the army was, and they did so, and thus the chief was slain. The chief was Soldan.

And when Arghun found that he was assured of the sovereignty, he gave orders to the army to march toward the court. It happened one day that Acomat was at court in his principal palace making great festivity when a messenger came to him and said: "Sir, I bring you news, not such as I would, but very evil. Know that the barons have freed Arghun and raised him to the sovereignty and have slain Soldan, your dear friend; and I assure you that they are hastening hither to seize and slay you. Take counsel immediately, what is best to be done."

When Acomat heard this, he was at first so overcome with astonishment and fear that he did not know what to do or say; but at last, like a brave and prudent man, he told the messenger to mention the news to no one, and hastily ordered his most trusted followers to arm and mount their horses. Telling nobody where he was going, he set out to go to the Sultan of Babylonia [Egypt], believing that there he would find refuge.

At the end of six days he arrived at a pass which could not be avoided, and the keeper of which knew that it was Acomat, and saw that he was seeking safety in flight. This man determined to capture him, which he could easily do, as Acomat had few men. He accordingly placed Acomat under a strong guard, and marching with him to the court arrived there just three days after Arghun had taken possession of it, and had been greatly mortified to find that Acomat had escaped.

When, therefore, Acomat was delivered to him a prisoner, he was overjoyed, and commanding the army to be assembled immediately, without consulting anybody he ordered one of his men to slay his uncle and to throw his body into such place as it would never be seen again. This order was immediately executed. Thus ended the affair between Arghun and his uncle Acomat.

After this, Arghun sent Casan [Ghazan], his son, with full thirty thousand horsemen to the Arbor Secco to protect his land and people. Arghun thus recovered his sovereignty in the year 1286, Acomat having held it only two years. Arghun reigned six years, at the end of which he died, as was generally rumored, by poison.

CHAPTER 9

How Kiacatu and Then Baidu Seized the Sovereignty

WHEN Arghun was dead, his uncle [actually his brother], named Kiacatu, seized the sovereignty, which he was easily able to do because Casan was at the Arbor

Secco. Casan was greatly angered when he heard of Kia-catu's action but he could not leave his post at that moment for fear of his enemies. He threatened, however, that he would revenge himself as signally as his father had done upon Acomat. Kiacatu held the sovereignty and all were obedient to him except those who were with Casan. He took the wife of his nephew Arghun as his own and enjoyed himself much with the ladies, for he was excessively given to his pleasures. Kiacatu held the sovereignty two years, at the end of which he was carried off by poison.

When Kiacatu was dead, Baidu, who was his uncle, and a Christian, seized upon the sovereignty, and all obeyed him except Casan and the army with him. This occurred in the year 1294. When Casan learned what had occurred, he was more furious against Baidu than he had been against Kiacatu, and resolved to march immediately against him.

When Baidu knew for certain that Casan was coming against him he assembled a vast number of men and marched for ten days and then waited for him to give battle. On the second day Casan appeared and immediately there began a fierce battle which ended in the entire defeat of Baidu, who was slain in the combat. Casan now assumed the sovereignty and began his reign in the year 1294. Thus did the kingdom of the Eastern Tartars descend from Hulaku to Abaga to Arghun to Casan, who now reigns.

CHAPTER 10

Concerning the King of the Tartars Who Rules the Far North

IT SHOULD be known that in the northern parts of the world there dwell many Tartars under a chief of the name of Kaidu, who is of the race of Genghis Khan and closely related to Kublai, the Great Khan. He is not the subject of any other prince. The people observe the usages and manners of their ancestors and are regarded as genuine Tartars. These Tartars are idolaters and worship a god whom they call Natigai, the god of earth, because they think and believe that this god has dominion over the earth and all things that are born of it. To this false god they make idols and images of felt, as described earlier in this book.

Their king and his armies do not live in castles or strong places, or even in towns; but at all times remain in the open plains, valleys, or woods, in which this region [Siberia] abounds. They have no corn of any kind, but subsist upon flesh and milk, and live among each other in perfect harmony. Their king, to whom they all give implicit obedience, has no object dearer to him than preserving peace and union among his subjects, which is the essential duty of a sovereign. They possess vast herds of horses, cows, sheep, and other domestic animals. In these northern districts are found bears of a white color, and of prodigious size, being for the most part about twenty spans in length. There are also foxes whose furs are entirely black, wild asses in great numbers, and certain small animals named *rondes,* which have most delicate furs, and are called zibelines or sables by our people. Besides these, there are various small beasts of the marten or weasel kind, and those which bear the name of Pharaoh's mice. The swarms of the latter are incredible, but the Tartars use such ingenious traps for catching them that none escape their hands.

In order to reach this country it is necessary to perform a journey of fourteen days across a wide plain that is entirely uninhabited because innumerable ponds and springs render it entirely marsh. In consequence of the long duration of the cold season, this is frozen over, excepting for a few months of the year when the sun dissolves the ice and turns the soil to mud, over which it is more difficult to travel than when it is frozen. But to enable merchants to visit their country and purchase their furs, in which all their trade consists, these people have exerted themselves to render the marshy desert passable by erecting a wooden house some height above the ground at the end of each day's journey. Here are stationed persons whose business it is to receive and accommodate the merchants, and on the following day to conduct them to the next station.

To travel over the frozen surface of the ground they

build a sort of vehicle not unlike that used by natives of the almost inaccessible mountains of our own country, which is termed a *tragula* or sleigh. It has no wheels, and is flat at the bottom but rises with a semicircular curve in front, which fits it for running easily upon the ice. To draw these small carriages, they keep in readiness certain animals resembling dogs, and which may be called such, although they are almost as large as asses. They are very strong. Six of them, in couples, are harnessed to each carriage, which contains only the driver who manages the dogs and one merchant with his pack of goods. When the day's journey has been performed the driver returns, while the merchant takes another sledge to the next station. The merchant returns with furs that eventually find their way for sale to our part of the world.

CHAPTER 11

Of Those Countries Termed the Region of Darkness

BEYOND the most distant part of the territory of those Tartars, whence come the skins that have been spoken of, there is another region which extends to the utmost bounds of the north and is called the Region of Darkness. During most of the winter the sun is invisible and the light is about the way it is at dawn of day when we may be said to see and yet not to see.

The men of this country are well made and tall but of a very pale complexion. They are not united under the government of a king or prince and they live without established laws or rules, in the manner of animals. Their intellects also are dull, and they have an air of stupidity.

The Tartars often go on plundering expeditions against these people and rob them of their cattle and goods. For this purpose, they avail themselves of those months in which darkness prevails. Being unsure of the direction in which they must return home with their booty, they provide against going astray by riding mares that have young foals, and these foals they leave behind. When their works of darkness have been accomplished and they want to return to the region of light they lay the bridles on the necks of their mares and allow them to take their own course. Guided by maternal instinct, they make their way directly to the spot where they had left their foals.*

The inhabitants of this region take advantage of the summer season, when they enjoy continual daylight, to catch multitudes of ermine, martens, foxes, and other animals of that kind, the furs of which are finer, and consequently more valuable, than those found in the districts inhabited by the Tartars. During the summer also, these people carry their furs to neighboring countries where they dispose of them most advantageously; and according to what I have been told, some of them are transported even as far as Russia, of which we shall speak in this concluding part of our work.

CHAPTER 12

Of the Province of Russia and Its People

THE province of Russia is of vast extent, is divided into many parts, and borders upon that northern tract which has been described as the Region of Darkness. Its inhabitants are Christians and follow the Greek ritual in their Church. The men are extremely handsome, tall, and of fair complexion. The women are also fair and of a good size, with light hair, which they are accustomed to wear long. The country pays tribute to the king of the Western Tartars, with whose dominions it comes in contact on its eastern border. Within it are collected in great abundance the furs of ermine, arcolini [unidentified], sables, martens, foxes, and other animals of that tribe, together with much wax. It contains several mines, whence a large quantity of silver is procured.

Russia is an exceedingly cold region and I have been assured that it extends even as far as the Northern Ocean where, as has been mentioned in a preceding part of the work, falcons are taken in vast numbers, and from there carried to various parts of the world.

*This seems to be a very old legend, appearing, for example, among the tales told of Alexander.

And now I will tell you about the Tartars of the Ponent, and the lords who have reigned over them.

CHAPTER 13

Of the Lords of the Tartars of the West

THE first lord of the Tartars of the West was Sain,* who was a very great and powerful king. He conquered Russia, Comania, Alania, Lac, Mengiar, Zic, Gucia, and Gazari. Before this conquest they were all Comanians, but they were not under one government; and because of that they lost their lands and were dispersed. Those who remained were reduced to serfdom under King Sain.

After King Sain came King Patu [apparently a compound error: "Patu" should be "Batu," and Sartak came after Sain]; after him, King Barka; next King Mongutemur; then King Totamangu; and lastly Toctai, who now reigns. Having thus given you a list of kings of the Tartars of the West, we will tell you of a great battle between Hulaku, Lord of the East, and Barka, Lord of the West.

CHAPTER 14

Of the War Between Hulaku and Barka

IN THE year 1261 a great quarrel arose between King Hulaku, lord of the Tartars of the East, and Barka, king of the Tartars of the West, on account of the province which bounded their territories, which both claimed and each refused to yield to the other. They defied each other; each declaring that he would take it, and would see who dared stop him. When things had come to this point, each summoned his followers, and within six months each had assembled full three hundred thousand horsemen. Hulaku, Lord of the East, now set out with all his forces. At length they reached a great plain between the Iron Gates [in the Caucasus] and the Sea of

*Batu Khan. He was also known as Sain, or "The Good" Khan. He led the Mongol drive westward into Europe in 1240, and founded the Western Tartar line.

Sarai [the Caspian], in which they encamped in good order, with many a rich pavilion and tent. And there Hulaku said he would wait to see what course Barka would follow, as this place was on the border of the two domains.

Now when King Barka had made all his preparations he also set out, and in due time reached the same plain, where his enemies awaited him. Barka's camp was quite as richly decked out as that of Hulaku, and his army was more numerous for it numbered full three hundred and fifty thousand horsemen.

When the day fixed for the battle arrived Hulaku called his men to arms, and when all this was duly arranged he ordered his troops to advance until they were halfway between the two camps, where they halted and waited for the enemy. On the other side, King Barka had drawn up his army exactly in the same manner as that of Hulaku's, and he also ordered his men to advance to within half a mile of the other, which they did. There they made a short halt, and then they moved forward again till they came to about two *arbalest* [crossbow] shots of each other.

After the two armies had remained a short while facing each other, the *nacars* [kettledrums] were at length sounded, upon which both armies let fly such a shower of arrows at each other that you could hardly see the sky, and many were slain, both men and horses.

The battle continued till dusk, when Barka began to give way, and fled, and Hulaku's men pursued furiously, cutting down and slaying without mercy.

Next morning Hulaku ordered the bodies of the dead to be buried, enemies as well as friends, and the loss was so great on both sides that it would be impossible to describe it. After this was done, Hulaku returned to his country with all his men who had survived the battle.

CHAPTER 15

How Totamangu Was Lord of the Tartars of the West

You must know that in the west the sovereignty descended to Tolobuga, who was young and unmarried. Then he was slain by Totamangu, a man of great force, with the assistance of another king of the Tartars, named Nogai. After a short reign, Totamangu died, and Toctai, a very able and prudent man, was chosen king.

Meanwhile, the two sons of Tolobuga had grown to be capable of bearing arms. These two assembled a very fair company and went to the court of Toctai and presented themselves, with so much courtesy and humility, on their knees, that Toctai welcomed them and told them to stand up.

Then the eldest said to the king, "Lord Toctai, I will tell you as best I can why we are come to court. You know that we are the sons of Tolobuga, who was slain by Totamangu and Nogai. Of Totamangu I shall say nothing, since he is dead; but we claim justice against Nogai for the murder of our father and we pray you as a righteous lord to grant it to us. This is the object of our visit to your court."

When Toctai had heard the youth, he knew that what he said was true and he replied, "Fair friend, I will willingly yield to your demand for justice upon Nogai, and for that purpose we will summon him to court and do everything which justice shall require." Then Toctai sent two messengers to Nogai and ordered him to come to court to answer to the sons of Tolobuga for the death of their father; but Nogai laughed at the message and told the messengers he would not go.

When Toctai heard Nogai's message he was greatly enraged and said in the hearing of all who were about him, "With the aid of God, either Nogai shall come before me to do justice to the sons of Tolobuga, or I will go against him with all my men and destroy him." When Nogai knew certainly that Toctai was preparing to come against him with so large a host he also made great preparation, but not so great as Toctai's, because he was not so great or powerful as the other.

When Toctai's army was ready, he marched at the head of two hundred thousand horsemen, and in due time reached the plain of Nerghi [apparently around the Don River], where he encamped to wait for his opponent. With him were the two sons of Tolobuga, who had come with a fair company of horsemen to avenge the death of their father.

Nogai also was on the way with a hundred and fifty thousand horsemen, all young and brave, and much better soldiers than those of Toctai. He arrived in the plain where Toctai was encamped and established his camp at a distance of ten miles from him.

Next day they prepared for battle. After a long and desperate battle in which the two kings, as well as the two sons of Tolobuga, distinguished themselves by their reckless valor, the army of Toctai was entirely defeated and pursued from the field with great slaughter by Nogai's men. Full sixty thousand men were slain in this battle, but King Toctai, as well as the two sons of Tolobuga, escaped.

CONCLUSION*

AND now you have heard all that I can tell you about the Tartars and the Saracens and their customs, and likewise about the other countries of the world as far as my travels and knowledge extend. Although I know it thoroughly, I have said nothing about the Greater Sea and the provinces that lie round it. But it seems to me needless to speak about places which are visited by people every day. For there are so many who sail all about the sea constantly—Venetians, Genoese, Pisans, and many others—that everyone knows all about it.

Of the manner in which we took our departure from the court of the Great Khan you have heard at the beginning of the book, in that chapter where we told you of the difficulty that Messer Maffeo and Messer Nicolo

---

*This conclusion appears only in two manuscripts of the work and may even have been added by a translator or transcriber, but it is very old and serves to round off the account with a suitable flourish.

and Messer Marco had in getting the Great Khan's leave to go; and in the same chapter is related the lucky chance that led to our departure. And you may be sure that but for that chance we should never have got away, and never returned to our country again.

But I believe it was God's pleasure that we should get back in order that people might learn about the things that the world contains. For as was said in the beginning of the book, there never was a man who traveled over so much of the world as that noble and illustrious citizen of Venice, Messer Marco, son of Messer Nicolo Polo.

Thanks be to God! Amen! Amen!

AFTERWORD

The Travels of Marco Polo is the second most influential ghostwritten book in the history of Western culture, after the Bible. Dictated to and transcribed by a fellow prisoner while Marco Polo was jailed by the Genoese years after his return to Venice, this account of his adventures brought a real report of the East, its people and cultures, to the West for the first time, a Discovery channel suddenly appearing on a cable system previously consisting entirely of religious broadcasting, local news and weather, and mindnumbingly repetitive (and grossly distorted) tales of the rich, royal and famous.

In the late thirteenth century, when the book was written, most of Europe knew nothing of the East, except for myth based on classical fragments and what was extrapolated from Christian teachings and legends. While there were, in fact, pockets of Nestorian Christians (heretics according to the doctrines of both the Greek and Roman church, who had settled outside of their reach) living as far away as China, and there had always been trade back and forth, for a thousand years Europe's understanding of the East was hermetic, almost completely untouched by fact. The story of Prester John, a Christian king who ruled in Asia, was widely circulated and taken as true (Marco Polo worked Prester John into his history of the Mongol empire); and the people east of the Holy Land were thought to include such oddities as a race of one-legged men, men without heads, and anthropophagi, cannibals; except for that last, which was no doubt as true in Asia at some point in history as it was at some point in Europe, these all were fairy tales left over from classical antiquity.

So the strangeness of the stories that Marco Polo brought back—of the hashish-smoking assassins of Persia, convinced they'd physically visited heaven; of the magic performed by Indian fakirs and Buddhist monks; and most of all, of the magnificence of Kublai Khan and his empire—was really of a piece with the strangeness of the stories that had preceded them. His stories were no more or less bizarre than what Europeans had thought for centuries, and since the earlier stories had the weight of tradition, the new ones were largely disbelieved.

Still though, the book was widely read in many languages, and was ultimately taken seriously enough that it helped to shape the age of exploration that was to follow two centuries later—Columbus, for example, carried a copy with him on his voyage to the New World—without which, of course, things would be very different today.

As you read these remarkably well-reported chronicles, two things leap out as glaringly absent. One is the Great Wall of China, which for some reason goes unmentioned, a surprising and still unexplained oversight. But even more surprising to a modern sensibility is the absence of Marco Polo himself. The book is a catalogue and travelogue, a bestiary and a geography; it contains history, sociology and anthropology, but it says almost nothing of the man who reported all of it.

It's impossible to imagine now what it was like for the young Marco Polo to journey to the court of Kublai Khan. There is nothing in our world that would appear to us as strange as these other ways of living would have been to him. We *do* have the Discovery channel, and *National Geographic*, and newspapers and the Internet, and even if we never leave the town in which we were born, we are exposed to images from the most obscure corners of the world. Modern communications have rendered even the surface of the moon more familiar to a middle-class teenager in an American city than China was to Marco Polo, a middle-class teenager from an Italian city-state when he set out.

It's just as hard to imagine somebody of our own time and place writing such a book and not making it as much about the writer's experience as the things that were experienced. In the contemporary tradition, when travelers return from other places and write books about spending a year in Paris or Provence or Tokyo, we expect them to interpret that experience for us, to bring a point of view to the story and talk about how the experience caused the writer to change. No matter where you go, somebody has been there before, and the only thing left to chronicle is the infinite minute variations of the inner world.

Everything strange has now been rendered familiar, and the essential differences of other people have become obscured by this superficial familiarity. When we think of people in other cultures, we believe that they are, deep down, just like us; it's only the trappings of their particular place and tradition that make them look odd, and as both people and ideas move about the world at an ever-greater rate, what differences remain are being reduced to superficial quirks and idiosyncrasies. We are all family, because everything is familiar; we are all related, because everything is relative.

In part, Marco Polo's near-absence from his own story can be understood as a continuation of centuries of publishing tradition. Personality was not much favored in books in the days between the Roman Empire and the Renaissance. Until Peter Abelard's twelfth-century memoir, *The History of My Calamities,* the approach to biographies and autobiographies was heavily Platonist, and tended to make the facts of a life—and they were largely royal lives, of course— conform to an ideal of how a Christian life should be lived. The degree to which the subject actually fell from that ideal, what we today would find most interesting and the reason we would be reading the book, was not mentioned at all.

But the absence of Marco Polo from his own story can just as much be attributed to the fact that he wrote at a time when things were not relative, before we had any idea that we were all related. There was no gene mapping to tell us that we were all descended from mitochondrial Eve, or paleontology to show us that we had all originated on the same African savannah. To Marco Polo, or any other Westerner of his day, other people *weren't* just like us. They could have been from another planet; they could have laid eggs, and it would not have contradicted their understanding of the world. When things are that uncertain, a traveler is too busy seeing what's in front of him to spend too much time contemplating his own inner life.

In the European experience of the thirteenth century, the primary relationship with another culture was the Crusades, a relationship of conflict. The continuing battle for control of the Holy Land (started by a smart pope who knew Europe would be a more comfortable place to live once he got some very aggressive, land-hungry noblemen to take it outside, as it were) did not allow for compromise, and the outcome was believed to have consequences reverberating into the next life. That made it a very us-or-them situation.

It should be noted that this attitude wasn't one-sided. It wasn't only the West that considered other people the Enemy, or not even people at all. Islam, China, the Mongols—all of them looked down on Europe at some point as backward, uncivilized, and barbaric, and not without some justification. In the twelfth and thirteenth centuries, the science and medicine being practiced under Moslem rule was considerably further along than anything in Europe, and works of Plato and Aristotle long lost to the West were part of the core curriculum; China had established effective empire-spanning administrative techniques when Rome was falling apart under the invasions of the northern tribes that would become the nation-states of Europe and continue fighting among themselves until, well, just yesterday, really; and the Mongols, a sort of magpie empire, instead of imposing their ways on their conquered people as we'd expect, were willing to adopt the best that each of them had to offer.

In fact, when Marco Polo's father and uncle made their first trip back to Europe from the court of Kublai Khan, it was at his behest; he had sent them with a message for the pope, requesting that one hundred of his best missionaries return with them. He wanted them to make the case for Christianity, and if they were persuasive enough, the Mongol empire would become another Roman franchise.

So while a world in which we are not all the same under the skin, where things aren't relative and there's no room for compromise, might seem primitive at first glance, consider whether any ruler today, let alone the most powerful man in the world, at the head of the most feared empire, would ever be so liberal-minded as to invite missionaries from a foreign land into his court to take their best shot at converting him to their beliefs. Or consider whether a Westerner today could travel Marco Polo's route from Venice to China and back—on foot, by boat, on camels, through present-day Turkey, Afghanistan, Iraq, and Iran, just to start—with a reasonable expectation of safety.

C. S. Lewis, a medievalist and one of the great Christian writers of the twentieth century, wrote some very persuasive and well-known essays, but his most widely read books are fiction, in which he creates allegories of his beliefs and arguments for a Christian understanding of the world. In his novel *Out of the Silent Planet*, Ransom, Lewis's hero and spokesman, travels to Mars—Malacandra to the natives. Here's what he has to say about why the three intelligent species of the planet don't keep pets:

> Malacandrans don't keep pets and, in general, don't feel about their "lower animals" as we do about ours. Naturally it is the sort of thing they themselves could never have told me. One just sees why when one sees the three species together. Each of them is to the others *both* what a man is to us *and* what animal is to us. They can talk to each other, they can cooperate, they have the same ethics; to that extent a *sorn* and a *hross* meet like two men. But then each finds the other different, funny, attractive as an animal is attractive. Some instinct starved in us, which we try to soothe by treating irrational creatures almost as if they were rational, is really satisfied in Malacandra. They don't need pets.

There's something of the medieval worldview in that passage, an enlightened, idealized version, of course, and nobody is suggesting that other people are animals. But there's a delight and an attraction available in the strangeness of other people when differences are not obscured, a valuable, seductive strangeness that seems to have gone out of the world; it's the strangeness and delight that caused Samuel Coleridge to write his poem about Xanadu and the pleasure domes of Kubla Khan while reading *The Travels of Marco Polo;* it's the strangeness and attraction that sent Columbus and uncountable other Europeans out seeking unseen lands after reading this book.

We live in a world where all the barriers between cultures are breaking down, where the language of rock and roll and the Internet is spoken everywhere, at a time when you can find mosques, temples, shrines and churches of all the world's religions all over the world. It's doubtful that anybody would want to turn the clock back to the time of Marco Polo and Kublai Khan (there's dentistry, if nothing else), but there's something to be said for a world that is full of abiding strangeness, a world where a traveler had reason to write about what he saw, rather than what he felt. It's likely something that will never be again, but, like readers for more than five hundred years before us, we can pick up *The Travels of Marco Polo* and, at least for a little while, see that world through those eyes.

—Howard Mittelmark

INDEX

293

READ THE TOP 25 SIGNET CLASSICS

ANIMAL FARM BY GEORGE ORWELL	0-451-52634-1
1984 BY GEORGE ORWELL	0-451-52493-4
HAMLET BY WILLIAM SHAKESPEARE	0-451-52692-9
FRANKENSTEIN BY MARY SHELLEY	0-451-52771-2
THE SCARLET LETTER BY NATHANIEL HAWTHORNE	0-451-52608-2
THE ADVENTURES OF HUCKLEBERRY FINN BY MARK TWAIN	0-451-52650-3
THE ODYSSEY BY HOMER	0-451-52736-4
FRANKENSTEIN, DRACULA, DR. JEKYLL AND MR. HYDE	
BY MARY SHELLEY, BRAM STOKER, AND ROBERT LOUIS STEVENSON	
	0-451-52363-6
JANE EYRE BY CHARLOTTE BRONTE	0-451-52655-4
HEART OF DARKNESS & THE SECRET SHARER	
BY JOSEPH CONRAD	0-451-52657-0
GREAT EXPECTATIONS BY CHARLES DICKENS	0-451-52671-6
BEOWULF (BURTON RAFFEL, TRANSLATOR)	0-451-52740-2
ETHAN FROME BY EDITH WHARTON	0-451-52766-6
NARRATIVE OF THE LIFE OF FREDERICK DOUGLASS	
BY FREDERICK DOUGLASS	0-451-52673-2
A TALE OF TWO CITIES BY CHARLES DICKENS	0-451-52656-2
OTHELLO BY WILLIAM SHAKESPEARE	0-451-52685-6
ONE DAY IN THE LIFE OF IVAN DENISOVICH	
BY ALEXANDER SOLZHENITSYN	0-451-52709-7
PRIDE AND PREJUDICE BY JANE AUSTEN	0-451-52588-4
UNCLE TOM'S CABIN: 150TH ANNIVERSARY EDITION	
BY HARRIET BEECHER STOWE	0-451-52670-8
MACBETH BY WILLIAM SHAKESPEARE	0-451-52677-5
THE COUNT OF MONTE CRISTO BY ALEXANDER DUMAS	0-451-52195-1
ROMEO AND JULIET BY WILLIAM SHAKESPEARE	0-451-52686-4
A MIDSUMMER NIGHT'S DREAM BY WILLIAM SHAKESPEARE	0-451-52696-1
THE PRINCE BY NICCOLO MACHIAVELLI	0-451-52746-1
WUTHERING HEIGHTS BY EMILY BRONTE	0-451-52338-5

Penguin Group (USA) Inc. Online

What will you be reading tomorrow?

Tom Clancy, Patricia Cornwell, W.E.B. Griffin,
Nora Roberts, William Gibson, Robin Cook,
Brian Jacques, Catherine Coulter, Stephen King,
Dean Koontz, Ken Follett, Clive Cussler,
Eric Jerome Dickey, John Sandford,
Terry McMillan...

You'll find them all at
http://www.penguin.com

*Read excerpts and newsletters, find tour
schedules, and enter contest.*

Subscribe to Penguin Group (USA) Inc. Newsletters
and get an exclusive inside look
at exciting new titles and the authors you love
long before everyone else does.

PENGUIN GROUP (USA) INC. NEWS
http://www.penguin.com/news

WITHDRAWN